LOVING WISDOM

Christ…in whom are hidden all the treasures
of wisdom and knowledge. (Col. 2:2b–3)

To Stuart C. Hackett—my first philosophy professor,
whose wisdom, intellect, and faithfulness to God
inspired me and so many others.

LOVING WISDOM

Christian Philosophy of Religion

PAUL COPAN

CHALICE PRESS

ST. LOUIS, MISSOURI

Cover art: © The Crosiers
Cover and interior design: Elizabeth Wright

Visit Chalice Press on the World Wide Web at
www.chalicepress.com

10 9 8 7 6 5 4 3 2 1   07 08 09 10 11 12

Library of Congress Cataloging-in-Publication Data

Copan, Paul.
  Loving wisdom : Christian philosophy of religion / Paul Copan.
      p. cm.
  ISBN 978-0-8272-2139-0
  1. Christianity–Philosophy. 2. Theology. I. Title.

  BR100.C77 2007
  230.01–dc22

                                                      2007007713

Printed in the United States of America

Contents

PART IV: REDEMPTION

PART V: RE-CREATION

Acknowledgments

This book is gratefully dedicated to Stuart C. Hackett—my mentally rigorous, strongly supportive, wildly dressed, and fun-loving philosophy professor and advisor while I was at Trinity Seminary. His religious epistemology class during my first semester—taught entirely in paragraph-long sentences—helped set me in a new direction. I am ever in his debt.

I'm grateful to Chad Meister for his valuable, detailed comments on the manuscript—and for the wisdom offered by Kevin Vanhoozer, David K. Clark, Charles Taliaferro, and Harold Netland. Thanks to my stimulating PBA philosophy of religion class (spring 2006) for their input: Kristin Atkins, Rebekah Blanco, Justin Borg, Nathanael Chenowith, Dustin Clinton, Maria Cocking, Chris Deutschle, Brian Dobrodziej, Shawna Durtschi, Nate Evans, Torie Fake, Scott French, Maria Gomez, Josh Leonard, Kris Lobasz, Joanna (Logan) Walter, Kyle Mains, Cory Mattox, Eamon McCaffrey, Patrick Moore, Julie Richards, John Robertson, Diana Varga, Valerie Villarreal, and Scott Wilson. Hearty thanks, as always, to my first-rate family for their patience and support.

Preface

The term "popularizer," philosopher Alvin Plantinga observes, is one of disdain among academics. However, Christian scholars shouldn't leave their work "buried away in professional journals,"[1] but make their work available to the broader Christian community and help Christians grapple with important questions and concerns: "If [Christian philosophers] devote their best efforts to the topics fashionable in the non-Christian philosophical world, they will neglect a crucial and central part of their task as Christian philosophers."[2] The *Christian* philosopher's task should be shaped, not by secular academia's concerns, but by the priorities of God's kingdom, all in the context of loving, trusting, and obeying God. This book is an attempt to take such an exhortation seriously.

Chalice Press has kindly invited me to write a user-friendly, Scripture-engaging Christian philosophy of religion book—a kind of launching pad for Christian leaders, students, and teachers in philosophy of religion as they think critically, instruct others, engage with non-Christians, and live their lives in God's presence. This book reflects themes I have found important and fruitful in my own spiritual and intellectual pilgrimage and in my interactions with those outside the faith in open forums and coffee shops.

My tornado-whipped editor, Trent Butler, told me he wasn't tied to a particular table of contents, nor was he interested in imitating another philosophy of religion volume. While he was hoping for an introduction that third-year college or seminary students could easily use in the classroom, his dream was for a user-friendly book such that a professor could model the teaching of the book and the student could then use that model as a framework to teach interested church members. "That is, the book and professor would help the student gain both information and teaching skill so that the student would feel confident to become a teacher." So hopefully both the novice and the initiated will profit.

Christian reflection on the philosophy of religion is deep and wide, so this book covers basic terrain, offering variation as well. I discuss key topics, address objections, note apologetically interesting themes, and offer practical pointers. At the end of the book are study questions for small groups and personal reflection.

The format follows the flow of biblical narrative: *God, creation, fall, redemption,* and *re-creation,* all within a relational Trinitarian framework.[3] Utilizing the backdrop of Scripture and themes in biblical and systematic theology, this book takes shape according to the triune *theodrama,*[4] in which a relational, self-contented triune God creates out of his goodness and freedom. He designs his image-bearers–priest-kings–to worship him and rule creation with him. Then, in the aftershocks of the fall, the creating, covenant-making God seeks to bring human beings into relationship with this "divine family"; the renewed creation will be fulfilled in the new heavens and earth when God dwells in the midst of his people. This restoration–this new creation and new exodus–is achieved through Jesus of Nazareth. He is both the second Adam, who creates a new humanity, and the beloved Son of God, who lives out Israel's covenant calling. In his life, death, and resurrection, he perfectly (and representatively) fulfills our vocation–and calls us to join in it–that God's fame and glory will be spread throughout the earth.

Christian philosophers, lovers of God's wisdom, won't get lost in abstractions, but will attend to the implications of the divine-human interaction–namely, love for God and neighbor, trust, humility, charitability, perseverance, and a host of other virtues necessary for the task.

Introduction

Philosophy under the Cross

"But may it never be that I should boast, except in the cross of our Lord Jesus Christ..." (Gal. 6:14a)

A "theology of the cross" (*theologia crucis*), as Martin Luther called it, is about a suffering God who reveals himself in humility, particularly in Christ. "Theologians of glory," proudly presenting confident, abstract "proofs," may be in danger of obscuring the cross (which casts "God's shadow") and a God who often veils himself. There is no salvation without humility. Human reasoning that seeks God without the aid of the cross and the Spirit of God will miss the mark.[1] Though Luther—hopefully only in his *pre*-mortem state!—would perhaps consider this book's philosophical discussion of the Trinity and Incarnation "sophistic," he rightly points us in a cruciform or crucicentric direction; indeed, the very wisdom of God is found in the cross.

When emphasizing the cross, though, we shouldn't forget the *entire* Christ-event: his *incarnate life* and *ministry*—indeed, his triumphant, *glorious resurrection* from the dead. The cross though remains a useful symbol to remind wisdom-seekers about humility, prayer, the Spirit's empowerment, and a life poured out for others.

This isn't a dispassionately written book. Thankfully, the New Testament authors wrote out of personal devotion and zeal for Christ, who had transformed their lives. Their passion didn't undermine their objectivity or twist the truth—no more so than did the passion of Auschwitz survivors Elie Wiesel or Viktor Frankl, who wrote with both fervor and penetrating insight about their experience and the human condition. Whether Holocaust survivors or New Testament witnesses, we're drawn to their writings precisely because they couldn't stop speaking about what they'd seen and heard. The charge of "bias" is often a truth-avoidance tactic, and the critic is still left holding his own bundle of arbitrary biases that needn't be taken seriously. No, certain perspectives ("biases")—even passionate ones—can be accurate, and we can many times recognize those that we should dismiss and others that we should affirm.

Though I write as an evangelical Christian, I hope this book serves not only the broader Christian community, but the inquiring non-Christian mind as well. After all, belief in God isn't private, inaccessible to public scrutiny. Speaking to King Agrippa, Paul asserts that Jesus' crucifixion and postmortem appearances—including Paul's Damascus road experience—

1

"were not done in a corner" (Acts 26:26). Yes, the glory of the triune, self-revealing God saturates the creation, is made known through historical events and in Jesus of Nazareth, and is available to all.

Good public reasons and arguments are important, though by themselves they don't guarantee participation in God's family. The Spirit, who can *use* evidence, assures us of such realities (Rom. 5:5; 8:15; Gal. 4:6), even if his divine influence and wooing can be stifled and resisted (Acts 7:58). We ultimately *know* the reality of God's presence and love by his Spirit's illumination and life-giving power—though we should be prepared to *show* people evidences and give reasons for the truth of the Christian faith.

Views differ on the relationship between Christianity and philosophy—or "faith" and "reason," and I don't wish to settle such large disputes here. According to Augustine and Aquinas, "philosophy" is the pursuit of wisdom by "unaided human reason." I'll be taking the view of church father Justin Martyr. Having gone from one philosopher to another in search of wisdom, he met an elderly man who told him about the Jesus of the Gospels; this led to Justin's conversion to Christ and his discovery of true philosophy. Philosophy wasn't the *means* to finding wisdom but the *goal.* True philosophy encompasses *all* wisdom and includes—indeed finds its climax in—God's revelation to us in Jesus of Nazareth, Wisdom incarnate—a wisdom that comes not through unaided reason, but by amazing grace.[2]

Philosophy and Religion

The fear of the LORD is the beginning of wisdom. (Ps. 111:10)

In [Christ] are hidden all the treasures of wisdom and knowledge. (Col. 2:3)

"Philosophy" is difficult to define. The academic, professional discipline involves hard and skillful thinking about ethics, knowledge, life's meaning, or what's real (metaphysics). The Greek word *philosophia* literally means "the love of wisdom"—which isn't a bad place to start.

Scripture takes wisdom to be more than intellectual, rational, and theoretical. It can involve having a Ph.D. or a high IQ, but it doesn't stop there. Wisdom involves knowledge that's immensely practical, relational, insightful, and virtuous: it is a God-centered and God-drenched engagement of the world and personal relationships. Wisdom (Latin *sapientia*) is *the skill or craft of living—intellectually, morally, emotionally, spiritually, and creatively—in right relationship to God, human beings, and the world around us.*

True wisdom begins with "the fear of the LORD" (Ps. 111:10; cp. Prov. 1:7; 9:10; 15:33)—a humble *submission to God's revealed will and purposes for us* (Prov. 15:33; 23:4; cp. Gen. 20:11).[3] Wisdom—living sapientially—centers on being mindful of God, just as he is mindful of us (Ps. 8:4). Wisdom comes through first saying *Yes* to God, by placing our will into his hands, reorienting our lives under God's direction and rule (God's "kingdom").

Jesus the Nazarene is no mere prophet, the Scriptures shout, but is rather God's own wisdom authoritatively revealed and embodied (Mt. 11:16–19;

cp. Jn. 1:1–18 with Prov. 8:22–31).[4] He epitomizes wisdom in his parables, sayings, and beatitudes–or, when enemies try to stump him, in declarations such as, "Give to Caesar what is Caesar's and to God what is God's" (Mt. 22:21, NIV). He makes this startling claim: "All things have been handed over to Me by My Father; and no one knows the Son except the Father; nor does anyone know the Father except the Son, and anyone to whom the Son wills to reveal Him" (Mt. 11:27). No wonder Jesus proclaimed himself greater than Solomon the wise (Mt. 12:42). Paul confirms this: all the treasures of wisdom and knowledge are hidden in Christ (Col. 2:3).

Despite baffling questions, mysteries, and conundrums, we can still embark on the life-long quest for ever-deepening wisdom, using heart and mind for God's glory and praise. With all of our limitations, wisdom-seekers can't afford to be anti-intellectual, which would be a rejection of God's gift to us. As hymnwriter F. R. Havergal wrote, "Take my intellect and use / every power as thou shalt choose."[5]

Many professional philosophers have offered astute, creative insights for us to think about and live out. Tom Morris, who once taught philosophy, is now engaged in helping businesspersons and CEOs understand the benefits of studying philosophy. Books such as *If Aristotle Ran General Motors*, *True Success*, and even *Philosophy for Dummies* help people apply concepts and insights of great thinkers across the ages in their day-to-day lives and work, resulting in much personal benefit and enrichment. The *discipline* or *profession* of philosophy at institutions of higher learning can offer understanding and sage advice–how to raise children to be virtuous citizens, how to judge between competing scientific hypotheses, how to relate to people, how to run a company. Whether believers or not, we all can make strides in gaining wisdom through God's gracious general revelation to all.

Biblically speaking, though, the true philosopher–the lover of wisdom–will at heart be a God-seeker (Prov. 8:17), not merely a lover of abstract ideas and arguments. True wisdom can't be detached from loving and knowing God; it will be *incomplete* if it doesn't lead to "salvation through faith which is in Christ Jesus" (2 Tim. 4:15). Though an atheist's knowledge may be encyclopedic and believers may benefit from his knowledge, he is detached from his Creator and Redeemer. Plenty of brilliant thinkers are unwise precisely because they're God-resisters. NYU philosopher Thomas Nagel candidly admits: "I hope there is no God! I don't want there to be a God; I don't want a universe to be like that."[6] He acknowledges a "cosmic authority problem" that governs much of academia:[7] many scholars, whether consciously or unconsciously, suppress God's self-revelation. Many intelligent–but spiritually unwise–academics pursue a wisdom devoid of God, the wellspring of all created reality. The psalmist gratefully recognized: "I have more insight than all my teachers, for Your testimonies are my meditation" (Ps. 119:99). *Wisdom* doesn't equal *well-educated*.

The quest for wisdom isn't merely intellectual fact-gathering; it's also a *virtuous* and *spiritual* endeavor, requiring certain attitudes and character qualities. Rightly received, education and scholarship enrich our lives and deepen our appreciation for God and the world he created. But as with wealth, good looks, and "natural" abilities, scholarship and learning may also hinder people from seeking God, because they trust in these gifts rather than the Giver. Without a humble disposition and seeking heart—a willingness to do God's will (Jn. 7:17)—we'll miss out on the very thing we were designed for: knowing and loving God, living God-saturated and God-affected lives.

Danish philosopher Søren Kierkegaard described humans as two-sphered creatures, designed to live in two realms—the *earthly* and *heavenly.* Many, though, are preoccupied with this-worldly concerns, whether crass pleasure-seekers or culturally sophisticated high-brows. Either way, they ignore the relating triune God, the I-You relationship they were intended for. People will devote their entire lives to mountain-climbing, perfecting their tennis serve, or playing video games—without taking half an hour to consider life's meaning or their relationship to God. However intelligent such people may be, they aren't wise—philosophers—in the biblical sense of the word.

True philosophy, loving wisdom, must be Godward—or "religious"—to be complete. The Bible speaks only incidentally about "religion" (*threskeia*). It can refer to a (God-centered) *belief-system*: Paul had once lived as a strict Pharisee within his "religion" (Acts 26:5). Unlike the view of the "unbeliever," "religion" includes an orthodox belief in the true God (e.g., 1 Cor. 14:22–23). True "religion" at its heart means *loving God* and *loving others.* "Pure and undefiled religion [*threskeia*] in the sight of our God and Father," according to James, involves caring for the helpless, guarding one's tongue, and maintaining moral integrity (Jas. 1:27–28).

Although the worship and love of God are central to scriptural religion, the contemporary, technical definition of "religion" is more elusive. One philosopher suggests that a religion "proposes a diagnosis of a deep, crippling spiritual disease universal to non-divine sentience and offers a cure. A particular religion is true if its diagnosis is correct and its cure is efficacious."[8] Of course, for Jains, Confucians, and Buddhists, religion doesn't necessarily involve belief in a God/deity and Creator. So some define religion more functionally—as a set of beliefs, attitudes, and practices that are centered on a person's conception of ultimate reality; as such, "religion" could include, say, atheistic humanism.[9] This broad sense implies that *all* people are religious; that is, they have a worldview or belief system around which they orient their lives, whether consciously or not. A *worldview*—which reflects a heart orientation or commitment—serves as a filter or grid by which we interpret the world and human experience. It shapes how we live and direct our lives. This doesn't mean people can't change their worldviews, but we should remember that a worldview encompasses more than just the intellect. As an aside, the worldview of naturalism or atheism is technically "religious"–an interpretive grid as well as a heart commitment; we could therefore distinguish between this and "traditional religion"–Hindu, Muslim, Christian.

(Incidentally, philosophers tend to distinguish between the more general discipline of *philosophy of religion* and the narrower, more specific sub-discipline of *philosophical theology*; the latter offers a philosophical analysis of specific doctrines or practices within a particular religion–in our case, the Trinity, Incarnation, resurrection, or prayer.)

Along these lines, another reasonable suggestion is that religion is "a form of life that seems to those who inhabit it to be comprehensive, incapable of abandonment, and of central importance."[10] A *form of life*, which is a pattern of activity that appears to its practitioners to have boundaries and particular actions that are bound up with it, has three characteristics:

- *Comprehensive*: It takes into account, and is relevant to, everything–a framework into which all the particularities of life can be placed–from how one dresses to the significance of marriage to moral actions.
- *Incapable of abandonment*: This religious stance/form of life defines the religionist's identity. A native English speaker, say, though he could learn another language, doesn't really think of himself as one who could readily abandon his deeply embedded mother tongue.
- *Of central importance*: This form of life is no mere add-on or extra; it addresses issues of paramount importance: *What is real? What is to be valued? What is my purpose?*

So as we do *philosophy of religion*, we seek to approach a comprehensive, centrally important matter with prayerful thoughtfulness, inspired by devotion to God.

Doing Philosophy as Christians

Philosophy of religion has come to be appreciated in a dramatic new way in the past forty years, as William Wainwright notes:

> [T]he current situation is very different. Important philosophers are now prepared to defend arguments for God's existence. Many argue that traditional concepts of the divine are not only meaningful but are also superior to alternatives. In their opinion, classical theistic metaphysics is still viable.[11]

One key figure, Alvin Plantinga, has led this renaissance, bringing the Christian faith to the broader academic philosophical community–a movement that continues to snowball. Plantinga has given some sage advice to Christian philosophers: Christians should do philosophy with a greater sense of independence, not slavishly following the criteria or demands of secular or non-Christian philosophers, who often operate with different standards and assumptions.[12] Thinking clearly doesn't involve being squeezed into the mold of unbiblical assumptions adopted by non-Christian thinkers, who may deny God's existence, life's purpose and meaning, the afterlife, the appropriateness of mystery, the possibility of miracles, and a host of other fundamental Christian assumptions. Yes, the Christian faith is publicly accessible and open to public scrutiny; it's not as though God has spoken into our ear and no one else can get in on the discussion! While, say, even the doctrine of the Trinity is specially revealed, it too sheds helpful light on important questions—for all to examine. As the theologian Anselm affirmed in his *Proslogion*, ours is a "faith seeking understanding" (*fides quarens intellectum*): "I believe that I may understand [*credo ut intelligam*]."

No one approaches these deep, far-reaching topics as a neutral, detached observer. Spectators need not apply! After all, *God* is far more than the subject of an abstract armchair discussion. As we begin or continue our wisdom-journey with our assumptions, a critical question to ask is: *Which outlook or philosophy of life does the best job of dealing with the range of available evidence and human experience?* Or, *Is my perspective consistent with my life philosophy's assumptions (e.g., regarding human rights or personal responsibility), or am I borrowing capital from another worldview to keep mine going?* A person's assumptions may twist the evidence or ignore the truth—or they may align quite well with the relevant evidence, which I believe the Christian faith does. We can present our case for the existence and nature of the triune God, offering responses to a wide range of otherwise unanswerable questions.[13] C. S. Lewis put it this way: "I believe in Christianity as I believe that the Sun has risen, not only because I see it, but because by it I see everything else."[14]

Unfortunately, some Christians speak disparagingly about philosophy, as though it's always done in an anti-Christian manner. They may cite Paul's caution, "Knowledge makes arrogant, but love edifies" (1 Cor. 8:1), or his warning against "philosophy and empty deception" (Col. 2:8). They may claim to promote a Spirit-given knowledge that seems foolish to the "natural" person (1 Cor. 1–2). While such passages remind us that our thinking shouldn't be detached from God's self-revelation and his Spirit's workings, they hardly undermine the importance of defending our faith in the marketplace of ideas and of engaging in the discipline of philosophy as Christians. Consider the following:

First, God created the mind, and it is simply non-Christian to be anti-intellectual. Loving God with all our *mind* (Mt. 22:37) means not justifying sloppy thinking because we "live by faith." We've been made in the image of a supremely wise Being, and it's dishonoring to God to squander mental gifts. Remember how Stephen's opponents "were unable to cope with the wisdom and the Spirit with which he was speaking" (Acts 6:10).

Second, the Scriptures themselves speak of defending the Christian faith in the marketplace of ideas. Jesus' half-brother Jude urges his audience to "contend earnestly for the faith" entrusted to believers (v. 3). In 1 Corinthians 15, Paul puts *everything* on the line by saying that if Christ hasn't been raised, Christians are believing a lie and should basically pack up and head to

Cancun or the French Riviera: let's eat, drink, and be merry, for tomorrow we die (v. 32). But Paul gives reasons for having confidence that Christ's body was raised: he appeals to a list of eyewitnesses who saw Jesus alive after his death (including over 500 believers, most of whom were still alive), and Paul himself encountered Jesus in a life-altering vision (which was different from Jesus' bodily appearances to his disciples). Jesus repeatedly showed that his physical body was gloriously raised by breaking bread (Lk. 24:30, 35), serving fish to his disciples (Jn. 21:13), and encouraging his followers to handle his flesh-and-bones body (Lk. 24:39; Jn. 20:27; cp. 1 Jn. 1:1). He didn't say, "Just believe," but he graciously gave evidence of this transformed physicality.

Throughout Acts, Luke uses words such as *reason, (trying to) persuade, eyewitness, witness, defense.* Paul is regularly *reasoning* with non-Christians (Acts 17:2, 17; 18:4, 19; 19:8, 9), seeking to *persuade* them (18:4; 19:8; 26:28; 28:23). The proconsul Sergius Paulus, "a man of intelligence" (Acts 13:7), seeing Elymas struck blind by Paul, "believed when he saw what had happened, being amazed at the teaching of the Lord" (13:12). At Athens (Acts 17), Paul is even portrayed as a Socrates-like philosopher: both of them "dialogue/discuss" in the *agora* (marketplace); both are said to proclaim "new" ideas and are accused of endorsing "foreign divinities."[15]

Intelligence doesn't oppose faith or trust in God. Christians must be prepared to give a *defense* of their faith, providing *reason* for the hope within (1 Pet. 3:15). This reasoned defense should spring from setting Christ apart as Lord in our hearts, and it should be done with gentleness and respect toward non-Christians. Defending our faith isn't operating by "works" rather than grace; it's a *prayerful* engagement that depends on God's Spirit, who can use reasons and arguments—as well as gospel presentations and personal testimonies of changed lives. Without the Spirit's working, no lives are changed and no minds persuaded.

Third, we'll likely be more bold and effective representatives of Christ if we're able to respond winsomely to objections and clarify misrepresentations of the Christian faith. Christians may be reluctant to talk about their faith because they're afraid to be questioned about it; however, they should instead welcome such inquiries and ask their non-Christian friends why *they* believe what they do. Sure, some non-Christians hide behind smokescreens and rationalizations. They might throw out some pretty lame, unimaginative slogans. Others, though, might be open to good reasons that God can use. If we're reasonably prepared to address important questions non-Christians typically ask, we'll likely communicate the good news of the gospel more confidently and effectively. While an effective Christian witness involves an array of factors—a listening ear, a gracious spirit, personal integrity, a loving Christian community—we should still be prepared to offer reasons for why people should prefer the person of Jesus over Muhammad's or Buddha's teachings. Good reasons for believing the gospel are part of its attractiveness.

Isn't reason limited? Aren't we fallen creatures? Yes and of course. But we are still endowed by God with the capacity to appreciate good reasons for belief. If Paul reasoned and sought to persuade others in the first century, why think that today God can't use good reasons for belief? It makes sense that God, in his multifaceted grace, can use good reasons—as well as loving relationships, dramatic beauty, a deep sense of shame or hopelessness—to awaken people to his spectacular reality.

Furthermore, where would the present church be without historic defenders of the faith—from the apostle Paul, Justin Martyr, Irenaeus, and Augustine, to G. K. Chesterton, C. S. Lewis, and Francis Schaeffer? God has blessed his church not simply with remarkable examples of courage, love, and self-sacrifice—like William Wilberforce, Dietrich Bonhoeffer, or Mother Teresa—but also with remarkably gifted minds that have used their intellect for God's glory to clarify, defend, and articulate the faith.

Fourth, we should consider how we are preparing the next generation of believers to defend and articulate their faith when it's challenged. Rather than helping their children think through their faith, too many Christian parents tell them, "Don't ask questions. Just believe," leaving them ill-equipped to give reasons for the Christian hope. In fact, 55 percent of American students who've grow up in Christian homes will end up rejecting their faith by the time they're done with college.[16] I've spoken with many dismayed Christian parents who've told me that their children have given up on the Christian faith at university. I've heard of scornful professors who toss Bibles out of classroom windows or make their freshmen students write a paper in defense of God's non-existence—no questions asked. How encouraging, then, is the news that the Christian faith has been believed and defended by rigorous minds to God's glory, and that heartening answers are available for serious questioners!

Fifth, engaging false ideas and misunderstandings of the Christian faith can help remove barriers that prevent people from taking the gospel seriously. In 1913, Princeton Seminary president J. Gresham Machen pointed out that false ideas are the greatest obstacle to the Christian faith. Our fervent preaching may bring in a straggler here and there, while our culture is controlled by ideas—consider *The Da Vinci Code*—that "prevent Christianity from being regarded as anything more than a harmless delusion."[17] Our failure to respond to caricatures of the gospel creates further barriers; this means non-Christians are even less likely to consider the Christian faith a serious intellectual option.

Doing philosophy of religion as Christians will mean keeping the great commandment—loving God supremely and loving our neighbors as ourselves. Everything hangs on this. If our philosophizing about God fills us with pride and self-sufficiency so that we lose touch with God and have no patience and grace toward others, then we are no longer lovers of wisdom.

1

Kings and Priests

"[Y]ou shall be to Me a kingdom of priests." (Ex. 19:6)

"You have made them to be a kingdom and priests to our God; and they will reign upon the earth." (Rev. 5:10)

Who are we? How are we to live? What is our purpose? Theories abound regarding human nature–Marxist, Darwinist, existentialist, Buddhist, postmodern. They may declare that humans are simply the product of economic, genetic, or cultural forces. Others question whether we can even speak of human identity; perhaps there's no enduring person–no "I"–but just a bundle of experiences or a stream of consciousness.

Ancient Near East kings were believed to be unique representations–"in the image"–of the gods. Scripture, however, affirms *all* humans as made in "the image of God" (Gen. 1:26–27; Gen. 9:3; Jas. 3:9)–his earthly representatives. They are first placed in the primeval garden-temple, where heaven and earth–God and humans–would meet. God's image-bearers have been made "a little lower than God [*elohim*]" (Ps. 8:5) and have been called to a dual vocation–as kings and priests:

(a) *Kings to rule with God:* God has called his image-bearers to be co-regents with him, to "rule over" creation (Gen. 1:26–28; cp. Ps. 8) as caretaking stewards–which was originally done by naming animals and working in the garden. Part of this calling was to be fruitful and multiply (Gen. 1:29; cp. 9:1)[1] and to put the finishing touches on God's good creation. In *working together with* God (cp. Hag. 2:4–5; 1 Cor. 3:4–9; 15:10; Phil. 2:12–13; Col. 1:29), humans are to extend the knowledge and glory of God to the ends of the earth.

(b) *Priests to worship and love God:* Humans were created to participate in the love of the triune God and the joy of his presence–to walk with

God and he with them (Gen. 3:8; cp. Enoch and Noah in 5:22, 24; 6:8–10).[2] The Hebrew verbs in Genesis 2:15–*work/serve* (*'abad*) and *guard* (*shamar*)–are probably best translated *worship* and *obey*,[3] a eucharistic and sacramental task. We're not simply "rational animals" or "thinking man" (*homo sapiens*). From the start, God intended for us to love and worship him (*homo adorans*).

From the beginning, we have a *democratization* of the elite role of priest and king: *all* human beings were intended to rule God's creation as priests and kings.[4]

God's Image Bearers on Earth: "Kings and Priests"

Priestly Role	Kingly Role
Worshiping, communing, "walking," and meeting with God as priests in the temple-garden at the center of God's creation.	Ruling the earth with God, naming animals, being fruitful and multiplying, and extending God's glory.

Both these roles are personal and relational. We're to love, think, relate, be creative, choose, and live wisely for the glory and praise of God. Jesus summarized our whole duty as loving God and loving others. We humans have been granted the privilege of participating in a dialogue and working together with the relating, triune God, who has made us for himself. As God speaks and acts on the stage of history, he involves us humans in this theodramatic story.

Along with Eve, God's first image-bearer, Adam–Luke 3:38 calls him the "son of God"–fails to live up to the priest-kingly calling. Instead of wisely reigning and evicting the subtle serpent, Adam and Eve allow it to "rule over" them.[5] Rather than trusting God's good intentions for them, they abuse their God-given freedom by taking the forbidden fruit. Believing themselves wiser than God, they became fools (cp. Rom. 1:22), damaging the very centerpiece of God's created order. Sin enters the stage, and humans become vulnerable to death–both physical and spiritual–danger; disease; and demonic powers. Humans become alienated from God, from each other, and from creation. They even become alienated within themselves, suffering from a dissonance of soul with twisted reasoning, will, imagination, emotions, and spiritual orientation.

Curse and death aren't the last word, though. God's plans from before the earth's foundations (1 Pet. 1:20) move forward toward a re-creation and a reestablishing of humans to their proper vocation as priest-kings. The man and woman's offspring will triumph over the fall and the powers of evil (Gen. 3:15). God chooses Abraham and his descendants (the particular), through whom "all the families of the earth" (the universal) will be blessed (Gen. 12:3). Scripture's earliest narratives and themes (*protology*) shape the patterns of God's ongoing work until they reach their climax (*eschatology*).

In the exodus, God delivers his people from Egypt (Ex. 14–15), portrayed as re-creation: God displays power over the "sea" (*yam*), dividing the waters (14:21) as he did at creation. God forms a people, the nation of Israel, God's new "son" (4:11; cp. Hos. 11:1). Like a new Adam, they are to be priest-kings–"you shall be to Me a kingdom of priests" (Ex. 19:4–6)–and a "light to the nations" (Isa. 42:6; cp. 49:6; 51:4) so that God's glory fills the earth. They are to be his people, to worship him and enjoy his presence as he "walks among [them]" (Lev. 26:11–12; cp. Ex. 29:45–6; Ezek. 37:27; Zech. 2:10–11). Biblical scholar N. T. Wright puts it this way: "Abraham's children are God's true humanity, and their homeland is the new Eden."[6]

National Israel, however, fails to live up to its calling. God, the wounded Lover, is "hurt by their adulterous hearts" (Ezek. 6:9). Despite God's repeated warnings and attempts to turn their hearts back (2 Chr. 36:15–16), they exasperate God: "What more was there to do for my vineyard [Israel] that I have not done in it?" (Isa. 5:4). So God sends his people into exile–the curse for disobedience to the covenant (Lev. 26; Deut. 28).

Again, God promises that curse and exile aren't the last word (Deut. 30:1–10). Many Old Testament scriptures anticipate (a) *a new exodus/a return from being in exile* and (b) *a new creation* (esp. Isa. 40–55). For example, Jeremiah 23:4 promises: "Then I will gather the remnant of my flock out of all the countries where I have driven them, and I will bring them back to their fold, and they shall be fruitful and multiply"–a new creation and new exodus. God's purposes for us are *that we might fully live out the divine image–as co-regents with God and as worshiping priests in his presence.* Jesus of Nazareth, God incarnate, lives out *Adam's* and *Israel's* story. He ushers in "a new creation" (2 Cor. 5:17) and gathers from the ends of the earth a new covenant people in a new exodus, delivering us from bondage to sin and Satan. Thus, in Rev. 15:3–4, the Song of Moses sung after the exodus (Ex. 15) is transposed into the Song of the Lamb.

Jesus is the *new–the second* and *last–Adam* who didn't fail (Lk. 3:38; Rom. 5:14–21; 1 Cor. 15:45–49) and the *new Israel–God's true son* that national Israel failed to be (Mt. 2:15; 3:17), leading a new exodus out of Egypt (Mt. 2:15; cp. Hos. 11:1), in which we outwardly participate in the waters of baptism (1 Cor. 10:1–4). Jesus' own baptism in the Jordan is a reenactment of the exodus:[7]

Creation	Covenant
As the new Adam, Christ is the head of a new humanity.	As the true Israel, Christ (the beloved "Son of God") is head of a renewed covenant (chosen) people.
Christ reverses the curse and brings about a restored creation.	Christ (as portrayed at his baptism) leads a new people out of bondage in a New Exodus.

Christ, the anticipated ruler-king (Gen. 49:8–12; Num. 24:17–19; Isa. 9:6) and priestly mediator (Zech. 6:12–13; Mal. 3:1–4), restores our fortunes as priest-kings. In his death and resurrection, he takes on himself Israel's—and by extension—humanity's exile and alienation (Isa. 49:6; 52:13–53:12), which comes from disobedience (Lev. 26; Deut. 28; Gal. 3:13). As our champion (Heb. 2:10; 12:2), Jesus' conquest becomes ours (Rev. 2:26–27; 3:21). As a result, we participate in the very life of the triune God, as "partakers of the divine nature" (2 Pet. 1:4) and sharers in God's "eternal life" (Jn. 17:3). The capacity to live out the divine image is restored through the One who is God's true image (2 Cor. 3:18; 4:4; Col. 1:15), the archetypal person.

Christ has made us—believing Jews and Gentiles alike—to be *kings* and *priests* to our God: "a chosen race" and a "royal" and "holy priesthood" (1 Pet. 2:9), "a kingdom and priests to our God" who will "reign on the earth" (Rev. 5:9–10; cp. Rev. 1:5–6; 20:4–6). Though partly realized now through *the giving of God's Spirit* (our identifying mark as God's people) and *the promise of resurrection in Christ* (a foretaste of the new creation to come), we await a new heavens and new earth (Rev. 22:1–5), where God will forever and perfectly dwell in the midst of his people: "Behold, the tabernacle of God is among men, and He shall dwell among them, and they shall be His people, and God Himself shall be among them" (Rev. 21:3). As in Eden, yet even more deeply, heaven and earth are united.

Addressing philosophy of religion questions without consideration of this sweeping picture of the triune God and his theodramatic workings through creation, fall, redemption, and re-creation will necessarily be deficient. The triune God is an engaging God of promise, interaction, and activity: he enters into this sin-soaked world, working through particular human beings like the patriarchs, the nation of Israel, and especially the incarnate Wisdom, Jesus of Nazareth, to bless all humankind. Our God is no generic Unmoved Mover or Ground of all being. To think more penetratingly and holistically about the philosophy of religion, we must involve ourselves in the biblical narrative. Without it, we are left with huge gaps, inadequate answers, and insoluble problems. John Calvin wisely wrote that to understand who *humans* are, we must first understand who *God* is. The wisdom of God in Christ offers us a far more plausible and adequate picture than the alternatives. This Wisdom incarnate has come into our midst, getting his feet dusty, his face sweaty, and his hands bloodied. He joins us in our suffering, faces and overcomes injustice and evil in his resurrection, and gives us hope and joy as we journey toward the fulfillment of God's creation and kingdom purposes.

2

The Need for God

Psychological Crutch or Argument from Desire?

As the deer pants for the water brooks,
So my soul pants for You, O God.
My soul thirsts for God, for the living God. (Ps. 42:1–2)

The Crutch Argument

We're familiar with the Bible's doubters—"Doubting Thomas," Job, and the cynical Preacher of Ecclesiastes. The lesser-known Asaph wonders why the wicked prosper and if his own efforts to do the right thing are pointless. In a moment of illumination, Asaph grasps the bigger picture. He confesses to God:

Whom have I in heaven but You?
And besides You, I desire nothing on earth.
My flesh and my heart may fail,
But God is the strength of my heart and my portion forever.
(Ps. 73:25–26)

God alone, Asaph realized, was the ultimate source of his well-being. His contentment didn't depend on the obliteration of God's enemies or his circumstantial success.

Critics consider such Asaphian thinking to be wish fulfillment. Humans who can't handle life's heat get out of its kitchen—and proceed to construct church buildings and chapels! Humans just make God in *their* image—not the other way around. The study of *God* (theology) turns out to be the study of *humanity* (anthropology).

Ludwig Feuerbach (1804-1872) wrote in his *Essence of Christianity,* "Religion is the dream of the human mind."[1] Austrian psychiatrist Sigmund Freud devoured Feuerbach's book and wrote another in its image—*Future of an Illusion.* Freud viewed religion as weak-minded and pathetic: "Religious ideas have arisen from the same need as have all other achievements of civilization: from the necessity of defending oneself against the crushing superior force of nature."[2] Religious beliefs are thus "illusions, fulfillments of the oldest, strongest and most urgent wishes of mankind….[T]he benevolent rule of a divine Providence allays our fears of the dangers of life."[3] Another Feuerbach fan, Karl Marx, called religion "the opiate of the people": belief in God is merely a painkiller to help people cope with difficult economic or material circumstances. In our day, philosopher Peter Railton speaks of the gods "to whom we have given life."[4] Zoologist Richard Dawkins finds a biological explanation for belief in God: it's the result of defective genes.[5]

This issue raises the realist/anti-realist question: Does "God" exist only because there are human minds that have "thought him up" (anti-realist), or does God exist as a mind-independent reality (realist)? That is, does the personal Creator of heaven and earth exist even if no human minds exist to think about the question? Of course, most religious adherents approach their own religion realistically: they assume that if the tenets of their faith are right, those disagreeing would be in error at those points. Throughout the book, we'll see that the Christian faith is true—and that public reasons can be given for it—whether people believe or not.

How then do we respond to those who try to psychologize our faith?

Responding to Religious Psychoanalysts

The discussion is illuminated when we ask: What if these psychologizers have gotten it backward? What if Asaph's insight was right—that religious devotion is an appropriate response to a God who is really there? What if the joke is really on Feuerbach and company?[6] Scripture indicates that we've been *created* with a longing for God because we've been *made for* God: "He has also set eternity in [the human] heart" (Eccl. 3:11). John Calvin called this the *sensus divinitatis* within every human soul; we were designed to believe in God, however sin's influence may obscure or distort this.[7] The quest for the transcendent need not be strictly "religious"; there can be "secular counterparts"—Nietzsche's Superman (*Übermensch*), Carl Sagan's "Cosmos," or scientists' and Romantics' "Nature" as the Ultimate.

What's more, psychologizers—or biologizers—of belief in God are just using a bad argument, attacking *the person* (*ad hominem*), not the argument itself. This argument commits the *genetic fallacy*—trying to prove or disprove a belief based on where it came from. That's like rejecting 2+2=4 based on a bad experience with a first-grade teacher. If I come to believe (or disbelieve) in God for certain motivations, how does the *origin* of my belief (or lack of it) show that God *actually* exists (or not)? The *motivation* for belief is a separate issue from the *truth* of that belief. Now Christianity lives or dies depending on whether or not Jesus died and lived: "If Christ has not been raised, your faith is worthless" (1 Cor. 15:17)—no matter how much comfort belief in Jesus might bring. As theological realists, we should distinguish between the *psychology* of belief and the *rationality* of belief. Whatever one's motivations, however interesting, reasons for belief in God are logically independent of them.

Ironically, the crutch-claim isn't very "scientific." Freud himself had no clinical evidence to support his claims, had little experience with genuine religious believers, and admitted that this was his own personal view.[8]

And *what's wrong* with comfort and solace? A belief that inspires courage and hope beyond the grave isn't necessarily false—not by a long shot. Human relationships, say, can and should bring comfort; a bowl of stew in a warm home on a cold wintry night does, too—both perfectly reasonable and healthy comforts. Why prefer a pessimistic, cynical, and depressing perspective over a more hopeful one?

What's more, many believers—hardly escapists—have faced incredible hardships, torture, and death precisely *because of* their faith. Though some have experienced miraculous deliverances, others have experienced mockery, ill-treatment, and ostracism (Heb. 11:32–40; cp. 2 Cor. 11:23–28). For many saints, it would have been much easier to abandon the narrow, less-traveled road of faith for the broad one of cultural conformity (Mt. 7:13–14).

The deeply religious impulse within human beings *may actually reflect that we've been made for relationship with God.* True, just because people *long* for the transcendent doesn't *guarantee* it exists. However, human longing for God may point to the reality of a relational divine Being. Perhaps we need God after all. Far from disproving God's existence, the psychoanalytic perspective may suggest a divine solution to our deepest yearnings. Acknowledging this need for "something more" may be the first step toward spiritual health.

If the skeptic persists in his fallacious argument, he should know we could turn it on its head. Just as Paul stooped to use the Corinthians' own fallacious assumptions against them, we could "speak as if insane" (2 Cor. 11:23; cp. 1 Cor. 4:10), applying the same argument to many hard-nosed atheists and skeptics of the past. David Hume, Baron D'Holbach, Ludwig Feuerbach, Karl Marx, Voltaire, Friedrich Nietzsche, Sigmund Freud, Albert Camus, Bertrand Russell, Jean-Paul Sartre, Madeline Murray O'Hair actually had negative or nonexistent relationships with father-figures in their lives.[9] What if *they* had subconsciously blamed God because of this significant absence in their lives? So why should *believers* be psychoanalyzed and not the hard-driving skeptic?

Indeed, it's not unlikely that one's background may make it difficult to trust in God when significant others become *unworthy of trust* or *are no longer present.* The secure love of Christian community can play a role to help restore that ability to trust in God. Despite a person's past, God's grace isn't far from any one of us. We're properly functioning when we worship and love God, finding our ultimate satisfaction and comfort in him alone.

These considerations can be worked into an *argument from desire*–one C. S. Lewis made famous. He speaks of "a desire for something that has never actually happened."[10] Humans have all kinds of desires–for sexual satisfaction, athletic success, exotic vacations, gourmet meals. But however enjoyable these experiences are, we aren't fully satisfied. We yearn for something *more*–something *beyond.* Lewis writes of seeking fulfillment in books and music:

> The books or the music in which we thought the beauty was located will betray us if we trust in them; it was not *in* them, it only came *through* them, and what came through them was longing. These things–the beauty, the memory of our own past–are good images of what we really desire; but if they are mistaken for the thing itself they turn into dumb idols, breaking the hearts of their worshippers.[11]

Our earthly enjoyments–God's common grace to all humans–aren't ends in themselves. Our unfulfilled desires can point us to something no earthly thing can satisfy.

Arctic terns annually travel 11,000 miles from the Arctic to the Antarctic regions and back again–often to the very same nests. Monarch butterflies follow their "homing devices," migrating each year to their nesting grounds in California or Mexico. Whether we realize it or not, we humans have a homing device for God. Though people may not care about God but instead fill their lives with secular substitutes, this doesn't mean that God's presence isn't their proper home, that his family isn't their true family. God in Christ offers us living water–the presence of the relating triune God in our lives, who can quench the thirst in our innermost being (Jn. 4:13–14; 7:37–39).

PART I

GOD

Who is like the LORD our God? (Ps. 113:5)

3

God Triune

the same Spirit…the same Lord…the same God. (1 Cor. 12:4–6)

Who exactly *is* God? In a post-September 11 world, we commonly hear the slogan, "Christians and Muslims worship the same God." Yes, Arab Christians used the term *Allah* for the triune God long before the time of Muhammad–and they still do! However, these two "Abrahamic faiths" diverge sharply: orthodox Christians affirm God's tri-unity (Trinity) as central while Muslims consider this heretical and blasphemous–*shirk*, ascribing partners to God.

Popular Western culture tends to assume "God" refers to a *supreme person.* Not a few Christian philosophers–I won't mention any names–have referred to God as "a person." This is misleading. There are *three persons*–Father, Son, and Spirit–who fully share in the *one true God's* identity. From eternity there has existed not one solitary *person*, but a God-in-relation–three divine persons fully loving and enjoying each other. Personal relationships didn't not come into existence when God created finite personal beings–angels and humans. Relationship has *always* existed in this triune divine family.

Christians shouldn't think of God apart from his self-revelation as triune. Sadly, many Christians give the impression that they are practical Unitarians. They often assume God is *a person*; confuse the persons of the Trinity–as though Jesus and the Father are interchangeable; or think that the Holy Spirit is an impersonal "It"–like a force or influence. Instead, a proper understanding of God as triune enriches our thinking about God and how we should live in the world and can also help overcome some theological caricatures about God that have built up over the centuries–that God is abstract and nonrelational or "wholly Other" and remote. This tri-personal God, though "over all" (*transcendent*), is also "in all" (*immanent*) and "not far from each one of us" (Acts 17:27, 28).

The triune God existed without the universe and without any need for it. Father, Son, and Spirit—the divine Family—have existed from eternity in their free, mutual self-giving and self-receiving love. Relationship or communion is intrinsic to this "household" (or economy) of divine persons who, though distinct from one another, are inseparably united in other-oriented love. This divine inter- (and inner-) connection of mutuality, openness, and reciprocity has no individualistic competition among the family members, but only joy, self-giving love, and transparency. Rather than being some isolated self or solitary ego, God is supremely relational in his self-giving, other-oriented nature. Within God is intimate *union* as well as *distinction*—an unbreakable communion of persons. The persons of the Godhead can be *distinguished*, but not *separated*. God is both *community* and *unity*.[1]

Although some analogies of the Trinity can be problematic (e.g., water's three states), certain analogies may prove useful and illuminating. Consider the mythological three-headed dog Cerberus that guards Hades' gates. Though a single organism (substance)—one dog (not three dogs)—he has three distinct centers of awareness, each with the same canine nature. Likewise, God is one immaterial soul (substance) with three distinct centers of consciousness, rationality, and will (persons) who are deeply interconnected.[2]

Because a relational God exists and chooses to create humans in his image, relationality is central to *our* identity as humans. No wonder the Ten Commandments divide into two tables—our relationship to God and to fellow human beings. Jesus himself summarizes our two-fold duty: "love the Lord your God" and "love your neighbor" (Mk. 12:28–31). We have been made for communion with God first and foremost, but how we regard fellow human beings reflects our spiritual condition (1 Jn. 4:20). We recognize what love is by the model of the self-giving God in Christ (1 Jn. 3:16).

Christians have long pondered the mystery of the Trinity, and we're not here trying to demystify the God whose nature and purposes can't be reduced to tidy formulas or manageable boxes. We should celebrate the unfathomable God, who's under no obligation to human demands to clarify everything about himself (Deut. 29:29). And why think our puny minds could grasp these "secret things" anyway?

Paul declared in his wonderment: "great is the mystery of godliness" (1 Tim. 3:16). "The great things of the gospel" (Jonathan Edwards' phrase) *are* astonishing, but Paul doesn't suggest divine *mystery* means *contradiction*. This applies to the divine Trinity as well. What then *do* the Scriptures mean when they tell us that God is both *three* and *one*? If Father, Son, and Spirit are divine persons, aren't there three Gods rather than one? Along with classical New England Unitarians—who stressed the fatherhood of God, the brotherhood of man, and the neighborhood of Boston (!)–today's Jehovah's Witnesses have suggested that many Christians just can't count: 1+1+1 equals 3!

Without trying to reduce God to human formulas and grids, how can we, in faithful humility, better grasp this central Christian doctrine of the Trinity? Perhaps the following considerations can assist us.

First, Scripture reveals both a oneness to God and a threeness. Jesus' first followers were Jews–orthodox monotheists: they were firmly committed to God's unique *oneness*, in contrast to the polytheism of the surrounding nations. Twice daily religious Jews would recite the *Shema* ("Hear, O Israel"), declaring God's *oneness*: "The LORD is our God. The LORD is one" (Deut. 6:4; cp. Mk. 12:29). An early Christian creed (53 C.E.) affirms Jesus' sharing in the divine identity as the "one Lord" (1 Cor. 8:4–7), while steadfastly declaring that "there is no God but one." Even the demons hold to an orthodox monotheistic belief (Jas. 2:19).

God's *threeness* is also apparent. In the "Great Commission" (Mt. 28:18–20), Jesus tells his disciples to go and make disciples of all nations, "baptizing them in the *name* [not *names*] of the Father, and of the Son, and of the Holy Spirit." At Jesus' baptism–a reenactment of the exodus–Father and Spirit are also present (Mt. 3:16–17). Paul's benediction expresses God's threeness: "May the grace of the *Lord Jesus Christ*, and the love of *God*, and the fellowship of the *Holy Spirit* be with you all" (2 Cor. 13:14; cp. 1 Cor. 12:4–6). So while God is one, three self-distinctions exist within the Godhead.

Second, God is one in essence or nature, but three in person. Three and one aren't in contradiction here; to be in conflict, *the same category or relationship* must be involved. But *threeness* pertains to persons; *oneness* pertains to God's very nature or essence. There isn't one divine nature *and* three divine natures; there aren't three persons *and* one person in the Godhead.

Now, a *nature* is *what makes a thing (or person) what it is.* God has certain characteristics that make him what he is. He can't *not* exist and is all-good, for example. And just as the earth's billions of humans possess a common nature that sets them apart from angels and aardvarks, the triune persons are equally and fully God, sharing in the same nature–though at a much-deeper, more-unified level than that of humans. Crucial to overcoming the contradiction charge in the doctrine of the Trinity is distinguishing between the only one divine *nature* and the three *persons* who possess it. There aren't three Gods, but one.

When Jehovah's Witnesses or Muslims ask Christians, "If Jesus was divine, to whom did he cry, 'My God, my God, why have you forsaken me?'" (Mt. 27:46), these questioners assume that if Jesus is God, then there can't be any other persons who possess the divine nature. We can reject this without inconsistency and even respond, "If the *Father* is God, to whom is he speaking when he says *to the Son,* 'Your throne, O God, is forever,' or, 'You, Lord,…laid the foundation of the earth'" [Heb. 1:8, 10]?"

Third, to distinguish between person and nature, we must keep in mind two ways to use "is"–identity vs. predication. Mark Twain is the pen name for Samuel Langhorne Clemens, the author of *The Adventures of Tom Sawyer* and a twenty-six-cigars-a-day smoker. There isn't a characteristic that Twain has that Clemens doesn't have. In other words, when we say, "Samuel Langhorne Clemens is Mark Twain," we can just as easily reverse the names: "Mark Twain is Samuel Langhorne Clemens." The "is" in each of those statements indicates identity: Mark Twain = Samuel Langhorne Clemens (and vice versa). The names, which refer to the same person, are interchangeable and thus identical.

When it comes to the Trinity, to say "Jesus is God" *isn't* identical to "God is Jesus." *Unlike* the Mark Twain example, "Jesus" *doesn't exhaust* what it means to speak of "God." *Jesus* and *God* are *not identical.* According to the Bible, Father and Spirit are called divine–just as Jesus is.[3] In the statement "Jesus is God," we use *is* to *describe* or *predicate*–not identify or equate: Jesus is God in that he shares in the nature that only two other persons share; so there isn't just one person who can properly be called God.

Again, *threeness pertains to persons, and oneness pertains to nature or essence.* There is only *one* divine *nature,* but there are three *persons* who share in it. For God to be God, he must possess certain qualities or properties–being all-knowing, all-powerful, and all-good. Only Father, Son, and Spirit participate in this divine nature and can thus be called "God." Each of these *three persons* is also a center of consciousness, responsibility, and activity and is *distinct* from the others; for example, Jesus *isn't* the Father; the Father *isn't* the Spirit. So there's simply no logical contradiction when Christians say, "Three *persons,* one *divine nature.*"

Fourth, the triune persons are deeply interrelated or mutually indwell one another, sharing a necessary, unbreakable oneness. We earlier noted that humans possess a common nature. You and I have the same nature as Plato and Socrates. This nature makes us what we are–human. When it comes to God, we need further clarification. Though I share the same human nature with my students, they are separate and distinct from me; it's possible for me to exist without them–or vice versa. The members of the Trinity, however, are inseparably related. One can't exist without the other two. A triangle, say, can't exist if we take away one of its angles; by definition, a triangle is tri-angular. Likewise, the Christian God by definition is triune. Unlike Unitarians, we can't have just the Father without Son or Spirit. The triune persons are necessarily and permanently interrelated.

Greek theologians used the term *perichoresis* (in Latin, *circumincessio*) to describe the Trinity's necessary interrelationships. Jesus spoke of being "in" the Father and the Father "in" him to describe their unique relationship (cp. Jn. 10:30, 38; 17:21). There's a "mutual abiding" in the Godhead unlike human relationships, however close they may be. The relationship of Father, Son, and Spirit is not some miscellaneous collection of distinct persons who just happen to share some generic divine essence ("God-ness") so that they can be classed together.[4] Rather, they *mutually, inseparably share* in the life of one another in a remarkable way—a life without isolation, insulation, secrecy, or fear. They enjoy a penetrating, transparent, mutual knowledge of the other as other, as co-other, and as loved other.[5] So while the divine persons each fully possess the same nature (each one can rightly be called "God"), more fundamental is their sharing a common, mutually indwelling unbreakable life together.

Consider the analogy of *the mutual interaction of the soul and the body.* The Scriptures speak of a *deep unity* between body and soul: the body interacts continually and deeply with the soul—and the soul with the body. If I feel nervous in my soul, my stomach starts churning. If I cut off my arm, my soul must make certain adjustments in light of this loss. So there's a kind of mutual indwelling or interdependence in this body-soul relationship. The soul may temporarily separate from the body at death—the believer's absence from the body means being at home with the Lord (2 Cor. 5:6–9). But there's normally a deep, interactive unity between them—they act as one.

Fifth, because the members of the Trinity share the same essence and mutually indwell one another, they also act as one and not in isolation from one another. All that the three divine persons do, they do as one in concert with one another. Whether creating, revealing, or redeeming, the three persons of the Trinity necessarily act as one. For example, when God creates, Father, Son, and Spirit are involved (e.g., Gen. 1:1–2; Jn. 1:3). Or when Jesus is raised from the dead, he is said to be raised by the Father (Gal. 1:1; cp. Acts 2:24, 32) and the Spirit (Rom. 1:4), but Jesus declares that he has authority not only to lay down his life but to take it up again (Jn. 10:18; cp. 2:19: "I will raise it up"). The persons of the Trinity also indwell believers (Jn. 14:16, 18, 23; Rom. 8:9). Even though each person has a distinct center of awareness or consciousness and a distinct will, only one harmonious will is expressed in divine action. Rather than acting as three independent persons (as with Greek and Roman gods), each member of the Godhead is equally present in every divine action.[6]

In the very depth of his being, God is *relational.* God is relating within himself, and he is relational towards us. This God is *for us.* He has created us to love him and to *cling* to him (Deut. 10:20; 13:4)—like a husband and wife must cling to each other (Gen. 2:24). When God came to this planet, he sat at table with the marginalized and outcasts of society, showing God's deep interest in them. When the Spirit brings us into God's family, he pours God's love into our hearts (Rom. 5:5), giving us the confidence that we're God's adopted children (Rom. 8:15; Gal. 4:5).

So these three divine persons are one in at least four important ways: (1) they share in the same divine nature; (2) they mutually indwell one another, being bound together in relationship; (3) they necessarily act in perfect harmony; (4) only one harmonious will is expressed in their actions. As we look at the story of Scripture, we can gather that, first, only one God exists and, second, three persons can legitimately be called "God." The Holy Trinity is indeed a mystery, but not an incoherent one.

The doctrine of the Trinity isn't just biblical and coherent. Its incredible richness can direct us to live sapientially—wisely—not only within a loving, relating Christian community, but also within society as public citizens, and within a pluralistic global village as witnesses to the great things of the gospel.

In the *public square* of Western democracies, people tend to view God as a singular, unitary person who is a rule-setting monarch endowed with sheer power to impose his arbitrary standards on humans. Obviously, many distrust and resist the idea of a God who only commands, calls for obedience, and judges the resistant. A doctrine of the Trinity, however, can enrich this barren ethical arrangement. What if people viewed God as triune, relating, self-giving, and other-centered by nature? What if God's rule includes not coercion or bullying but a desire for friendship with humans? What if God reveals and commands so that humans may freely "choose life" (Deut. 30:19) and experience it "abundantly" (Jn. 10:10)? And what if rather than portraying a unilateral, top-down arrangement, we can present a relational God who wants none to perish, but rather to experience the holy warmth of his company (2 Pet. 3:9). So if people continue to resist God's wooings (Acts 7:51), they will not only damage themselves, but they have the capacity to separate themselves from God, who reluctantly allows them to go their own way forever. In the public square, Christians should proclaim a relating God who is the foundation for ethics and personal responsibility, for human dignity and rights, for reason and truth, and for tolerance and cooperation.

Trinitarian doctrine can give the Christian valuable insights in *dialogue with other religions.* Today's "unknown God" (cp. Acts 17:22–23) is "something out there" that's unknown and unknowable; yes, "It" may be the cause of the universe's existence and remarkable arrangement, but that's all. But surely we can go further. Although Eastern or New Age philosophies often espouse an abstract, impersonal view of the Ultimate Reality, why think an *impersonal* entity or force offers a secure basis for the *personal* virtues—love, humility, kindness, compassion—elevated within such views? How can "It" serve as a foundation for human rights and personal dignity? In the monistic all-is-one philosophies of the East, there are no real I-You relationships, no distinctions between the compassionate and the pitied, between good and evil. All differences are illusory (*maya*). And why think this impersonal "God" is responsible for creating and sustaining the world we experience? It can't create anything that's not-God or act on anything since there's nothing to act on.[7] Even if Eastern religions stress *duties* or *societal roles* rather than *rights*, their emphasis on not harming others but respecting them still takes human worth and dignity for granted–an assumption that an impersonal metaphysic can't easily accommodate.

We naturally give priority to persons over impersonal objects in our everyday lives: "The most important things in life aren't things." Why then favor some Eastern ideal of "nothingness" (*sunyata*) or pure consciousness (Brahman) that's beyond personality or beyond good and evil? By contrast, the triune God offers a more fruitful context to ground and make sense of loving human relationships and interpersonal virtues–in addition to the existence of a finite universe.

Also, *feminist philosophers* have objected to a power-asserting "male," "hierarchical" conception of God in Western philosophy. But the biblical God, who makes male *and* female in his image, is a relational, personal Being without gender. And although male pronouns are used in many instances to refer to God, Scripture contains metaphors of God's motherlike actions and emotions as tender, care-giving, compassionate, and protecting: giving birth to Israel (Deut. 32:18); a nursing mother (Ps. 131:2); a mother in labor (Isa. 42:4); a mother bear and lioness (Hos. 13:8). In addition, God's essentially other-oriented relationality goes a long way in addressing certain concerns–and misconceptions–feminists raise regarding an autocratic, dictatorial male deity.

Finally, the Trinity contributes to a resolution of *the problem of the One and the Many*–what philosopher William James called philosophy's most central problem. The ancient philosopher Heraclitus said that ultimate reality is *many* and *changing*–that is, *no unity*. On the other hand, Parmenides claimed that reality is *one* and *unchanging*–that is, *no plurality*. We live not in a *multi-verse* but a *uni-verse*–a unity holding diverse things together, and the three-in-one God furnishes us with resources to account for both unity and plurality.[8]

4

Talking about God and Knowing God

He made known His ways to Moses, His acts to the sons of Israel.
(Ps. 103:7)

Philosophers of religion have asked whether we speak *intelligibly* or *accurately* about God. Can we truly refer to God *coherently*? Can our language describe God *truly*?

Is the Idea of God *Intelligible?*

'Twas brillig, and the slithy toves
Did gyre and gimble in the wabe:
All mimsy were the borogoves,
And the mome raths outgrabe.[1]

Critics have claimed that the statements "God loves us" and "God created the world" make as much sense as Lewis Carroll's poem above: they're meaningless– incoherent gibberish and pure nonsense. Using such God-talk, we're told, is like saying that "drogulus" (A. J. Ayer) or "teavy" and "toovy" (Rudolf Carnap) created the universe.

This issue–"the problem of religious language"–arises because statements like "God is love" can't be positively verified or "scientifically" shown to be meaningful. After all, what empirical evidence would show that God, if he exists, *couldn't* be love? What amount of evil would it take to falsify this statement? If the believer can't show this, then his belief is meaningless. Scottish skeptic David Hume said that any theology book making claims that can't be proven empirically (scientifically) is mere "sophistry and illusion." Hume's recommendation is, "Commit it then to the flames."[2]

Or some might protest that they just don't know what is meant by "God" since this concept doesn't remotely resemble anything we experience in everyday life. Atheists Paul Edwards and William Rowe have asserted that every person we observe has a body; the idea of a "disembodied personal being" is meaningless. And besides, how could something *immaterial* produce a *physical* world? Another example comes from D. Z. Phillips, who asked: Why think *everlasting objects* exist when all the objects we know of are *contingent* or *dependent?* "God," then, can't exist in any objective sense.[3]

Theists offer important criticisms of this school of thought.

First, not all nontheists seem to have this problem; they appear to have a basic idea of what believers mean when they say "God." Obviously, plenty of well-informed believers have no problem understanding religious language as truly referring to objective realities such as God, salvation, or incarnation. Intelligent nonbelievers also seem to grasp what we're talking about. For instance, atheist philosopher J. L. Mackie didn't find religious language or descriptions unintelligible and literally meaningless: "There is really no problem about this," he insisted. Even though the only persons we're acquainted with have bodies, "there is no great difficulty in conceiving what it would be for there to be a person without a body." We can conceive of a personal spirit that is "present everywhere" or that "creat[es] something where there was nothing."[4] So despite questions about religious language having meaning, skeptics themselves often seem to have a basic grasp of what they're criticizing!

Second, the problem with this demand of scientific verifiability is that it's arbitrary. Why think that *science* is the only legitimate source of knowledge? Science isn't going to help us to determine whether right and wrong exist—not to mention the soul or angels or laws of logic. This demand involves a number of *philosophical assumptions,* not scientific observations.

Third, this standard doesn't practice what it preaches; insisting on this standard renders it incoherent. How can we scientifically verify that all our beliefs should be scientifically verifiable? There's just no way science (empiricism) can show that all beliefs should be scientifically provable. How can we show that there's no other reality—God, the soul, free will, life after death— besides the physical? Insisting that there is none actually goes against this scientific standard. How so? Because the standard is a presumed philosophical outlook, not the result of scientific research. Behind this allegedly "scientific" standard are philosophical presuppositions that aren't themselves scientifically verifiable.

Fourth, believers in God tend to be in a better position than nonbelievers to determine whether or not the idea of God is intelligible. According to whose experience is God unintelligible? The skeptic's experience will be far too limited, as he hasn't tasted and seen the Lord's goodness (Ps. 34:8), nor does he trust God's character.

Fifth, we shouldn't call into question God's existence simply because we can't give an exhaustive definition or description of him—and why think we should?

We can still have a basic idea of what "God" means. Many people have a difficult time defining black holes, art, or knowledge; but that doesn't mean we deny their existence. A child of tender age knows its mother by voice or appearance—even if he can't perfectly describe her. Similarly, we can know to varying degrees what "God" means and basically describe him (i.e., the eternal Creator of the universe who has manifested himself in Jesus of Nazareth to redeem human beings)—even though many of our theological descriptions will always be incomplete and may simply serve as pointers in the direction of God. This "rule" of needing to define or describe God before we can talk about him is flawed and arbitrary; we don't normally operate this way in other spheres of life. That may be one way to talk about something, but hardly the only way.[5]

Finally, even though scientific confirmation or support isn't everything, it still plays a useful role. Indeed, there is much empirical support available for the biblical God's existence. In 1 Corinthians 15, Paul stakes the Christian faith itself on the empirically supportable historical event of the resurrection. Archaeology and historical research offer much confirmation for Scripture's many other historical claims.[6] Additionally, the Christian faith finds empirical support from scientific discoveries such as the universe's beginning and its delicately balanced conditions for biological life. The list of such evidences goes on. But scientific confirmation, while helpful, isn't the only guide to consider when it comes to making sense out of God-talk.

Can Our Descriptions of God Be *Accurate*?

Aren't feeble, lisping human words utterly incapable of describing God? When we say, "God is wise," does "wise" mean the same sort of thing in the sentence as "Johanna is wise"? Some Christian philosophers, such as the Aristotle-influenced Aquinas, have argued that we can't say what God is *like* (positive or *cataphatic* theology), only what God *is not like* (negative or *apophatic* theology): "Now we cannot know what God is, but only what he is not."[7] So we use words beginning with *un-*, *in-*, or *im-*: God is *un*created, *in*corporeal (having no physical body), *im*passible (not able to suffer), *im*mutable (not changeable). We can't speak of God's positive attributes—of what God is in himself—"God is good"; rather we use the "way of negation" (*via negativa*)—"God is not evil." So Aquinas used the method of *analogy* for referring to God. When our language refers to God, it is somewhere between the *univocal* and the *equivocal*—that is, between the precise or exact sense and the imprecise or inexact. God's goodness may bear a resemblance to human goodness, but it is still in a class by itself. (Compare "Jim is a good man" to "Fido is a good dog.")

Now Christian apophatic ("negative") theologians rightly remind us of God's unsurpassable greatness and "otherness." This emphasis implies the need for humility before an untamable God, who "moves in a mysterious way His wonders to perform."[8] The Scriptures themselves speak of God's ways as *un*searchable and *un*fathomable or *in*scrutable (Rom. 11:33). We're also reminded of the dangers of idolatry—creating false gods according to our human categories.

However, it appears that certain Greek conceptions of God—from Plato, Plotinus's Neoplatonism, or Pseudo-Dyonisius—have strongly influenced some forms of negative theology.[9] The typical Greek gods, like Zeus and Poseidon, possessed very human traits, seeming all too human (*anthropomorphized*)—rather like flawed and dysfunctional human beings though possessing special powers. So, various Greek philosophers tried to improve on the concept of "God." Not surprisingly, these revised conceptions of the divine tended to be *impersonal, lifeless, inactive,* and *abstract.* The updated Greek views were far removed from the biblical understanding of God. The Greek philosophers did not emphasize God's *holiness, love,* and *relationality.* Greek philosophical descriptions of the Divine are a far cry from the *inherently personal, vibrant, willing, acting,* and *history-engaging* triune God. Biblically rooted Christian philosophy sees humans made in God's image as his co-regents and priests. Jesus, the very image of God who fulfills the vocation of humanity and the people of God, shows us who God is with clarity. God's transcendent otherness notwithstanding, our being made in God's image not only opens the door for our speaking accurately about God; it also makes possible the Incarnation of God's very Image.

Furthermore, this tradition emphasizing only God's otherness seems to imply we can't know *anything true* about God as he really is—which means we can't speak truly about him either. What's more, this view seems to negate the Spirit's work to freely reveal something of God to us (1 Cor. 2:12). The God of Abraham, Isaac, Jacob, and Jesus can't be reduced to rational descriptions, but perhaps the goal of modesty in certain strands of apophatic theology turns out to be an unintentional *resistance* toward God's enthusiastic self-revelation.[10] Thankfully, the high and exalted God condescends to the weak and flawed (Isa. 57:15). He even wraps his message in words we can understand, speaking into the thus-and-so-ness of human culture.[11] As a result, we can grasp something of his greatness and love. God's Spirit graciously ensures our personal *knowledge* of God; we can *grasp* what he is truly like in his very nature and in what he has done for us. Exhaustively? Hardly. Adequately? Definitely! God created the material world—downplayed or rejected by Greek thought—as good. He was even willing to take on human flesh in the Incarnation of Christ. God's image suggests some *resemblance* between God and us: we *rule with God* over creation, and *God shares in* our humanity in Christ's Incarnation. While Paul speaks of the "mystery" of the gospel, he notes that this mystery has been *revealed* (Eph. 3:1–12). Such divine acts of creation and Incarnation should remind us of God's deep desire to communicate himself to us.

Consider divine and Christian love in 1 John 3–4. We know what *love* is because of God's *love* for us in Christ, who laid down his life for us (3:16). Again, "Beloved, let us *love* one another, for *love* is from God; and everyone who *loves* is born of God and knows God" (4:7, my emphasis). The text adds, "If God so *loved* us, we also ought to *love* one another" (4:11, my emphasis). Though our love pales in comparison to God's, *it's still love,* and we know God's own love by his revealing Spirit (4:13).

The Bible bends over backwards to tell us that *we can genuinely know God!* Our knowledge of God, though *limited,* is *true.* We can know something of God *as he really is* through his historical acts and speech-acts; his Son Jesus has accurately interpreted him for us (Jn. 1:14, 18). To see Jesus is to see the Father (Jn. 14:9).

5

The Attributes of God (I)

For great is the Lord and greatly to be praised;
He is to be feared above all gods.
For all the gods of the peoples are idols,
But the Lord made the heavens. (Ps. 96:4–5)

"Who is like You?" the awe-struck biblical poets ask (Ex. 15:11; Ps. 35:10; 71:19; 89:8). The answer—as though there needs to be one!—is, "There is none like You" (Jer. 10:6, 7). Biblical writers regularly express wonder at God's magnificent greatness. The New Testament affirms that Jesus reveals what God is really like (Jn. 1:14, 18; 14:9). God's greatness is revealed in humility, condescension, love, and grace—an important consideration to keep us from lapsing into abstraction and depersonalization when discussing the divine attributes.

Anselm said that God is the greatest imaginable being—the being "than which nothing greater can be conceived." This is what we mean by God's being *infinite.* Contemporary theistic philosophers speak about God as "maximally great," "supremely excellent," and the "most perfect" or "absolutely perfect" being. However, many critics have argued that the concept of God is incoherent.[1] That's a problem. It's possible for something—like a fairy tale—to be coherent *and* false, but if something is incoherent, it's *definitely* false.

So is a *necessarily existent being* incoherent? If God made the universe, then who made God? Can God make stones too big for God to lift? If God *can't sin* and *can't keep from* doing what's just and right, does God really have freedom? If God knows what we're going to do, do *we* have freedom?

Theologians and philosophers have weighed in on these questions, offering a wide range of responses. While this can be confusing, we should maintain a certain flexibility of interpretation on God's attributes. While skeptics—or believers themselves—may critique one view on, say, omniscience, three or four other views may be left to examine. Unfortunately, we can't survey the different approaches and then weigh the merits of each. We'll explore some of the philosophically rich, often-discussed views about this worship-worthy Being, focusing on answers that I myself have found fruitful and most satisfying.

God's Necessity and Self-sufficiency

Of old You founded the earth,
  And the heavens are the work of Your hands.
Even they will perish, but You endure;
  And all of them will wear out like a garment;
Like clothing You will change them and they will be changed.
  (Ps. 102:25–26)

You alone are God. (Ps. 86:10)

The universe's existence depends on something outside itself. Not so with God, who exists necessarily and self-sufficiently. Theologians call it divine *aseity* (*a se* = [being] by itself). So great is this God that he *cannot not exist!*

Keep in mind that *everlasting* doesn't mean *necessary.* Various medieval theologians like Aquinas thought it logically possible that the universe could have been created out of nothing *from eternity* by God and thus everlastingly dependent on God. Though such a possibility may seem odd to us, such thinkers insisted that just because something is everlasting, that doesn't mean it exists necessarily. It can exist but only in dependence upon something else—namely, God's sustaining power. What is necessary has an existence in and of itself, and it exists in every conceivable or possible world—which we'll look at below.

Philosopher Immanuel Kant believed the idea of "necessary existence" was a contradiction in terms. "Existence" isn't included in the definition of anything, including God. After all, plenty of people don't find the statement "God does not exist" to be self-contradictory. So why think "God exists" is a logically necessary statement?

Such an objection doesn't have much power to it, though. Some philosophers have responded to Kant by utilizing the language of possible worlds (modal logic). By *possible worlds,* we don't mean "logically possible *physical* universes," but simply states of affairs or configurations of reality. So a possible world could be utterly empty, except that God exists within it; or in another possible world angels might exist with God—and nothing else.

Now, by definition, necessary truths or basic logical laws exist in all possible worlds—for example, the law of non-contradiction ("a statement and its opposite can't both be true"). There's *no* possible configuration of reality in which such laws wouldn't be true. (These laws, of course, are themselves rooted in God's mind.) So if there's no problem with logical laws being necessary in all possible worlds, then it's certainly not incoherent to say "God exists" is true in all possible worlds. Just as basic logical laws by definition would exist in all possible worlds, it's hardly incoherent that God by definition would exist in any of them. There can be no God-less possible world. To the "Kant-rary," it's simply question-begging—assuming what one wants to prove—to say that a necessary being can't exist.[2]

Furthermore, prior to the twentieth-century discovery that the universe began to exist a finite time ago, a lot of people in the past assumed the universe existed eternally—and, for some, necessarily—and thus didn't need any explanation. That being so, we can, all the more, say this of God, whose very nature *requires* that he exist—unlike a universe that didn't *need* to exist.

God's self-sufficiency speaks to the question of why God created human beings. God wasn't lacking anything so that he felt compelled to create out of some inner need. The doctrine of the Trinity *strengthens* the concept of God's self-sufficiency—that he is perfectly complete, content, and joyful in himself, as Father, Son, and Spirit. He didn't *have* to create, "as though He needed anything" (Acts 17:25). God, the source of all things (Rom. 11:35–36), freely and graciously created us out of his goodness so that we might be partakers in the very life of the triune God's love and joy (2 Pet. 1:4). God wants as many people as possible to get in on what the three-in-one God has enjoyed all along.

Process theology or panentheism—"God in the world"—declares that God *needs* the world. As a soul has a body, so the world is God's body; they are eternally and necessarily dependent on one another. This view, though, isn't well-rooted in Scripture, which sees the universe (heavens and earth) as capable of perishing or enduring (Ps. 102:25–26). God alone endures from everlasting to everlasting (Ps. 90:2). To its credit, panentheism emphasizes God's relationality and his interaction with creation, but the doctrine of the Trinity already suggests this. The triune God is both distinct from the world (transcendent) but deeply present within it (immanent).

Now some feminist theologians similarly suggest that the world is God's body—a model they claim avoids problems created by traditional Western theology: a God who sovereignly ("monarchistically") rules over creation only encourages tyranny and oppression of the weak. The feminist model, they suggest, promotes peaceful relations rather than oppressive ones; it encourages humans to care for the world, not exploit it.

We've already noted important trinitarian responses to such charges. Also, if God is triune and relational by nature, we don't need to resort to such world-as-God's-body images. What's more, such interdependence models of God and creation dramatically conflict with the consensus of science—that the universe had a beginning a finite time ago. This conclusion is supported by the fact that the universe is expanding and that it is also winding down—without the ability to wind back up (the second law of thermodynamics).

Physicist Paul Davies sees the clear implications of the question, What caused the Big Bang? "One might consider some supernatural force, some agency beyond space and time as being responsible for the big bang, or one might prefer to regard the big bang as an event without a cause." However, "we don't have too much choice": it's either "something outside of the physical world" or "an event without a cause."[3] The universe hasn't always been around. It isn't God's body.

Divine necessity and self-sufficiency suggest the doctrine of creation out of nothing and that God sustains all things in being. Challenging that, Mormons and classical panentheists claim that the Divine and the world have been eternally related and that God created from eternally preexisting matter. Mormons assert that God *can neither* create nor annihilate matter. He's merely the Organizer, not the "Originator," of these primal elements.

Again, such a view not only flies in the face of contemporary scientific discovery, which points to a beginning of the universe from nothing without the existence—and assistance—of matter, energy, space, and time. (More on this later.) It also diminishes God's self-sufficiency and power. That is, if God wanted to create a cosmos but had no preexisting materials "lying around," then he wouldn't create a universe because he couldn't. So it was just a fluke—lucky chance—that God happened to have the right materials handy, waiting to be used! God's self-sufficiency and all-powerful nature are most adequately reflected in the doctrine of creation out of nothing (*ex nihilo*).[4]

Excursus: "If God Made the Universe, Who Made God?"

In "Why I Am Not a Christian" (1927), Bertrand Russell quotes philosopher John Stuart Mill, who wrote in his autobiography: "My father taught me that the question 'Who made me?' cannot be answered, since it immediately suggests the further question, 'Who made God?'" Persuaded, Russell concluded: "If everything must have a cause, then God must have a cause."[5]

Children frequently ask parents, *If God made the universe, who made God?* Though it may seem baffling—to some, self-contradictory—that *anything* could exist from eternity, Mill and Russell are left with more difficult problems if "everything must have a cause."

First, God is by definition uncaused and uncreated and therefore is the cause of everything outside himself. To ask, "Who made God?" amounts to asking, "Who made the Unmakable?" or, "Who brought into existence the Source of all existence?" It's a confusion of categories—like wondering how the color green tastes or whether J. S. Bach's *Coffee Cantata* smells like coffee.[6]

Unlike his creation, God doesn't exist by something else. If something had a beginning, then we're not talking about God!

Second, this "everything must have a cause" assumption is implicitly atheistic and therefore begs the question, assuming what one wants to prove. Whether he knows it or not, the questioner assumes atheism: if everything needs a cause, then God would too, which means he's not really God at all, but something finite and dependent. We should question the hidden assumption that "everything must have a cause." The right-thinking person—whether atheist or not—has very good reason to believe that whatever *begins* to exist has a cause. But why think everything must have a cause? Russell got it wrong when he assumed that.

Third, it's just not obvious that everything has to have a cause, nor is it counterintuitive that something could be eternally existent. The notion that everything must have a beginning and that nothing can be necessary and eternal is of relatively recent vintage. Many philosophers across the ages, including Plato and Aristotle, believed the universe to be eternal rather than its having begun a finite time ago. So while it's difficult to grasp how something could be eternally existent, this doesn't mean it's self-contradictory.

Fourth, if eternally existent or beginningless logical laws exist, then why can't an eternal God? Consider the law of identity, $A = A$ (e.g., Jonathan's leopard gecko is Jonathan's leopard gecko), and the law of non-contradiction, $A \neq$ *non-A* (Jonathan's leopard gecko is not Peter's bearded dragon). Such laws never *began* to exist but are necessarily and everlastingly true. And what of Russell's principle that everything must have a cause—is *that* eternal, or was it caused a finite time ago? No, something's being eternally existent isn't counterintuitive at all.

Fifth, contemporary cosmology's findings plausibly suggest a cause external to the universe, which readily implies that not everything must have a beginning. Studying the history of the universe has yielded a fairly wide consensus that it began a finite time ago.[7] But if all matter, energy, space, and physical time began to exist, how did it ultimately get started? We're left with two simple options: (a) it came from nothing, or (b) it came from something. Option (a) presents a huge problem: Can something come into existence, uncaused out of nothing when there isn't even the potentiality to produce anything at all? Could a redwood forest or Komodo dragons suddenly appear from absolutely nothing? The metaphysical fact is: something doesn't come from nothing at all; something comes from something. Being comes from being, not from nonbeing. Even Scottish skeptic David Hume considered the idea of something coming uncaused from nothing as "absurd."[8] The chances of something coming from nothing are precisely zero. (The possible suggestion that the universe was self-caused is a nonstarter: something has to exist first before it can exert any causal influence.)

The philosopher Leibniz asked, *Why is there something rather than nothing at all?* If a self-sufficient God doesn't exist, there's no reason *anything* should exist. God's necessary existence makes sense of the existence of everything else. So, though we find the question of God's existence from eternity hard to fathom, we know the finite universe couldn't have come from absolutely nothing. We're pointed in the direction of a cause outside the universe, and denying this leads to far more difficult problems.

Divine Eternity

From everlasting to everlasting, You are God. (Ps. 90:2b)

"God is outside of time," Christians commonly affirm. "God sees past, present, and future all at once—in the 'eternal now.'" In his *On the Consolation of Philosophy,* medieval theologian Boethius (c. 480–524) refers to God's eternity as the "simultaneous and complete [*totum simul*] possession of infinite life," completely grasping past, present, and future all at once. Is this *really* so? Is God *outside* time (timeless) or *in* time (temporal)? What *is* time? While the variations and details would bog us down,[9] here's a brief attempt to discuss the topic.

Time is, someone remarked, what keeps everything from happening all at once. Time is the succession of events or happenings, and it is characterized by "before-ness" and "after-ness." So without the change of events, time wouldn't exist. Some have distinguished between "lived time" and "measured/clock time." Though time continues to move along apart from our perceiving it (it is objective), "lived time" reflects our experiencing time, not simply measuring it. So when we think of the "present," we don't view it as balanced on a knife's edge between past and future—that's more a feature of measured time—but rather in terms of *moments* or experiential *happenings.*

What is God's relationship to time, though? Though Scripture uses words such as *forever, everlasting,* or *eternal,* such words by themselves don't tell us whether God is in time (temporal) or outside of time (eternally timeless).[10] Consider: God's being omniscient involves his knowing all truths—including tensed facts such as "I *am* (now) *typing* these words on 28 May 2006," "Julius Caesar *was killed,*" or, "Jesus *will return.*" It seems counterintuitive that God would know all truths but not be able to distinguish between past, present, and future. But if God is in the "eternal now" and "sees all events at once" (the *static* rather than the *dynamic* theory of time),[11] then he can't distinguish between tenses. All that God can know is tenseless truths such as, "Jesus is born in 5 B.C.E.," or, "The American Revolution begins on 19 April 1775." If all events are simultaneous to God, as some claim, then God couldn't know *when* an event is actually occurring. If outside of time, how would God be able to differentiate between past, present, and future, or how could we say that God knows something *at this time* that will *no longer* be true as a *present*-tense statement tomorrow? For God to be omniscient, he would have to be *in* time to know *tensed* facts. Apart from such a view, God's creating out of nothing or becoming incarnate in Christ wouldn't make sense. After all, this "eternal now" perspective suggests that God and the universe coexist statically or tenselessly—and that leaves us wondering: Why does the universe exist rather than nothing at all?

Imagine you're looking at a mural portraying a sequence of Civil War events: the pre-Civil War raid on Harper's Ferry by John Brown, Lincoln's being elected as the sixteenth President, the attack on Ft. Sumter, the First Battle at Bull Run, then Antietam, Gettysburg, Sherman's "March to the Sea," and Lee's surrender to Grant at the Appomattox courthouse. Now imagine that the Civil War is actually raging beyond the walls of our mural in the round. You can see the sequence of events on the mural before you, but you can't know which ones have already taken place, which are taking place now, and which will take place. This illustrates the sort of problem that emerges if God is "outside of time." In the "eternal now" view, God knows the (static) sequence of all events across history (*Paul Copan is typing on 28 May 2006*), but not the (dynamic) awareness of what events are past, present, or future (e.g., *Paul Copan is now typing*) since present events ("is now") are constantly becoming past ("was then"). For God to know all things, he would be aware of when the present changes into the past and the future changes into the present.

Some philosophers claim such a dynamic view doesn't square with God's unchanging nature (immutability), since change must be from perfection to imperfection or vice versa. God's omniscience (being all-knowing) and immutability are therefore incompatible. However, this view of immutability seems problematic since it incorrectly assumes that *change* must imply something *negative*. There can be *neutral* changes—like the South Pole's temperature fluctuation or a chameleon's color alteration. God's awareness of changing events seems inescapable if we're to preserve the notion of omniscience.

Also, this dynamic change in God's temporal awareness isn't an *intrinsic* change—namely, in God's nature, which is fixed and stable—but a change in God's *relationship* to creation. It seems that denying God's omniscience itself is more problematic than denying that God's knowledge changes as time progresses. God's knowledge isn't *necessarily* unchanging. Consider this: through creation, *God has come to know us as his creatures*—this is something he didn't know apart from creating. If God had freely refrained from creating, then he *wouldn't have* had this knowledge that we are his creatures. That is, if the creation is contingent, then God's knowledge of his creation—once he actually creates—is also contingent. By creating, God comes to know, "My creation now exists."[12]

So the timeless triune God, at creation, enters into time because he is truly related to happenings within creation. The beginning of the universe is the beginning of God's time. So Christ's return is still in God's future whereas Christ's death is in God's past. The view we're suggesting is that God is *timeless*–and changeless–*outside* the universe, but *in time*–and changing in tensed awareness–*with* the universe.[13] But some lingering questions remain.

Doesn't God's being "in time" limit or "trap" him? Not at all. Though God is *in time*, he still perfectly knows all events, including *future* ones. He isn't caught by surprise. And he's still omnipotent and perfectly good. If anything, eternal timelessness would limit God since he couldn't know what is happening at present, but only what event precedes or follows another. *There's no theological need* to say that God must be outside of time. His being *temporal* (with the creation-event)–along with his *possessing complete foreknowledge* of all that will transpire and his *dynamically interacting* with his creation–offers us a biblically robust approach to God's relationship to time.

Isn't there a "before" creation and "after" creation, which suggests time prior to creation? Time is the succession of events, the series of happenings; so technically there isn't any (physical) time without the universe's existence.[14] To talk of God's being timeless "before" creation is like saying that it's physically impossible for temperatures to actually go "below" absolute zero (0° Kelvin or -273.15° Celsius) even though we use the term "below" as a manner of speaking. So we should *reject* the temporal language of "before" and "after" creation. It's clearer to speak of God existing timelessly or atemporally *without* the universe and temporally *with* the universe. God is *causally* prior to creation, not *temporally* prior to it. From eternity, God timelessly willed to freely create and redeem. (Think of a person sitting from eternity who freely chooses to stand up.)

This also means that without the universe, we shouldn't speak of the creation as being "future" to God (just as we should reject the language of God's determining something "before" he created the universe). There is no literal future in God's existing without the universe since time doesn't exist in such a scenario. Without creation, there just is no time, and without time, there can be no future-tensed events.[15] (Think back to the example of not being able to go "below" absolute zero.)

How can God, without the universe, exist in a changeless state? Critics have argued that a being can't be both timeless *and* personal; they claim that *personhood* presupposes *time.* But why think personal beings must have a succession of thoughts or that knowing something involves an earlier and a later time? Must all knowledge–or awareness in general–involve time?

Philosopher of mind Daniel Dennett–hardly sympathetic to belief in God–has laid out various "conditions of personhood": being rational, capable of verbal communication, self-conscious, and several others.[16] What's significant for us is that *temporal succession in thought doesn't figure into this definition*: that is, it's just not intuitively obvious that personhood *necessarily* involves temporal mental succession even if this is how human thinking operates. So we should be careful about how we define personhood lest we diminish it. For example, while we typically say that consciousness is a condition of personhood, we don't say that personhood ceases while we are in a dreamless sleep or are unconscious!

Admittedly, since we *associate* personal consciousness with sequences of events, thinking about God's own timeless awareness without the creation is difficult to grasp. Timeless personal existence is hardly incoherent, however. Without the universe, the mutually indwelling persons of the triune God delight in the sublime, eternal exchange of love in a kind of transfixed gaze of pure joy. It is like lovers who, simply by looking deeply at each other, communicate mutual concern, joy, and contentment—quite unlike the impersonal, detached "God" of certain Eastern philosophies. So, we can think of the infinite, perfect, interpersonal, and transparent love of the Trinity as being mutually and telepathically communicated—all without any need for change.

Divine Omniscience

> *Even before there is a word on my tongue,*
> *Behold, O LORD, You know it all. (Ps. 139:4)*

God is omniscient (Latin *omnis*–"all"; "*sciens*"–"knowing"); he "knows all things" (1 Jn. 3:20) and is "the only wise God" (Rom. 16:27). God knows the details of our lives better than we do (Ps. 139)—even down to the very number of hairs on our heads (Mt. 10:30); he is aware when the humble sparrow is sold or falls to the ground (Lk. 12:6; Mt. 10:29). God knows everything within the universe: "I know every bird of the mountains, and everything that moves in the field is Mine" (Ps. 50:11)—or the momentum and location of every subatomic particle in existence. God's omniscience means that *if something is true, then God knows it.* If something happens, he is aware.

But some skeptics claim that God's omniscience means he must experience lust or envy;[17] it seems odd and counter-intuitive that humans would know what it's like to lust or envy, but that God doesn't (not knowing would mean he's not omniscient). And if God *does* know these things, then he can't truly be God (he's not all-good). Here's one such argument: "Since God has all of men's knowledge and more, He must know lust and envy. But to say God has known lust and envy is to say that God has had the feelings of lust and envy. But this is incompatible with God's moral goodness. Hence God does not exist."[18]

We can easily shrug off such criticisms, though. For one thing, they fail to take seriously the Scriptures, which lay out some important parameters regarding God's omniscience. God's knowledge doesn't mean *having the experience of* envy or lust. Yes, God knows humans perfectly and how sin operates, but being all-knowing just doesn't require having *experiential* knowledge of sin.

The biblical God is morally perfect; he doesn't need to *be* immoral to know what is immoral and what immorality can do to a person. God's being all-knowing means that *God knows all truths.* Because God's omniscience can't be separated from his goodness, neither can it be reduced to sheer information storage. Of course, God knows *much more* than all truths: he knows us *as persons*; he experientially knows *what it's like to be God*; neither of these can be reduced to a set of true propositions.

In addition, God's maximal greatness means he knows or grasps all truths *immediately*—not to mention having deep and immediate access to the experiences and thoughts of his creatures. Say that a non-divine person comes to know a vast sum of truths and human experiences, but he comes to know them only circuitously or indirectly—perhaps through lots of study, learning by trial and error, and so on. That kind of knowing is inferior to knowing accurately and directly. So an important aspect of God's knowing everything is not just *what* God knows (the content), but *how* he knows it (the means).

Some skeptics insist that for God to be omniscient, he must know

- all truths (*propositional* knowledge);
- how things are done (*procedural* or *skilled* knowledge);
- all things by direct acquaintance (*experiential* knowledge).

We've seen that God's supremely good knowledge excludes *immoral* experiences such as envy or lust. Here the critic makes philosophically problematic demands that result in *metaphysical* (real) contradictions. If, say, an omniscient God must know exactly *what* you know *in the exact way* you know it, this leads to metaphysical confusion. Why? You alone—and no one else—have a private ("first person") perspective or "inner feel"; only you know what it's like to be you. While God knows what goes on in your mind better than you do yourself, he knows it as an "outsider" while you know it as an "insider." It's a simple metaphysical fact: God *doesn't* have the knowledge that, "I am Alexander the Great," or, "I wrote *The Scarlet Letter.*" If so, that would mean God would believe he is someone else—a serious problem indeed! *You* alone know the "feel" of what it is to be you, and it's metaphysical silliness to demand that God have direct acquaintance of what it's like to experience life as *you.*

That said, God is "intimately acquainted" with all our ways, knowing our thoughts "from afar" and our words before they're on our tongue (Ps. 139:2–4); though God doesn't have our experiences, feelings, and thoughts, he has *immediate and deep access* to them. God's understanding is much richer than knowing all truths. But it's a phony challenge to say God has to know (a) *everything* that (b) *any* person knows (c) *in an identical way.* Yes, if something is true, God knows it intimately. However, insisting that "God must know all that humans know in the way that they know" is nonsensical—metaphysically absurd. As we'll see with other attributes, we shouldn't separate or isolate one attribute from another—like God's knowledge from his goodness; the very *integration* of all of God's great-making attributes is essential for a proper understanding of maximal excellence.

Excursus: Omniscience and Human Freedom

Some theologians and philosophers of more recent vintage have questioned whether God can know the future free acts of human beings. If he *knows* what they'll do, are they really *free?* And if those acts are truly free and if it's *up to humans* to choose, *how* can God know these choices in advance? Maybe God just has complete knowledge of all necessary truths as well as truths about the past and present, but just can't know future human choices *since they don't yet exist.* Such a view, however, is problematic for a number of reasons.

First, Scripture indicates that God, by his very nature, knows the future free choices of human beings. He knows what we'll say even before we speak (Ps. 139:4, 16). Jesus was aware that people would crucify him, that Judas would betray him, that Peter would deny him three times. God *knew* humans would freely sin *before* they actually did; that's why Jesus' atoning sacrifice was "foreknown before the foundation of the world" (1 Pet. 1:19–20).

God even knows *hypothetical situations* of what human beings *would* do if placed in certain circumstances. In 1 Samuel 23:6–10, God knows that if David *were* to stay at Keilah, King Saul *would* pursue him. If that *were* the case, Keilah's inhabitants *would* hand David over to Saul. Based on God's knowledge of future hypotheticals and his revealing this, David and his men leave and are safe from danger. Jeremiah gives Judah's king Zedekiah the Lord's message: if he *would* surrender to the king of Babylon, his entire family would be spared, and Jerusalem wouldn't be burned with fire. But if Zedekiah *wouldn't* surrender, he wouldn't escape; and the city would be burned (Jer. 38:17–18), which is what indeed happened. Other such examples appear in Scripture.[19]

How then does God know human future free choices if it's truly up to human beings to do the choosing? Of course, knowledge of *all* events—past, present, and future—is *essential* or *innate* to God; without it, he wouldn't be a maximally great being. In Isaiah 42–44, God challenges Babylon's gods (idols) to make known what will take place in the future—something only Yahweh can do; that's what makes God God—even if we don't know how he knows. We may not be able to explain *how* God is all-powerful, though it's essential to God. Likewise, we may not be able to tell *how* God knows future human choices, though this, too, is innate to God.

Some thinkers refer to God's knowledge of future human choices using a *perceptual* model. Aquinas refers to God's "divine sight," seeing the whole sequence of future events at once: "Just as he who goes along the road does not see those who come after him; whereas he who sees the whole road from a height sees at once all those traveling on it."[20] This model raises the question of how God could "see" past, present, and future events taking place all at once since they don't all *now* exist. Perhaps a more accurate portrayal—a *rational* model—is this: Since God *by his nature* innately knows all truths, including truths about the future, God must know what will take place.[21]

Second, we should distinguish between what will *happen and what* must *happen, between what is* certain *and what is* necessary. If God knows that my wife and I will go out to the Breakers Hotel for an anniversary breakfast, then it *will* happen. Now it doesn't logically follow that this *must* happen. If we had freely chosen to go another time or to a different place, then God would have known *that*. So if God knows what we'll choose, then it's *true* that the event *will* happen—that it's *certain*. But it's *false* that it therefore *must* happen—that it's *necessary*.

Third, God's knowledge of future actions doesn't by itself hinder human freedom since knowledge doesn't actually cause *anything*. God's foreknowing what we freely choose to do is caused by or grounded in what we'll freely choose to do. God's knowledge of a future event doesn't cause this event. A psychic may have an accurate intuition of a future event (cp. Acts 16:16)—say, that a murder will take place down the street tomorrow. Someone is murdered, but the psychic's knowledge didn't actually *do* anything. The psychic's awareness doesn't mean the murder *necessarily* occurred—nor that the awareness *caused* it to take place. The murderer acted freely. It would seem strange to claim that simply knowing something will take place actually causes it to happen. Why should things change if God is the knower? His knowing a murder will occur doesn't mean he caused it.

What *grounds* God's foreknowledge of what we freely choose to do is that we will freely choose to do it! What humans will freely choose to do is the basis of God's foreknowledge.

Fourth, God not only knows what we will do in the future, but he also knows what he *will do in the future*. Does this mean that God isn't free? The triune God isn't hemmed in or constrained by outside forces; he is free to act as he wisely chooses. From eternity, the triune God decided to freely create humans and graciously rescue them from their desperate plight. But if God knew what he would do, was he determined to act as he did simply because he knew his own future actions? In one of his earlier writings, "On the Free Choice of the Will," Augustine addressed this: "Don't you see that you will have to be careful lest someone say to you that, if all things of which God has foreknowledge are done by necessity and not voluntarily, his own future acts will be done not voluntarily but by necessity?"[22] God's foreknowledge of his own actions doesn't cause him to do them; rather, he does them freely. So God's simply knowing what I'll do in the future need not cause me to do something either.

The subject of *prayer* is relevant here: "Why pray if God knows what's going to happen anyway? Does prayer really accomplish anything?" The biblical picture suggests that *God, who knows that we will pray, may bring about certain events that wouldn't have taken place had we not prayed.* James 4:2 indicates that we "do not have" because we "do not ask." Setting aside the matter of God's ability to raise the dead, consider this further step: You hear a friend of yours is in an auto accident, but you don't yet know whether he's alive or not. What good will prayer do since he's in fact either alive or dead? Well, God knows how you'll freely pray in response to hearing the news of this accident; so, in his foreknowledge, he may have worked out his purposes in advance so that your friend would live in direct response to the prayer you offered up—but die if you hadn't.[23] The prayer of a righteous person can accomplish much (Jas. 5:16)!

Fifth, God knows the array of possible worlds and ones he could feasibly create, and he knows what free creatures would do in particular circumstances. He thus chooses to create this (actual) world to bring about his wise purposes without undermining human freedom. God arranges the details of the actual world in light of his knowledge of what human creatures would freely do in whatever world they would happen to exist. So God arranges the details of the actual world without eliminating or undermining our freedom. While certain narratives in Scripture portray God as surprised or regretful or changing his mind, as we'll see below, we shouldn't assume that God didn't know what would happen; in other places, the Bible tells us otherwise (e.g., Peter's three denials; finding a colt for Jesus [Mk. 11:1–6]; preparing a room for Passover [Mk. 14:12–16]). Rather, such narratives nicely illustrate the divine-human interaction and God's engaging humans on the stage of history.

This topic of God's foreknowledge also relates to the question of the saved, the lost, and the unevangelized. In keeping with his goodness, God created a world in which *as many persons as possible are saved* and *as few persons as possible are lost.* In light of God's desire to save any and all who would freely respond to him, perhaps it's the case that anyone who is lost would have been lost through his own free rejection of God's initiating grace—in any world he could have existed. As we'll see later, no one is separated from God's glorious presence because he was born at the wrong place and at the wrong time, but from freely rejecting God's initiating grace.

6

The Attributes of God (II)

Divine Omnipresence

Where can I flee from Your presence? (Ps. 139:7)

After Hagar, Sarah's handmaiden, was obviously expecting her (and Abraham's) child– Ishmael–Sarah oppressed her so that she fled into the wilderness. God met this desperate woman there, assuring her that he had not abandoned her and offering promises regarding her son. She replied with these wonderful words, "You are a God who sees" (Gen. 16:13).

God is "omnipresent" (Latin *omnis*–"all"; *praesens*–"being before/at hand"); everything is present to him. The psalmist muses: "Where can I go from your Spirit?" (Ps. 139:7). In his temple dedicatory prayer, Solomon declares: "Behold, heaven and the highest heaven cannot contain You" (1 Kings 8:27). Paul would later tell the Athenians: "The God who made the world and all things in it, since He is Lord of heaven and earth, does not dwell in temples made with hands" (Acts 17:24). God is intimately aware of all that takes place–and is able to act anywhere–in the universe; this can bring great comfort to the believer, Ps. 139 suggests; it should also prompt us to pay careful attention to the state of our hearts.

God's omnipresence reminds us that the cosmos isn't cold and hostile. Rather, the Father of lights fills it with his personal, glorious presence (Jas. 1:17). Of course, God's omnipresence can also trouble those who don't want him to have access to or charge of their lives.

God's presence everywhere isn't like some ether gas that permeates the entire universe, his presence physically spreading out as the universe expands! After all, the existence of space depends on objects (space has to do with *in-betweenness*), and God, the Creator of all *physical* objects—not to mention nonphysical ones—existed *spacelessly* without creation. Space came into being with the creation of these physical objects. So God's omnipresence, more accurately, refers both to (a) *God's perfect knowledge or awareness* of every facet of his creation, including nonphysical angelic powers, and (b) his *being causally active (and interactive) at every point in it*.[1] Everything everywhere is known to God's mind, sustained by his power (Col. 1:17; Heb. 1:3).

In light of Einstein's work on the Special Theory of Relativity, some might wonder whether there *can* be any privileged access—a vantage point for judging whether or not two events are simultaneous, or an object is in motion or at rest. Contrary to popular belief, Einstein didn't do away with Isaac Newton's claim that an absolute frame of reference existed—a divine one. God isn't just another observer within the universe; all created things are simultaneously "present" to him. Einstein rightly spoke of *our* limited frame of reference as finite observers. So *we* may not be able to tell what events are simultaneous and which aren't—especially since all objects in space are in motion. What is "now" to us (seeing an exploding star) may have occurred millions of years ago. Or when a clock is traveling at the speed of light, the time on a clock actually slows down or stretches out (known as "time dilation") in comparison to a stationary clock or one traveling at less than 186,000 miles per second.

God, however, isn't locked into a finite (relative) framework; all events throughout the universe are immediately accessible to him. The immediacy of these events to God can be compared to the cosmic background radiation—the hissing after-effect of the Big Bang—that permeates the universe. To further illustrate this point about God's awareness of what is going on at every point in the universe, we could refer to the model of ether gas, which many scientists of yesteryear believed pervaded all space. (Though outmoded, the ether model still offers a helpful picture of how God's presence could permeate the entire universe simultaneously.) These examples serve as an analogy of God's objective privileged access to every point of the universe; that is, God (a) has a cosmic perspective over everything in the universe, (b) sustains all things in being, and (c) can readily act upon them.[2]

Divine Incorporeality

"God is spirit, and those who worship Him must worship in spirit and in truth." (Jn. 4:24)

The Scriptures affirm that, Christ's Incarnation aside, the triune God is spirit. The "eternal King" is "invisible" (1 Tim. 1:17), dwelling in "unapproachable light," whom no one "has seen or can see" (1 Tim. 6:16). Christ himself is the image of "the invisible God" (Col. 1:15). Being spirit means more than just "disembodied" or "immaterial." That is, God isn't confined to one sphere of existence—say, the physical universe—but transcends such limits and fully penetrates every dimension of reality: visible and invisible, earthly and heavenly (Col. 1:16).

Atheist Kai Nielsen wonders if the idea of a disembodied personal being is coherent: "But it makes no sense whatsoever to say something is indirectly observable, if it is not at least in theory or in principle directly observable as well."[3] We can't encounter a transcendent being because we can't *directly* observe God or note his existence. Similarly, Bede Rundle considers it unintelligible that an eyeless, earless being can watch the world or listen to prayers.[4] Or how can someone act *justly*, *lovingly*, or *forgivingly* without a body?

Orthodox believers, however, assume that God's seeing or hearing simply refers to his *awareness of* activity in the world and that he doesn't need physical organs to detect it. Think about the claim that a person can't act lovingly or forgivingly without a body. Yes, we typically *recognize* human forgiveness or love through bodily actions—hugs, spoken words of affirmation—but we also know people can *act* one way but *think* or *feel* the opposite. Someone may *pretend* to forgive another—complete with bodily actions!—but still remain bitter and unforgiving in her soul. Persons are more than their bodily actions. While helpful, bodily actions don't *necessarily* give us direct access to love, forgiveness, or justice. Later on, we'll explore the very possibility of the soul's disembodiment—another support for the coherence of God's incorporeality.

Some may wonder whether a spirit being can act on physical objects, whether planets or molecules. But if all matter, energy, space, and physical time began to exist a finite time ago, we have very legitimate reason for thinking that an *immaterial* or *spirit* being brought them into existence. So even though God is spirit, he leaves indicators or traces of his existence throughout creation.

Divine Omnipotence

"Is anything too difficult for the LORD?" (Gen. 18:14)

Scripture portrays God as "the Almighty," who does what humans can't, who accomplishes the impossible: "Behold, I am the LORD, the God of all flesh; is anything too difficult for Me?" (Jer. 32:27). The angel Gabriel tells Mary about her miraculous virginal conception, "For nothing will be impossible with God" (Lk. 1:37). After Job's overwhelming encounter with God, Job affirms, "I know that You can do all things" (Job 42:2).

What does it mean that God can "do all things" or is "omnipotent" (Latin *omnis*—"all"; *potens*—"powerful")? Can he undo the past—say, Napoleon's death or Julius Caesar's crossing the Rubicon—as though it never happened? Can he make square circles? Can he cease to exist?

French philosopher René Descartes believed that the Almighty, if he wants, has the power to make $2 + 2 = 5$, change laws of logic, or alter the basic structure of morality.

When people discuss God's power, they commonly raise the "stone paradox": *Can God make a stone so big that he can't lift it?* After all, he can do *anything*, right? If he *can't* make such a stone, he's not all-powerful. If God *can* make such a stone, then he's still not all-powerful since he can't lift it! This apparent dilemma, however interesting, is flawed. No being, great or not, can do something *self-contradictory* or *nonsensical.* Can God, for whom no stone is too great to lift, make a stone too great to lift? The question answers itself. C. S. Lewis said:

> I know very well that if it is self-contradictory it is absolutely impossible….His Omnipotence means power to do all that is intrinsically possible, not to do the intrinsically impossible. You may attribute miracles to Him, but not nonsense….It remains true that all *things* are possible with God: the intrinsic impossibilities are not things but nonentities….[N]onsense remains nonsense even when we talk it about God.[5]

Just as there's no possible world in which God doesn't exist, there can be, by definition, no God-defying rocks. The stone question is meaningless. Similarly, no power can undo the past, making it *un*-happen. How could an event that *has* occurred *not* have occurred?

Another consideration: Does God have power to do *wrong*—even if he chooses not to use it? The Scriptures suggest that God by his very *nature* can't do the immoral—not just that he *won't* or *chooses not to* do evil. It's *impossible* for him to lie (Titus 1:2), to be pulled down by sin (Jas. 1:13), to break his promises (Heb. 6:17–18), or to change in his good, holy character (Hab. 1:13; Mal. 3:6; Heb. 13:8). If God can't sin, he may be perfectly good; but is he truly *all-powerful* or even *free*? Here's the apparent dilemma: (a) If he can potentially sin, then he appears not to be perfectly *good*; but (b) if God can't sin, then it seems that he is not really *free* or *all-powerful,* since there's at least one thing God can't do. How do we begin to resolve this matter?

First, we can't separate God's goodness from God's power—or any of his other attributes because this supremely great Being possesses these great-making qualities together. An evil powerful being who is his own "brute squad"[6] wouldn't be worthy of our worship. God is by definition worship-worthy. Just as God's omniscience is more than sheer information-storage, God's omnipotence is more than brute power. Sheer power itself doesn't make its possessor supremely excellent. Rather, goodness is a kind of hub that connects and holds together the various divine attributes.

Second, the "power to sin" turns out to be powerlessness. Anselm argued that if God were able to sin, this would be a deficiency since "[God's] powerlessness puts him in another's power."[7] The ability to sin reveals a deficiency in God's character, making him less than necessarily good. It would also undermine God's full power. How? To say of the world-conquering Alexander the Great, "He *cannot* lose in battle," doesn't reveal a deficiency in *him* but rather in his *enemies*. As Anselm put it, "Thus when I say that I can be carried off or conquered against my will, this is not my power, but my necessity and another's power. For to say, 'I can be carried off or conquered,' is the same thing as to say, 'Someone is able to carry off or conquer me.'"[8] Said Aquinas, "To sin is to fall short of a perfect action; hence to be able to sin is to be able to fall short in action, which is repugnant to omnipotence."[9] God's inability to sin—a metaphysical impossibility—doesn't undermine his omnipotence any more that a general's inability to lose a battle should be seen as a lack of power or ability.

Third, God's power doesn't undermine human freedom but works with it. As we'll see in the chapter on evil, God takes human freedom seriously and works out his purposes without undermining personal agency and responsibility. He doesn't trample upon creaturely freedom.

Fourth, skeptics may make faulty assumptions about or artificial demands of divine omnipotence. Michael Martin insists that God's omnipotence entails his doing something that wasn't done by God. God's being omnipotent means that he could, say, create a certain state of affairs—namely, the flooding of Hidden Valley that is brought about directly or indirectly by a *non*-omnipotent being.[10] But this turns out to be confused—a misplacing of focus. Rather than focusing on the actor, Martin's scenario raises problems with who the agent actually is—God or a non-omnipotent being—rather than the *act* itself or the states of affairs produced. The latter is the relevant issue; the former creates metaphysical confusion. God *can* flood a valley, and we know that human agents can *also* flood valleys, but not *both* flooding the same valley at the same time. Focusing on the state of affairs produced rather than on the actors dissolves the omnipotence puzzle.[11]

Finally, omnipotence involves God's having the greatest possible scope of power—"maximal power." Perhaps the following set of descriptions will help us form a coherent understanding of omnipotence:[12]

Omnipotence will involve *bringing about certain states of affairs that are logically possible.* Such power isn't simply "the ability to do anything at all"—God's making himself cease to exist or creating square circles would be silly or incoherent. No power, however great, can produce something self-contradictory. Also, God's power is *bound up with his goodness.* Not *every* ability to do something should be considered worthy of divine power.[13] It would be wrong to worship a being with raw power but horrifically evil; worshiping the supreme, intrinsic Good who is also omnipotent is a different story.

Omnipotence will take into consideration *the world God has freely chosen to create from among other possible worlds that God chose not to create.* God has both chosen to create and chosen a particular world to create a world in which God weaves the free choices of human beings into the intricate tapestry of his overarching and glorious purposes. Because of the wisdom and power God exerted in creating the actual world, it would be an inappropriate expectation that God *change course* and shift from the actual world to bringing about another world that God *could have* created but, in his wisdom, chose not to.

Omnipotence doesn't involve the ability to alter the past (a metaphysical impossibility). God shouldn't be expected to change events that have already occurred–the assassination of Abraham Lincoln or the Hundred Years' War (1337–1453). While God could erase all *memory* of such events, that still wouldn't undo those events. Now, God does have the power to bring about some present or future states of affairs. That means he would also have *foreknown* them and thus would have brought about certain states of affairs that preceded them. This scenario has a bearing on whether God really answers prayer. As we've noted, prayer makes a difference: "You do not have because you do not ask" (Jas. 4:2). God, knowing the various states of affairs and human choices in the possible worlds he could have created, creates a world in which he responds to certain prayers he knows will be prayed. God, knowing what we would pray in advance, configures a world so that our prayers can have a genuine impact on the world.[14]

God is certainly *free* to act–say, to create a world rather than not–and exert his power. But we must take care to understand what God's being all-powerful truly means.

Divine Immutability

"I, the LORD, do not change." (Mal. 3:6)

Aristotle called God the "Unmoved Mover." Theologian Paul Tillich called God "the Ground of all being." Throughout church history, theologians have often portrayed God as absolutely changeless. *Any* change is presumably negative, implying God isn't perfect. Such portrayals of God, though, sound more like a static, impersonal, abstract, or mathematical principle rather than the dynamic, living, acting, history-engaging personal Being of Scripture. Theologian Colin Gunton has reminded us not to separate God's *act* from his *being.*[15] God's action reveals something of who he is, and he is not absolutely changeless. Any change on God's part wouldn't involve moving from perfection to imperfection. God can move from *not* being Creator to *becoming* Creator without diminishing his supremacy. God shifts from *not being* incarnate to *becoming* incarnate in Jesus of Nazareth. God's necessary goodness, power, and knowledge aren't affected at all by his acquiring these new characteristics–ones he didn't have before.

Absolute immutability doesn't describe the biblical God. God *comes to know* what it's like to be Creator. On having created, God *obtains* an awareness of tense or the passage of time. God's knowledge of what is actual changes with the passage of time. So even if God never freely created a world, it would still be the case that absolute changelessness isn't an *essential* feature in God. It's still *possible* that God could change.[16]

As historical theologian Jaroslav Pelikan has shown, God's immutability in Scripture, contrary to certain theological portrayals, refers to his *promise-keeping covenant faithfulness* and *reliable character.*[17] God's character, being the source of all good things, can't produce evil (Jas. 1:13). Unlike humans, God isn't fickle; he won't "repent" or "change His mind" (1 Sam. 15:29; cp. Mal. 3:6).

Why then does the Bible elsewhere tell us that God *does* "change his mind" or "repent"?[18] Or why is God "grieved" or "sorry" (*nacham*) he made humans (Gen. 6:7)? First, we're not speaking of a change in God's nature or character. Second, the words for "repent" or "be sorry" have a *range of meanings* depending on the context in the Bible. They can refer to the *experience of emotional pain or regret,* suggesting the dynamic relationality of God. While God isn't being fickle or wishy-washy, he is a being engaged with his creation, not aloof from it.

Moses pleads with God not to destroy Israel (Ex. 32:12, 14), and God relents. God, who sends Jonah to Nineveh, threatens to judge it, but God "changes his mind" or "repents" of what he had said, sparing the city. "Repent" (*nacham*) in this context (Jon. 3:9–10) refers to *relenting or changing from a stated course of action because of the recipient's change of heart.* Repenting means "retracting blessing or judgment" based on human conduct. *A change within the recipients after a threat renders blessing or judgment no longer appropriate.*[19] Although Jonah confidently proclaimed, "Yet forty days and Nineveh will be overthrown" (3:4), he *already knew* that God, being gracious and compassionate, was capable of showing mercy (4:2)–*if* there was repentance. That's why he didn't want to warn Israel's enemies! David, while fasting and weeping in hopes that his illegitimate son would live, reckoned, "Who knows, the LORD may be gracious to me" (2 Sam. 12:22).

There's often an underlying conditionality behind God's warnings: judgment *will* come *unless* we repent:

> "At one moment I [God] might speak concerning a nation or concerning a kingdom to uproot, to pull down, or to destroy it; if that nation against which I have spoken turns from its evil, I will relent concerning the calamity I planned to bring on it. Or at another moment I might speak concerning a nation or concerning a kingdom to build up or to plant it; if it does evil in My sight by not obeying My voice, then I will think better of the good with which I had promised to bless it." (Jer. 18:7–10)

During the time of Noah, Moses, and Jonah, God knew exactly what he was going to do–though this meant "relenting" or "repenting" in response to how humans acted. When biblical narratives portray God changing his mind, they appear to *ignore* the question of whether God knew this change would take place. God even seems surprised at times. Why? The biblical authors use a *literary means* to depict an interactive God who takes the divine-human drama seriously. Think of the literary device used in Job: God makes a bet with Satan and is portrayed as not knowing the outcome, but that would ruin the story line! Despite God's eternal awareness of human prayers and responses, the Scriptures capture God's dynamic historical engagement.

While God's faithful character and promise-keeping don't change, he still experiences changes. The triune God isn't the static, untouchable deity commonly associated with sophisticated Greek philosophy. He's a prayer-answering, history-engaging God.

Divine Impassibility

How often they…grieved Him in the desert. (Ps. 78:40)

Related to the question, "Can God change?" is the question, "Can God suffer?" Traditional Christian theology has held that God can't suffer (impassible): he can't be acted on by his creation. The Scriptures, though, present a God who is able to suffer. God can be "grieved in His heart" (Gen. 6:6). His Spirit can be quenched and resisted. God movingly declares about unfaithful Israel, "how I have been hurt by their adulterous hearts which turned away from Me" (Ezek. 6:9). Biblical scholar D. A. Carson asks, if God doesn't suffer, "Why does the Bible spend so much time depicting him as if he does?" Indeed, the "biblical evidence, in both Testaments, pictures God as a being who can suffer."[20] Here's Jaroslav Pelikan again: "It is significant that Christian theologians customarily set down the doctrine of the impassibility of God without bothering to provide very much biblical support or theological proof." This concept came into Christian doctrine from Greek philosophy.[21]

God's sovereignty and unchanging nature imply that God *isn't* at the mercy of his creatures' actions, nor does he lack control of his emotions. Advocates of God's absolute impassibility are right to protect this emphasis. On the other hand, though, God isn't indifferent to creaturely attitudes and actions. Perhaps it's more helpful to distinguish between God's being emotionally *touched* by human suffering, repentance, and grief and his being emotionally *crushed* by human experiences and actions. Of course, God is perfectly happy in himself, the knowledge of his good creation, and his directing history to completion (cp. Ps. 50:7–15).[22] But God truly does suffer—particularly in the incarnate Christ on the cross. As Plantinga observes, "Some theologians claim that God cannot suffer. I believe they are wrong. God's capacity for suffering, I believe, is proportional to his greatness."[23]

Is God *play-acting* in his suffering since he *knows* what is going to happen anyway? Not at all! We may know that a loved one is going to die in the near future, but that doesn't eliminate the experience of pain and sorrow once he or she passes away.

Also, suffering isn't *imposed on* God from outside. God suffers because of his sovereign decision—something that comes from *within* the triune God, something God *determines* to accept.[24]

Divine Humility

"I dwell on a high and holy place,
And also with the contrite and lowly of spirit." (Isa. 57:15)

Some people charge that God seems so egotistical and attention-seeking. Atheist Bede Rundle puts it this way:

> If you are going to make your god in the image of man, you might at least filter out some of the less desirable human traits. God should be above any sort of attention-seeking behaviour, for instance, and an insistence on being told how unsurpassably wonderful one is does not rate highly. As Hume, in the guise of Philo, observed: "It is an absurdity to believe that the Deity has human passions, and one of the lowest of human passions, a restless appetite for applause." True, this objection assumes that God commands us to worship him in order to gratify some self-regarding desire on his part, when it could be that the point of singing God's praises was protective—to propitiate a God who could be angry or jealous, for instance—but this hardly shows God in a better light.[25]

On closer scrutiny, the Scriptures actually reveal a humble God, not a vain one. As the philosophical and theological literature does not discuss this important topic, we'll devote a little more space to it here.[26]

First, humility involves an appropriate acknowledgment and realistic assessment of oneself; pride, on the other hand, is an inflated view of one's self or accomplishments. So "pride" or "vanity" doesn't accurately describe God, who has a realistic—rather than inflated—view of himself. Vanity is an overblown self-perception. Yes, God knows himself to be maximally great. Denying this would be a denial of reality—like a world-famous concert pianist saying, "I don't play piano all that well." But God doesn't take credit where credit isn't due: he doesn't take credit for making humans freely choose this or that, since it's up to humans to do the choosing; or, even though God's purposes can't be thwarted and he can use evil choices or circumstances for his ends, he doesn't take credit for evil (Jas. 1:17). God knows the extent of his greatness, his esteemed place in the order of things; however, that doesn't spill over into reality-denial. His self-awareness is absolutely accurate. And his concern that we give him "glory"—due honor, credit, and acknowledgment—stems from his being in touch with reality. To diminish the credit this maximally great God deserves—not to honor him—is to enter the realm of reality-denial.

Second, the triune God is intrinsically other-centered within himself. Because many people don't think of God as essentially triune, they more easily fall prey to the notion that God is vain. No, God is by nature other-centered in the self-giving love within the Trinity. Within God, no vanity exists, only mutual, other-oriented love.

Third, God's making us in his image isn't a mark of inappropriate divine pride. Our being God's image-bearers is a gift he bestows on us—one we should receive gratefully so we might share in the divine life. Being made in God's image and receiving his salvation are expressions of divine kindness, not arrogance. God's making humans in his image, some charge, is like a vain toymaker creating objects to look just like him. God's creation of humans is quite the opposite: (a) God creates humans to enjoy and share in his goodness and triune life, the divine family; (b) in creating us, God graciously and uniquely equips us to rule the world with him (sharing in his kingly role) and to worship and relate to him (a priestly role). Being made in God's image as priest-kings brings with it the ability to love God, think rationally, make moral decisions, express creativity, and care for creation. God lovingly bestows his image on us—with the Creator's high compliments, having been made "a little lower than God" (Ps. 8:5).

Fourth, worshiping God doesn't diminish our humanity, but rather fulfills it, helping us realize our very purpose—a relationship with God. Such worship realistically reflects our place in the universe: that we are creatures/sinners and God is Creator/Savior. To worship God is to acknowledge his "worth-ship"—a mind-set of self-forgetfulness as we remember and acknowledge God.[27] Worship not only humbles us, but this highest of human pursuits also exalts and transforms us into what we were designed to be. Biblical scholar Richard Bauckham astutely notes:

> For a human being to seek such universal and eternal fame would be to aspire to divinity, but God must be desired to be known to be God. The good of God's human creatures requires that he be known to them as God. There is no vanity, only revelation of truth, in God's demonstrating his deity to the nations.[28]

Acknowledging God's worship-worthiness is to be in touch with reality and to embrace what is ultimately for our own benefit. The logic of evangelism—telling the good news of Jesus—is essentially a call for people to get in touch with reality—to come into intimate personal contact with the triune God.

Fifth, God's jealousy isn't attention-seeking vanity; it is aroused when humans turn creatures or false ideas into God-substitutes. Jealousy isn't always bad—a husband's jealousy for his wife's affections, say, when another man seeks to come between this couple. Like God, he won't share his glory with another (Ex. 20:5)!

Contrary to caricature, God's jealousy is noble and virtuous. It doesn't spring from an inferiority complex that makes prideful, selfish demands, but *from a denial that God is God and that a relationship with the one true God is optional for human flourishing.* Scripture refers to divine "jealousy" in the context of idolatry and false worship.[29] Choosing this-worldly pursuits or various God-substitutes over against a relationship with God not only brings us harm, but also causes us to commit spiritual adultery (Jas. 4:4; cp. 2 Cor. 11:2).

Sixth, God's authority and human freedom aren't opposed. Rather, God's designs and commands have our best interests in mind—"for your good" (Deut. 10:13; cp. 8:16; 30:9).[30] God's relationship to us isn't primarily commander to commandee. He doesn't coerce, overriding human choice and agency. Rejecting God is ultimately a life-denying lifestyle, not a life-affirming one. When we realize God's intentions and designs for us and attend to divinely given boundaries, our lives flourish through loving, trusting relationships with God and with one another. When we live life God's way, not only is "the name of our Lord Jesus...glorified" in us, but we are "glorified in" him (2 Thess. 1:12). Like the moon reflects and shares in the sun's glory, we, too, are praised or exalted by God himself. The other-centered God delights in *praising humans* who seek to please him: our "praise" isn't from humans "but from God" (Rom. 2:29)—yet another expression of divine humility!

Seventh, when the Scriptures enjoin us to praise God, it isn't God who commands praise, but creatures spontaneously urging one another to recognize God's greatness, goodness, and worth-ship. Naturally flowing praise simply completes and expresses the creature's enjoyment of God. Praise to God in Scripture isn't God's fishing for compliments or flattery. A cursory examination of Scripture reveals a self-sufficient, self-contented triune God who doesn't need frail humans for an ego boost. That would be pathetic: "If I were hungry, I would not tell you; for the world is Mine, and all it contains" (Ps. 50:12).

Against popular misconceptions, praise isn't commanded by God. *Creatures* are caught up with God's greatness, power, goodness, holiness, and love. They fittingly erupt in praise, spontaneously beckoning the rest of us to do the same. Praise is the climax of realizing God's excellences,[31] which C. S. Lewis learned well:

> But the most obvious fact about praise—whether of God or any-thing—strangely escaped me. I thought of it in terms of compliment, approval, or the giving of honor. I had never noticed that all enjoyment spontaneously overflows into praise....The world rings with praise—lovers praising their mistresses, readers their

favorite poet, walkers praising the countryside, players praising their game....I think we delight to praise what we enjoy because the praise not merely expresses but completes the enjoyment; it is appointed consummation.[32]

Indeed, "it is good to sing praises to our God." Why? "For it is pleasant and praise is becoming" (Ps. 147:1).

A related point: when we creatures show love for God, we don't (or shouldn't) do so because of a crass desire for reward or avoidance of punishment. The sheer enjoyment of God's presence–our greatest good–and the pleasure of his approval is reward enough. Again, Lewis offers a delightful picture:

> Money is not the natural reward of love; that is why we call a man mercenary if he marries a woman for the sake of her money. But marriage is the proper reward for a real lover, and he is not mercenary for desiring it....Those who have attained everlasting life in the vision of God know very well that it is no mere bribe, but the very consummation of their earthly discipleship.[33]

Eighth, God himself is humble and continually manifests his humility in his interactions with human beings. Jesus of Nazareth turns out to be a remarkable example of the humility of God, who comes to serve us. Jesus describes himself as "gentle and humble in heart"–in the very same context as (a) his declaration of uniquely knowing, relating to, and revealing the Father and (b) the one who alone can give the weary rest for their souls (Mt. 11:27–29). Jesus' greatness and humility don't contradict each other but accurately reflect reality. Though "Lord" and "Teacher," Jesus takes the role of a slave who serves his disciples (cp. Jn. 13:1–20). He is "among you as the one who serves" (Lk. 22:27), having come to "serve" and "give His life a ransom for many" (Mk. 10:45).

Though "equal with God," the Son of God didn't clutch or grasp onto his glorified status, but humbled ("emptied") himself, becoming a slave who died in great shame and humiliation (Phil. 2:6–8). God is humble in his very nature. The Lord is not only "high above the nations," but "humbles Himself to behold" things in heaven and on earth (Ps. 113:4–6). Similarly, Isa. 57:15 affirms that the "high and exalted God" also dwells "with the contrite and lowly of spirit."

Ninth, divine humility is most evident in the humiliating and degrading death of Jesus of Nazareth on the cross; this is, simultaneously, God's greatest, most glorious achievement. The God who "became flesh, and dwelt among us" (Jn. 1:14) dined with society's undesirables and outcasts. Furthermore, divine greatness and humility are marvelously demonstrated in Jesus' own crucifixion–a display of God's shameful, degrading, naked, public, and cursed humiliation. This event turns out to be God's own mark of distinction and moment of glory! This is how low God is willing to go for our salvation!

John's gospel shows that Jesus' being "lifted up" on the cross (Jn. 12:32; cp. 3:14–15; 8:28) as both *literal* (being physically raised up onto a cross) and *figurative* (spiritual exaltation/honor from God, involving the drawing of the nations to salvation [12:32]). The moment of Christ's humiliating death is precisely when he is "glorified" (Jn. 12:23–24; 13:31–2). John's theological point? That God's great moment of glory is when he experiences the greatest humiliation and shame–when he takes the form of a servant and suffers a shameful death on a cross. According to theologian Colin Gunton, "It is as truly godlike to be humble as it is to be exalted."[34] The triune God's other-centered character within himself and toward us reveals that he is indeed humble.

Excursus: Divine Simplicity

The doctrine of divine simplicity tends to be one of the more obscure and debated aspects of the divine nature. Many Christian theologian-philosophers across the ages have held this doctrine; others have found it curious, elusive, incoherent, and unbiblical! Simplicity (or "simpleness") hasn't been uniformly defined in the history of Christian theology. Given its notable lineage, we want to mention it and offer a few thoughts for those with ears to hear!

Many theologians have considered God's simplicity to be his defining feature–what sets him apart from his creation. Now, this term is used in at least *eight* different senses–some of them being much stronger than others.[35] According to some interpretations of simplicity, God literally has *no* distinct attributes or characteristics. Unlike God, we're *compound* beings: we have (a) *essential* qualities, which make us what we are–such as the capability to think and choose; and (b) *accidental* ones–qualities or properties that could have been different, like being snub-nosed or brown-eyed.

Simplicity entails that God doesn't *have* properties; he just *is* those properties. His attributes are one: for God, *wisdom = love = holiness = justice = omnipresence = omnipotence.* God's *existence* is identical to his *essence* or *nature.* That is, God's nature demands that he exist necessarily whereas any creature's essence or nature is contingent (that is, it's logically possible that no creature exist). Everything about God is essential to him; there's nothing nonessential or "accidental." In my Aquinas philosophy class at Marquette University, a student joked: "Why does God have low insurance rates? Because he has no accidents!"

Also, creatures can *actualize* or realize their *potentiality*–like an acorn having the potentiality to become an oak. But there's no potentiality in God. God is "pure act(uality)" (*actus purus*).

A brief response: We can affirm something that some versions of simplicity try to preserve–that God's nature demands that he exist necessarily; there's no world in which he doesn't exist. We can also affirm that God isn't a being who just happens to have all the right attributes that make him supremely excellent. He doesn't have "generic deity" characteristics, as though another being could be omniscient or omnipotent but not be God.

However, some versions of divine simplicity look to be more an exercise in Greek metaphysics than a description of Scripture's robust, history-engaging triune God. Not only does it seem *really* hard to derive certain notions of simplicity from Scripture; they also seem philosophically problematic, for the following reasons:

- God's love, holiness, and omnipresence are *distinct* properties, even if they're possessed by the same being. Being a husband and being a father are clearly *distinct*, though the same man can have both characteristics. Or, some properties may always go together in all possible worlds (they are "co-extensive")—a triangle's trilaterality and triangularity, say—but these properties aren't *identical.* So God's omniscience or goodness always coexist in any possible world, but they're not identical.

- If God is simple, then, in some versions of simplicity, God really doesn't seem to be a *personal agent.* If God *is* his properties of omnipresence and wisdom and love, then he's more like an abstract object—like *triangularity* or *evenness*—which can't act or do anything.[36]

- If everything about God is *absolutely essential* to him, not accidental or contingent, then God apparently can't know things he *could* and *should* know—like possible worlds he could have created. It seems that whatever God does, he *had* to do. His choices and actions are necessary, not free. However, it's because of the *free exercise of God's will* or eternal determinations that certain contingent characteristics come to exist in God—God as Creator or Redeemer. There is some potentiality[37] in God *in the sense that he is free* and that he can bring about a contingent state of affairs—such as creation—if he so chooses.

- Aquinas claimed God *isn't really related to* his creatures; rather, his creatures are related to *him.* This was an attempt to preserve God's perfect similarity across all logically possible worlds. But this simply won't work. God very clearly has the quality of *being the Creator,* but without the universe, the triune God didn't have the quality of being Creator. So we have two *distinct* states in the divine life—one in which God knows, "I exist alone," and another in which God knows, "I have created creatures."[38] It seems strange to say that God's act of power ("pure act") is the same in all possible worlds, if, say, human creatures exist in some worlds but not others. Isn't God's free choice the very *reason* he created something contingent? If God chooses to create, then *contingency* is introduced into God. Through creation, God acquired an accidental (or non-necessary) characteristic of being Creator and then Savior. We could also add that by creating, God becomes temporal. Even though God doesn't change in his nature, non-necessary change is introduced. So perhaps those insurance rates *should* be raised!

- The doctrine of the Trinity seems problematic for certain versions of simplicity since there *are* distinctions within God. The Father, Son, and Spirit have their respective person-defining relationships and characteristics that distinguish each divine person from the other. The Father's relation to the Son is really *different* from the Son's relation to the Spirit. And there's something about the Father that makes him the Father and *not* the Son or Spirit. All attributes within the Godhead *aren't* equivalent.

7

The God of Truth

"Only fear the LORD and serve Him in truth with all your heart; for consider what great things He has done for you." (1 Sam. 12:24)

Jesus said to him, "I am the way, and the truth, and the life; no one comes to the Father but through Me." (Jn. 14:6)

"...the Spirit of truth, whom the world cannot receive." (Jn. 14:17)

"Sanctify them in the truth; Your word is truth." (Jn. 17:17)

The faithful triune God is the author of truth—the Father's "word is truth"; Jesus is "the truth" who faithfully reveals God's character; and "the Spirit of truth" has come as "another Helper" in Jesus' stead. There's nothing inauthentic or faithless about God. Jesus, "the truth," has come to "set you free" (Jn. 8:32). Satan, the "father of lies" (Jn. 8:44), seeks to distort our perceptions of what is authentic, life-imparting, and freeing. Unlike flawed humans, God is trustworthy: "let God be found true, though every man *be found* a liar" (Rom. 3:4).

A soul-destroying mind-set is gradually overtaking the West. With pseudotolerant airs, people apathetically declare, "Whatever!" or, "That's true for you but not for me," or, "That's just your perspective." Professing Christians, influenced by the spirit of the age, have become timid about truth. One Christian professor writes that he has an almost physical reaction to the word *truth*—an unfortunate response to (perhaps) arrogant, Bible-thumping "truth" tellers. Christians should view themselves as mere beggars, graciously and humbly telling other beggars where to find bread. That said, some Christians, even the most scholarly, seem so reluctant to talk about truth and knowledge—rather *unlike* the earliest Christians who lovingly proclaimed the truth of the good news with conviction and boldness. Today's timidity isn't the stuff of persecuted saints and martyrs. So how did this new mood weasel its way into our culture?

What Is Postmodernism?

Before the 1960s, the above attitudes were a lot less common. The new mood of *postmodernism* has descended, and Christians can't ignore it if we want to connect with this generation. Still, Christians must remember that while postmodernism can instruct us and reveal blind spots, its influence can be spiritually corrosive.

Before the 1600s, Westerners generally believed that *God* supplied the basis for moral value, human dignity, reason, and truth—the starting point for wisdom and knowledge (*premodernism*). God helped make sense of things, providing the filter, grid, or lens to interpret reality and human experience. Anselm's statement, "I believe that I may understand"–or, if you want to get fancy, "*credo ut intelligam*"–characterized this mind-set. Faith in God enables us to understand the world rightly.

Roman Catholic philosopher René Descartes (1596–1650) lived in a day of skepticism—both *philosophical* and (due to the Protestant Reformation) *theological.* In a quest to silence all skeptics and ground knowledge on absolutely certain foundations, his first step was to doubt everything: "Maybe an evil genius is messing with my mind—or, the world could just be an illusion." Descartes came to realize he couldn't doubt that he was doubting—a form of thinking. He confidently concluded: "*Cogito, ergo sum*"–"*I think; therefore I am.*" So Descartes unwittingly would remove God from center stage, and the individual human thinker ("I") would become the starting point for knowledge. Modernism had begun.

Europe's Enlightenment (c. 1650–1800) reflected this shift—optimistic about human progress, human potential, and reason, but skeptical about church authority, state churches, and Christian doctrine—"dogma." Modernism idealized neutral, unbiased knowledge and absolute certainty. It defended many noble ideals—reason, truth, goodness, human dignity—but without God. *Rationalism,* with its confidence in reason's supremacy, was one modern philosophy. Others included *Romanticism* (feelings); *Marxism/communism* (economics, labor, a classless society); *Nazism* (German nationalism/domination, Aryan purity); and *scientism* ("science" alone as the source of knowledge and, for some, human hope). Such God-substitutes, which presented stiff challenges to the Christian faith, furnished people with new "authoritative" starting points for understanding, living, and finding meaning.

In the wake of two World Wars, confidence in human progress and autonomy was shattered on the rocks of Auschwitz and Soviet gulags. Modernistic systems—these *metanarratives* (French *grands récits*)—ended up oppressing "the other," excluding or marginalizing Jews, capitalists, religious believers. But these systems proved to be total failures. A postmodern climate started to settle in that now questions any grand story. It tends to assume God's *non*existence; it's skeptical of certainty about *any* universal truth, reason, morality, or grand story—whether God- or human-oriented. Such perspectives are inherently oppressive. So all we're left with are fragmented perspectives or mini-narratives. If the storming of the Bastille during the French Revolution (1789) symbolizes the shift to *modernism,* the Berlin Wall's fall exactly 200 years later (1989) symbolizes the rise of *postmodernism.*

Postmodernism emphasizes our *limitations*: we're finite, biased, and embedded within a historical-cultural context. Knowledge and truth aren't neutral. They're a matter of perspective—often used in the service of political power or personal agendas. Truth is *created,* not *discovered.* Those in power get to make the rules and determine what is "true" and who is the "other," the outsider. Nietzsche, a favorite of postmoderns, sums it up: "There are *no eternal facts,* just as there are no absolute truths."[1]

Unquestionably, postmodernism has struck a nerve, exposing deep flaws in modernism. Despite some of its own incoherencies, postmodernism can teach us much.

- *We have our limitations, biases, and perspectives.* We don't enter the world as a blank slate (*tabula rasa*), but with a context—"baggage"—and a place in history. These influence thought and act. Truly, Paul noted, we "know in part" and "see in a mirror dimly" in this life (1 Cor. 13:9, 12). While we have confident assurance by God's Spirit that we're his children, we must communicate the gospel graciously and humbly. We note the context of others, being quick to listen and slow to speak (Jas. 1:19). Each of us is capable of self-deception and rationalization. We're not the purely rational persons we often believe ourselves to be.

- *The culturally or politically powerful—even the "religious"—often attempt to redefine ("spin") the truth or reality to suit their agenda.*

- *Metanarratives often do alienate and marginalize "others" or outsiders.* Postmodern thinker Emmanuel Levinas (*not* an atheist) rightly emphasized the place of "the other"—the defenseless orphan, widow, or stranger. The other-oriented God, who isn't willing that any perish (2 Pet. 3:9) but that all share in his eternal life and love, opens his arms to all. No one is beyond the reach of God's love. Those who resist God's grace marginalize or exclude *themselves* from God's presence.

- *The quest for absolute certainty in every area of life is impossible and unnecessary.* We can know many things—like the expansion of the universe or that that various planets orbit the sun—even if we don't have 100 percent certainty. Between (a) absolute, mathematical certainty and (b) utter skepticism are degrees of knowledge—the highly (im)plausible, the (im)probable, the (un)reasonable. The skeptics' demand to "prove that God exists" is problematic: What do they mean by *prove*? Do *they* live by the same standard of proof they demand of others? Also, this demand overlooks the importance of personal trust and the legitimacy of mystery and of hope.

While Christians *can* give strong reasons for the hope within, we don't do so as neutral, dispassionate, context-free observers.

Finding Truth as Limited Knowers

Despite these lessons, the fundamental problem with postmodernist thinkers is ultimately *theological*:[2] *they actually substitute one authority or metanarrative for another.* Their outspokenness against metanarratives becomes self-refuting: they themselves promote a grand story that attempts to make sense of human experience—*a grand story that questions grand stories*! They reveal truth's unavoidability!

No wonder—God has made us truth-seeking beings. We can't escape truth and reality. In denying the truth, we implicitly admit to it: *"It's true that there is no truth."* To deny a mind-independent reality (or that we can have access to it) is to assert belief in a mind-independent reality (or that at least *we* have access to it): *"We make up our own reality, and I'm not making that up!"* We keep on *bumping up against reality.* Traffic jams, exams, headaches, death are part of the thus-and-so-ness of life—its unavoidable "givens." World religions scholar Huston Smith correctly notes that we require "eco-niches"—a grid or worldview that enables us to make sense of reality and human experience. If we've been made in God's image, this isn't surprising: we'll seek a sense of place and meaning rather than feeling isolated and anxious (signs of a poor fit between our minds and reality). A good fit will be evidenced by the world's making sense.[3]

What is truth? Philosophically speaking, truth is the proper relationship to or match-up with reality—like a socket wrench fitting onto a bolt: (a) beliefs, ideas, propositions, stories, or claims are true if they match up with (b) reality—the way things are. "The moon is made of cheese" is false; it's a mismatch with the way things really are. It's false that Abraham Lincoln died of natural causes. And by its very nature, truth excludes something—falsehood.

While we're *biased* and *sinful* and though we view life from a certain *perspective*, we can still get things right. Thankfully, we can *truly know*, though not *exhaustively* or *perfectly*. God's image-bearers are truth-seeking beings by design. Attempts to avoid the truth can only end in massive inconsistency and dysfunction. If someone claims, "it's all a matter of perspective," well, isn't that just *her* perspective? If it's just her perspective and nothing more, then it's *trivial*—just one of many ultimately irrelevant perspectives. If it's not just her perspective, the belief is *self-refuting.* She is making a sweeping, universal statement that applies to all persons and cultures. This inescapable dilemma applies to those who assert the following slogans:

- "There are no facts, only interpretations": Is this a fact or just another interpretation?
- "There is no reality, only appearances": Is this statement reflecting reality, or is it just an appearance?
- "We shape reality any way we want—like a lump of clay": Is this idea just the result of trying to shape reality, or is this one abiding feature of reality that can't be manipulated any way we want?
- "It's all relative": Is this statement universally *true for all people,* or is it just *relative to the individual?* This raises the question: Why should relativists get upset with another's bigotry or intolerance if everything is relative? Isn't this just wrong for them?
- "Everything we think and do is the function of our genes/nervous system": Is this belief itself just the result of genetic/neural activity? If so, why trust it—or any belief we have? If your belief happens to be right, it's just by accident.
- "We can't get outside our context": Is this statement context-bound, or does it speak about all contexts?

Usually, people making these sweeping claims believe themselves to be exceptions to their own rules!

Relativists—who believe something can be true for one person but not for another—are quite *selective* about what's relative: questions about morality or God are typically relative (*God exists for you, but not for me*), but *not* stock exchange numbers, a city's average annual rainfall, or sports scores. (*The Cleveland Browns may have lost for you, but they won for me.*) In fact, relativists will probably give universally true and undeniable reasons to support their view: "Lots of people hold lots of different beliefs." *And* they believe that relativism *logically follows* there being so many diverse beliefs!

Ultimately, people aren't relativists for *intellectual* or *rational* reasons, but *personal, moral* ones. Philosopher John Searle notes the "much deeper reason for the persistent appeal" of views like relativism: "it satisfies a basic urge to power. It just seems too disgusting, somehow, that we should have to be at the mercy of the 'real world.'"[4] Of course, *inferior motivations* don't refute relativism, but their existence and use help keep before us the reality that most relativists aren't too concerned about consistency anyway. They don't *want* God to be in charge or to acknowledge the need for salvation. Most relativists don't need arguments; they need a moral and spiritual *cure.* Relativism rejects (a) any *universal truth* or *moral standard,* which implies that there's no need for (b) *repentance,* and thus there is no possibility of (c) finding *salvation.* However, experiencing the practical, authentic, relational, loving witness of the Christian community can help people more readily realize the hollowness of their self-centered relativism. Relativists remind us that matters of truth are deeply personal and hardly disinterested.

In biblical perspective, the faithful revelation of God's truth, beauty, and goodness isn't reducible to mere propositions—a list of truth-claims. Scripture's story, its genres of poetry or parables or prophecy, its commands and other speech acts, its powerful expressions of emotion and beauty can't be captured "in a nutshell." As the beauty of Bach's First and Second Orchestral Suites or Mozart's *Requiem* defies description, the Scriptures' rich, beautiful, and startling story—though *true*—isn't a set of facts stitched together. While propositions help us anchor the Bible's story to reality, God's faithful character and self-revelation can't be reduced to them.

Jesus' self-declaration as "the truth" (Jn. 14:6) is an affirmation that he is the genuine, trustworthy revealer of God's own character, the measure by whom all truth-claims are judged, and the test for the self-proclaimed seeker: "For this I have been born, and for this I have come into the world, to bear witness to the truth. Everyone who is of the truth hears My voice" (Jn. 18:37). Scripture views truth holistically—personally, intellectually, practically, relationally, and transformationally—not as detached, theoretical, and abstract. Being a person of truth requires more than holding correct beliefs. Being a person of truth also involves virtuous character—humility, charity, trust(worthiness), perseverance, and wisdom in judgment.

Truth and Skepticism

"The truth may exist, but can we know it?" the skeptic asks. Taoism's purported founder, Lao-Tzu, asked, "If, when I was asleep I was a man dreaming I was a butterfly, how do I know when I am awake, I am not a butterfly dreaming that I am a man?" Maybe we're just brains in a vat receiving signals through electrode hook-up so that our eating steak or winning the World Series is "virtual reality," not actually real? *Can* we truly trust our senses or our reasoning abilities?

Now skepticism can be *healthy* and *constructive*. After all, we shouldn't be gullible and naïve, believing everything we hear or read. Scripture takes a commonsense view here—a "critical realism": a world exists *independently* of human minds (*realism*), but *sifting, judging,* and *discerning* (*critical*) are often required in the knowledge process. This sifting enables us to discern between *appearances* (mirages, optical illusions, dreams) and the way things *are,* between *truth* and *falsehood.*

Then there's *unhealthy* and *corrosive* skepticism. "Global" (total) skeptics completely reject (the possibility of) knowledge. "Local" skeptics may doubt we can have knowledge about *certain aspects* of reality, but global skepticism is impossible and incoherent. *"We can't know"* is a statement of knowledge: "I know that we can't know." Ironically, such skeptics aren't truly skeptical about two fundamental things they take for granted: (a) the *inescapable logical laws* that they're constantly using or (b) that *their minds are properly functioning* so that they can draw their skeptical conclusions!

The skeptic will point out that people regularly get things wrong and fall prey to error and deception. However, this argument *already assumes knowledge* of the truth to be able to detect mistakes and deception. Furthermore, the skeptic often wrongly assumes that if another alternative is even *logically* possible, then you should question your beliefs, no matter how well-grounded. But it doesn't follow that if it's *possible* I'm wrong, therefore I *am* wrong. What's more, lots of things are *logically* possible but highly unlikely—swimming across the Atlantic or jumping to the moon.

We've seen that being less than 100 percent certain doesn't mean we can't truly know. We can have highly plausible or probable knowledge, even if it's not 100 percent certain. We can know *confidently* and *truly,* even if not *absolutely* or *exhaustively*. The problem with global skeptics is they set too high a standard for knowledge, which ironically leads to skepticism! But why should we reject many things we really do know, but with less than 100 percent certainty? Instead of accepting the skeptic's assumption, we can ask: "Can you know *with 100 percent certainty* that *100 percent certainty* is required to know something?" The honest answer is *no*—and that's okay. There are *degrees* of knowledge—what's probable, beyond reasonable doubt, evident, obvious, or certain. The skeptic incorrectly suggests that if we can't know with 100 percent certainty, then the only alterative is skepticism. But if that's the case, then we can't distinguish between *plausible* and *ridiculous* views, but that's clearly silly. Certain beliefs may require *further investigation* before they can be truly called knowledge, but that doesn't mean we reject whatever doesn't immediately have strong warrant.

In everyday matters, we're right to follow the "credulity principle"—all things being equal, our senses or reasoning abilities are innocent until proven guilty. We typically follow this "commonsense realism"; there's no reason to reject what seems so obvious to us in favor of less-obvious alternatives. Of course, our proneness to sin and self-deception—of which extreme skepticism is a symptom—tends to emerge with issues that *deeply involve us as persons*—belief in God or in right and wrong. Like relativism, skepticism tends to eliminate personal or moral responsibility since it systematically ignores or evades *truth*, which is a crucial component of knowledge. If nothing will persuade the global skeptic anyway, perhaps his position is less rational and more personal. Skepticism can be an easy way out of making commitments, being morally responsible, and pursuing God.

Motives, of course, don't prove or disprove a position, but we should consider personal stumbling blocks that may be driving the skeptical enterprise—issues that only grace and humility can help dislodge. Philosopher Dallas Willard notes that a comprehensive skepticism is *an affliction of the mind for which treatment is appropriate,* but it can't be advanced as a *rational* ground for anything.[5]

We must never forget that commitment to truth involves virtue or character. While *skepticism, cynicism,* and *suspicion* may define postmodernism or may characterize a Godless perspective, *trust* and *charity* should be the Christian's stance. We're persons made in a relational God's image; therefore, *trust* in a faithful heavenly Father and the cultivation of trusting and faithful relationships in our individualistic, self-sufficient age are utterly fitting. And unlike the postmodern approach, *charity* is another virtue we must cultivate—namely, giving the benefit of the doubt and a listening ear. Faith(fulness) and love are profoundly bound up with commitment to truth.

Assessing Worldviews

See to it that no one takes you captive through philosophy and empty deception, according to the tradition of men, according to the elementary principles of the world, rather than according to Christ. (Col. 2:8)

Another concern with skepticism is its failure to take seriously the inference to the best explanation: Which worldview does the best job of explaining reality—why things are the way they are? Skepticism offers little guidance on this important question, but we should explore it.

We find ourselves facing *baffling questions* that have no easy answers—in addition to the tangled conditions of our own hearts, prone to *idolatry* and *self-deception.* Even so, we can observe certain features of our world to help us get a foothold or vantage point from which to assess belief-systems.

Why be a *Christian* rather than a Muslim, Buddhist, or atheist? Ultimately, because the Christian faith is *true.* If Christ's body hasn't been raised, our faith is false; and we have no hope. How then do we determine whether a worldview or philosophy of life is more likely true than another? There's no algorithm or precise mechanical formula to follow, but some pointers and guideposts can help us on our journey. Humility, perseverance, charitability, and wise judgment will also be required.

I've heard critics claim that if we "find the truth," then spiritual journey somehow stops—"What then?" Truth, however, isn't something to simply discover, but to explore, enjoy, and love. When we find the truth in the person of Christ, we enter into a living and vital relationship with the triune God. The critics' objection turns out to be misguided—like asking, "Once you find a life-partner and get married, what then?"

The Christian faith focuses on Jesus of Nazareth, as Scriptures attest. We have an immediate starting point to investigate whether there is a ring of truth to Jesus' person and work. Generally speaking, we could propose some guidelines for assessing rival views. These criteria don't necessarily receive *equal* weight; some will be clearer and more fundamental than others. For example, a worldview's match-up with reality (#1) should be weighted more strongly than practical livability (#5). After all, if Jesus didn't rise from the dead, then the claim that "Jesus makes me happy and gives me purpose" is sorely misguided and out of touch with reality.

1. *A worldview is more likely to be true if it's factually supportable and matches up with what we know to be real.* The Qur'an claims Jesus didn't die on the cross: "they slew him not, but Allah took him up unto Himself" (Sura 4:157–58). If true, this would undermine the Christian faith. Jesus' death is mentioned in various extrabiblical documents, though, and no history-of-Jesus scholar takes seriously the Qur'an's guidance. Or, though the Qur'an is purportedly eternal and without alteration throughout its history, then the strong evidence of human editing and even expunging certain sections appears to negate this.[6] And Muslims claim that the original Law (*Taurat*) or Gospel (*Injil*) has been corrupted—contrary to the historical and textual evidence.[7]

2. *A worldview is more likely to be true if it is coherent or internally consistent rather than self-contradictory.* A truly self-contradictory view—like relativism—is certainly false. Philosophies or religions that speak of the ineffability (or utter indescribability) of the Ultimate Reality are wrong in that it can be described as indescribable.

3. *A worldview that's likely to be true must not only be internally coherent, but must also have greater explanatory power than others.* Coherence is necessary for a view to be true, but the truth of a view involves more than coherence. Coherence is a necessary component of truth, but doesn't constitute truth. Tolkien's Lord of the Rings trilogy is remarkably internally coherent, but this doesn't mean that Middle Earth, orcs, or hobbits actually exist. Two mutually opposed belief systems—however internally consistent each is—can't both be true. A preferred worldview must not only be coherent, but must do a better job of explaining the world and human experience. When a worldview borrows from the metaphysical capital of another to hold itself together (e.g., proclaiming humans have value and dignity despite a context of valueless processes), it reveals a glaring weakness. The Christian faith, on the other hand, puts the pieces together for us, offering a natural context for explaining consciousness, rationality, objective moral values, human dignity, beauty—not to mention explaining Jesus' empty tomb or the emergence of the early church. By the Christian faith, we can truly see everything else.

4. *If a worldview neglects or denies good and evil or morality and virtue, it is fundamentally flawed.* There's a basic, undeniable reality to certain objective moral values—the goodness of kindness and self-sacrifice or the wrongness of raping, committing adultery, and torturing babies. Some Eastern philosophical views or Christian Science deny the reality of evil, distinctions between good and evil, or even individual human dignity. They fail to account for a key feature of our existence, diminishing their plausibility.

5. *A worldview is more likely true if it is livable. If it is impossible to carry out in everyday life, it is likely false.* The view of pragmatism says, "If it works, it's true." Of course, depending on your *goals*, a lot of ideas can "work" but be false or immoral. Hitler's anti-Semitic goals or Stalin's anti-private property collectivization goals may have appeared to "work," but we know there's more to truth than what works. What "works" may not match up with reality. While "working" doesn't *constitute* the truth, it may often be an *indicator* of the truth. If relativists get upset when someone violates their rights, steals their property, or even disagrees with their views, this suggests a deep defect because relativism can't be carried out in everyday life. David Hume confessed that his skeptical ideas couldn't be lived out practically; this caused a kind of an internal clash in his mind. Dinner with friends followed by backgammon would provide a kind of escape from this conflict between his philosophy and everyday life. Eastern monists who claim the world is illusory (*maya*) still live as though it isn't: they read books, eat, get stuck in traffic, and relieve themselves. They repeatedly bump up against what their worldview denies. So all things being equal, we should prefer a view that can be lived out consistently over one that simply can't. When possible, wholeness is to be preferred above compartmentalization and fragmentation.

In summary, we can ask:

- Does the worldview take reason seriously? Is it logical?
- Does it take empirical facts seriously? Is it factual?
- Does it best explain the broad range of human experience and the world we live in? Is it illuminating?
- Does it take right/good and wrong/evil seriously? Is it moral?
- Does it take everyday experience/livability seriously? Is it practical?

While we shouldn't apply these guidelines mechanically or rigidly, our innate desire for coherence, lack of contradiction, moral soundness, and connectedness to everyday life is *deeply embedded* within us. We can ill-afford to be without them—for many reasons.

PART II

CREATION

For since the creation of the world His invisible attributes, His eternal power and divine nature have been clearly seen. (Rom. 1:20)

8

Proofs or Pointers?

Natural Theology and the Evidences for God's Existence

The heavens are telling of the glory of God. (Ps. 19:1)

On TV talk shows, the Christian participant might say, "But the Bible says—." The host or fellow panelist might reply, "I respect your right to believe, but I just don't accept the Bible as authoritative. And what about the Qur'an or Bhagavad Gita?"

While Christians can encourage and even warn fellow believers based on Scripture's authority, where do we begin with the unchurched who don't accept it? First, we can offer good reasons for treating the Bible, not necessarily as an inspired holy book, but as *generally historically and textually reliable.* This investigation can lead to taking Jesus' message seriously.[1] If the biblical authors prove reliable where verifiable, we have good grounds for giving the benefit of the doubt where we can't verify—say, miracle-claims or authoritative statements of Jesus.

Second, God has given us *two books*—God's *Word* and God's *world.* There are *two* kinds of revelation: *special*—in Christ and the Scriptures—and *general*—in nature, reason, and conscience. We don't appeal to the Bible with non-Christians, particularly nontheists, but to God's general revelation—something more basic and accessible to all people. God isn't limited to using Scripture to bring people to a deeper awareness of himself. He can graciously use natural revelation as well—*if* people are open to good reasons for embracing the God who seeks them.

Christians can build important bridges with atheists or Hindus, who have been made in God's image but don't accept Christ's unique authority. *All* people have access to God's general revelation; they're obligated to respond to the light of God's gracious revelation that they might seek for him and find him (Acts 17:27–28). Though they had some lessons to learn, Job and his friends still understood a good bit about the universe's Creator, Sustainer, and Source of goodness. God's encounter with Job (Job 38–41) impressively depicts God's great power, intelligence, artistry, imagination– even a certain playfulness. The heavens declare God's glory (Ps. 19:1–2); God's revelation in creation and conscience is available to all (Rom. 1–2). So the prayerful Christian can talk with non-Christians about God's world, appealing to public reasons and plausible evidences from science, history, human experience, and philosophical and ethical insights.

Romans 1:20–21 affirms: "since the creation of the world [God's] invisible attributes, His eternal power and divine nature, have been clearly seen, being understood through what has been made, so that [people] are without excuse." The appropriate response to God's self-revelation in nature is to "honor Him as God or give thanks" (1:21). Paul tells his pagan audience in Lystra that God, the Creator of heaven and earth, "did not leave Himself without witness": God "did good and gave you rains from heaven and fruitful seasons, satisfying your hearts with food and gladness" (Acts 14:17). He later tells the Athenians that God is the self-sufficient being on whom we wholly depend: "in Him we live and move and exist." God's intentions for us are *relational*–that we "would seek God, if perhaps they might grope for Him and find Him, though He is not far from each one of us" (Acts 17:27–28). So if God calls on all people everywhere to *repent,* then he must have *taken initiative* to help all of us see our need and make indications of his presence universally available. The Belgic Confession (1561) sweetly speaks of God's signposts in creation: "before our eyes as a most beautiful book in which all created things, whether great or small, are as letters showing the invisible things of God to us."

Some philosophers of religion aren't so sure; they claim the world is *religiously ambiguous.*[2] Given our various human perspectives, a religious *or* naturalistic explanation and way of life could offer equally plausible and consistent interpretations of the evidence (known as the "epistemic parity thesis"). Add to the mix the world's religious belief systems, and we apparently get further theological fuzziness. We can't conclude that one religious or philosophical tradition is more obviously true than another.

Paul, who acknowledged that "now we see in a mirror dimly" (1 Cor. 13:12), along with other biblical writers firmly believed the created order tells us some important things about a personal God. Detecting God's "fingerprints" in creation assumes that we're *responsive* to God's gracious self-revelation and Spirit-promptings, that we're not *suppressing* the truth (Rom. 1:18).

This brings us to the matter of *natural theology*. This is the formulation of philosophical arguments regarding *the existence and nature of God* without specifically appealing to special revelation. *Natural theology* has gotten a bad name with talk of "proofs" for God and irrefutable conclusions ("deductions"). Aquinas' arguments for God ("the Five Ways") conclude with "this all men speak of as God" or "this we call God."[3] This suggests that no other options are possible. So let's try to get clear on what we mean—and don't mean—by "natural theology."

1. Successful arguments aren't *knock-down, air-tight, and non-negotiable "proofs" or "self-evident" reasons with mathematically certain conclusions.* The aim of these arguments regarding God's existence and nature is more modest than this—namely, to show that their conclusions are *more plausible or reasonable* than their denials, that they're highly probable and offer the best explanation for important features of our universe or human experience.[4] Actually, we can't even "prove" that other minds exist—or that the universe is more than five minutes old: perhaps the universe only appears to be ancient, and we came equipped with an entire set of what appear to be memories. However, the existence of minds and the ancient history of the universe form a commonsense or basic belief—one quite reasonable to hold. We should probably speak of *pointers* and *signposts* for God's existence—*echoes* of God's voice (Ps. 19:2)—not "proofs."

2. Good arguments should be presented in an environment of prayer and dependence on God's empowering Spirit, engaging personal relationships, Christian character, and loving Christian community (1 Pet. 3:15; Jn. 13:35).

3. These arguments aren't just relevant *for atheists* (conscious *dis*believers in God) and *agnostics* ("not-knowing" *non*-believers), as books and debates in the West have typically assumed; they apply to *nontheistic religionists*—Buddhists, Hindus, Jains, Shintoists. We can offer reasons from the created order for the existence of a good, powerful Creator—that is, reasons for *not* being Buddhists, Confucians, or Jains.

4. Given God's reconciling intentions and self-revealing actions toward the world through Christ (Jn. 3:16–17; 1 Tim. 2:4; 2 Pet. 3:9), persuading people to believe in God, though important, is still incomplete. *If a good, powerful God exists, people should seek to discover whether this God has made provision to help humans in their miserable condition.* Arguments can show the reasonableness of God's existence, but we must move beyond intellectual debate and discussion, working with the triune God to bring people into a reconciled relationship with him through Christ.

5. Such arguments don't furnish an *exhaustive* understanding of God—why think they *should?* But we can have an *adequate* understanding of God the Creator so that we can recognize our personal, moral accountability to this self-revealing Being. To say, "But this Being *may not* be the God of the Bible" won't do. If such a God exists, then this demands further prayerful searching, exploration, and reflection.

Whose Deity? Which God?

Then you call on the name of your god, and I will call on the name of the
LORD, and the God who answers by fire, He is God"....When all the people
saw [the fire], they fell on their faces; and they said, "The LORD, He is God;
the LORD, He is God." (1 Kings 18:24, 39)

Wouldn't it be terrific if God, as in Elijah's day, silenced all skeptics
with such displays of divine pyrotechnics, leaving no doubts about his
existence? Despite Elijah's victory on Mount Carmel, when Yahweh
overpowered Baal and his prophets by sending heavenly fire, the success
proved short-lived. Queen Jezebel's hostility toward Elijah continued,
as did Israel's waywardness. If we may not be able to have a heavenly
fireworks display for doubters everywhere, what about some knock-'em-
dead arguments—"proofs"—to convince them of God's existence? Why do
the critics say, "Arguments for God's existence don't work"? Of course, a
lot depends on what they mean by "work."

Critics commonly ask, *"Exactly what kind of God are we talking about?"*
After all, various theistic philosophers have claimed that their "proofs"
point to a single personal God. Why can't the arguments point to *many*
gods—polytheism—or maybe to some *abstract Principle* or *Pure Consciousness,*
as in some Eastern religions? What about a *Deistic God,* who winds up the
universe and then lets it "tick" on its own—without any miraculous acts in
history or special revelations? Or maybe God is just a powerful *evil deity*
who crushes all who don't submit to him. Antony Flew, once a prominent
atheist, has come to believe that a Deistic "Jeffersonian deity" must exist
because of the scientific discoveries for the universe's beginning and its
being finely tuned for life, neither of which can be naturalistically explained.
However, Flew still has problems with a God who allows evil or hell.[5] So the
standard theistic arguments seem rather incomplete; they don't necessarily
point us to the triune God.

There's another criticism. Perhaps an argument is successful in
showing a powerful cause of the universe exists (cosmological argument)
or that there's a designer of the universe (teleological argument). This still
doesn't show that this First or Uncaused Cause and the Designer are *one*
and the same—or that either is morally *good* and *worthy of worship.* In fact,
a cosmological argument may show that a powerful creator exists, but
not necessarily *all*-powerful. Some natural theologians have given the
impression that their arguments establish a "robust theism"—the existence
of a full-blown omniscient, omnipotent, omnipresent, omnibenevolent, self-
sufficient, and self-explanatory divine Cause. In fact, the results are much
more modest—a "thin theism." Let's respond to some of these criticisms.

First, if it's reasonable to believe that "Something is out there," we shouldn't
dismiss the evidence simply because this "Something" isn't as clear as we'd like it to
be. If a Being outside the universe exists, this fact itself is hugely important.
Maybe this Being is connected to the meaning of our existence. Maybe this

Being is self-revealing in fairly specific ways and has even acted in human history. Maybe this Being expects us—to the best of our ability—to actively reach out and seek a greater understanding of this Being and, perhaps, of the key to our existence. Maybe we can see pointers and fingerprints of this Being's nature and existence as gifts to be gratefully received rather than skeptically and suspiciously handled.

Second, if this "Something out there" started and designed the universe, then we live in a "haunted universe" that not only calls for an explanation, but also undercuts atheistic or nontheistic alternatives.[6] Any such plausible evidence would undercut atheism—whether one is a scientific naturalist, a Buddhist, or Confucian. Such indicators would also eliminate from consideration an impersonal or abstract "Ultimate Reality" within various Eastern philosophies. The universe's beginning out of nothing, its vast beauty, and its incredible life-sustaining intricacy as well as our existence as personal, moral, valuable, free, creative, and reasoning beings point to a purposeful, personal universe—not a coldly impersonal, hostile, abstract, or purposeless one. A personal God—especially a relational triune Creator, from whom and by whom are all things, and for whom and through whom we exist (1 Cor. 8:6)—provides a context for affirming this. We've noted that the tri-personal God—as opposed to an impersonal Ultimate Reality—offers a stronger foundation for personal virtues such as love and compassion.

Available reasons for a personal Creator's nature and existence indicate that ours is a supernaturally "haunted" universe; thus nontheistic viewpoints—including Buddhism or Shintoism—are in error on this point. Such an observation should prompt further probing and whole-hearted seeking, not casual dismissal.

Third, on closer scrutiny, the proposed alternatives to the biblical God aren't all that impressive. David Hume wondered why *one* God explains the design of the universe. If *lots* of people—not just one—make obviously designed skyscrapers, cars, or computers, why not *lots* of designing deities? Or what if a Deistic God, an evil deity, or some other entity created or designed the world? Some of these alternatives that various skeptical philosophers have suggested appear in the following list.

- **Alternative 1: Many gods (polytheism)?**
  Response: The principle of simplicity or economy helps here: if just one God will suffice, why resort to many gods to explain the universe's existence or design? An additional concern is the interrelationship of these multiple deities: how do these distinct, independently minded beings work together? Again, one God is a simpler explanation.
- **Alternative 2: A powerful evil deity?**
  Response: If "God" suggests a worship-worthy Being, then an evil deity wouldn't be worthy of our worship and shouldn't be called "God." We intuitively prefer goodness over evil. A cosmic bully or

evil deity wouldn't legitimately command our grateful respect and loving worship.

- **Alternative 3: A Deistic deity?**
  Response: The Deistic God is inferior to the triune God. The Deist's God isn't intrinsically relational or deeply involved in creation (or immanent). He winds up the universe, lets it go, and leaves humans with no concrete guidance–no miraculous signs, no redemption, no special revelation, no engagement with humans (e.g., in the Incarnation). Deists reject miracles since they make God appear inept, needing to adjust the universe periodically to keep it running well. However, miracles don't supply what nature lacks. They display God's grace and concern for us.

- **Alternative 4: An abstract impersonal Principle?**
  Response: Abstract principles or objects (numbers, logical laws, mathematical theorems) can't produce anything, let alone generate and sustain a universe. Abstractions do nothing. Not so with an intelligent personal Agent! Also, if the universe came into existence a finite time ago out of nothing (as Big Bang cosmology suggests), a personal cause–not an abstraction–is a more likely explanation.

These alternatives don't exhaust the list of "Ultimate Reality" candidates, but you get the idea.

Fourth, theistic arguments shouldn't be considered in isolation from, but in combination with, one another. Bracketing the ontological argument (for a maximally great Being, whose nonexistence can't be conceived), each successful theistic argument suggests various features about God:

- **Cosmological argument:** A very *powerful personal Cause* of the contingent universe exists; the fact that the universe began to exist a finite time ago suggests a *personal* Agent who brought something from nothing.
- **Teleological argument:** An *intelligent* designing–and thus *personal–Agent* exists, who intends certain ordered ends for creation. Though not every aspect of creation is orderly, such as the quantum world, order can incorporate and accommodate randomness.
- **Moral argument:** A *personal, intrinsically good* Being exists–rather than a impersonal monistic "One" beyond all distinction and beyond good and evil.
- **Argument from consciousness:** A supremely *self-aware* Being exists–rather than some abstract principle or force.
- **Argument from reason:** A *truthful, rational* Being exists.
- **Argument from beauty:** A *beautiful* and *alluring* Being exists.
- **Argument from religious experience:** A *transcendent, awe-inspiring Presence* exists whom many persons have encountered, further reinforcing the weight of other theistic arguments.

- **Argument from miracles:** An *engaged, concerned personal Agent* exist. If certain events—say, Jesus' resurrection—are better explained within Israel's religious context of divine activity rather than within a naturalistic one, we have reason for believing in the triune God. Although this is technically "special revelation," we can still appeal to such miracles as publicly accessible and worthy of historical investigation.

Aside from the argument from miracles, the critic typically ignores a more holistic approach to these arguments, which furnishes us with a more filled-out understanding of God and would *even more* successfully challenge alternative religious and philosophical positions. While one version of the *cosmological* argument, say, may allow for a Deistic God who creates and then withdraws, adding the *moral* argument for a supremely good God would undermine Deism's morally inferior deity, who doesn't engage the human situation.

It's logically possible to infer a distinct entity from each successful theistic argument (one from each). However, "Ockham's razor"—the principle of economy— suggests that if the conclusions of these arguments for God don't involve mutually conflicting attributes, then why involve more entities unnecessarily? Unless we have further evidence for multiple deities, the simpler, less-convoluted alternative is one God.

Despite all this, natural theology typically *falls short* of the robustly triune theism within Scripture—"thin theism" vs. "thick theism." Still, successful arguments are adequate pointers to warrant a personal response to the Creator and even to hold human beings accountable to him. While successful theistic arguments don't give as many specifics about God, *they shouldn't be dismissed as inadequate or insufficient.* Rather, *they at least present a reasonable basis for believing in the existence of a transcendent Being (a) with whom we have to deal, (b) to whom we should be rightly related, and (c) who has a rightful claim on our lives.*

The Scriptures themselves suggest that encountering God's self-revelation through nature, reason, and conscience is ample for us to recognize God as Creator, thus having a claim on our lives. When biblical writers speak of the Creator, they are referring to the one, true, worship-worthy God. Yahweh is the true God who made the heavens and the earth—in contrast to idols, or false gods (Jer. 10:10–12; cp. Isa. 45:18). The One who formed the mountains and the earth is fittingly called "God" (Ps. 90:2).

Those dismissing such arguments because "they don't prove the God of the Bible" move too quickly. A *wiser* response calls for further examination of the interrelations between natural theology's lessons and special revelation's offerings. Rather than ending the discussion with lines like, "The universe's designer might *not* be omnipotent or omniscient," the lover of wisdom will want to explore the nature of this designer, particularly in connection with the illuminating specifics of special revelation.

*Fifth, whether a believer or not, one's expectations for what counts as a "proof"
for God's existence and nature should be a bit more modest.* We've said that
successful theistic arguments, evidences, and pointers are more reasonable
than their denials.[7] The sapiential life—the love of wisdom— while full of
conviction, calls for humility and modesty. Rather than speaking of "proofs"
and "refutations" that can be demonstrated with mathematical certainty, we
should seek to show why Christian theism in particular is not only credible,
but is more likely to be true than its alternatives.

*Sixth, despite the skeptic's use of the principle of economy (Ockham's razor), God
simply isn't an additional, unnecessary entity; rather, God's nature and existence
do a lot of explanatory work.* Earlier we talked about preferring one God
(monotheism) over polytheism (many gods) because, all things being equal,
there's no reason to prefer many gods when one God will do. Atheists or
skeptics, however, will say that a universe by itself is simpler than a universe
plus God. In response, it's highly unlikely that we can have a universe
without God. Consider: spontaneous generation (i.e., maggots simply
appear on rotting meat) is "simpler" than the actual process (involving
adult flies laying eggs) in that it involves fewer entities—just as a universe
appearing uncaused out of nothing is "simpler" than if God created it. But
the chances of a universe coming from nothing are exactly zero. To get rid
of God in the name of simplicity is to get rid of much explanatory power,
as we'll see in the next two chapters.

*Seventh, taking a personal Creator seriously has very practical implications
that we should consider.* In the book's final chapter, we'll note that practical
considerations can't be evaded. Though not a logical point, God's existence
and nature press us to be serious-minded rather than casual about such
weighty matters. Too much is at stake. For example, Buddhism's Dalai
Lama declared: "The purpose of reincarnation is to fulfill the previous
[incarnation's] life task."[8] But, practically speaking, this is a massive gamble.
What if only one life is *all* we have before our final state (Heb. 9:27)? Hoping
for "another shot" to get things right may be false comfort. Some things
just can't wait a lifetime—or more.

Moving beyond a Generic Deity

The universe isn't "religiously ambiguous." If we have good reasons
for believing in a personal, powerful, wise, and good God, then *many* other
worldviews—"religious" or not—are removed from our radar screen. When
we humbly, prayerfully offer an inquirer reasons for believing in God, we
engage in an important and legitimate task. But we can't stop here. If such
a God exists, *then we should ask: Has he done anything to address the problem
of human misery, evil, alienation, fear, shame, and despair?* Has this good
personal Creator to whom we're accountable gotten his hands dirty and
made any provision to rescue us from our desperate condition? Has he
sought to replace our sin, estrangement, and humiliation with forgiveness,

reconciliation, and dignity? Perhaps *redemption* and *hope* are part of our story, not simply distress and anguish.

In the rest of Part II, we'll look at reasons for believing a good, powerful, intelligent personal God and Creator exists—indeed, the triune God of Scripture. We'll observe how this powerful, wise, good personal Being offers us the best explanation of things. Though no small matter, any "bare" or "minimal" theism must give way to considering *the human condition*—the evil, suffering, misery, alienation, shame, despair, sin, error, and fear of death we are subject to—and *what God has done about it.* We'll look specifically at miracles—indicators of the misery-ending God's interaction with humans in history. While Part III goes into detail about our fallenness, Parts IV and V more closely examine how God reveals himself uniquely in Jesus of Nazareth, through him bringing light, help, and hope to human blindness, frailty, and despair.

The story that best helps pull the disparate strands together involves the triune God—not some generic God of thin theism—whose story includes his creation of all things; a creaturely falling away from him; his acting in and through Israel's history, bringing redemption and restoration through Jesus' death and resurrection; and then the final re-creation and the establishment of God's righteous reign. The rich resources of this story provide reasons for embracing Christ over against his rivals. God has left widely available indicators of his presence in nature, reason, and conscience. As we study nature and psychology, philosophy and ethics, history and the arts, the triune God brings illumination to our path.

9

Arguments for God's Existence

The earth is full of the lovingkindness of the Lord. (Ps. 33:5)

"The whole earth is full of His glory." (Isa. 6:3)

As we look at arguments for God's existence, we'll note some *good reasons* for noticing and seeking God; these questions can't be separated from the call to cast ourselves on his mercy and call him Master of our lives. While people may ignore these evidences and signposts, they're readily available to *all* who are interested. God isn't far from each one of us. As we'll see, God does leave enough obscurity in the world so that people can find loopholes or reasons for disbelief. An important consideration is: How does a person respond to the light or revelation that he or she *already* has? The humble seeker, grateful for any evidences God may give of himself, will appropriate such reasons for belief. Here are some such reasons.[1]

The Cosmological Argument: The Universe's Contingency, God's Necessity

In the beginning God created the heavens and the earth. (Gen. 1:1)

"Why is there something rather than nothing at all?" the philosopher Leibniz asked. Advaita Vedantan Hindus would deny a mind-independent universe exists at all since the universe itself is illusory (*maya*). They are *monists,* believing all apparent differences—between trees and chairs or you and me—aren't real. Differences are only "apparent," like a wrinkle in a carpet; this "difference" isn't anything separate from the carpet. However, why deny differences since they seem so obvious and commonsensical? Monists themselves assume this world exists in their day-to-day activities.

So in this argument, we're taking for granted the existence of a world outside our minds.

In a 1947 BBC debate, atheist Bertrand Russell responded to Christian philosopher Frederick Copleston's question regarding how the universe got here: "I should say that the universe is just there, and that's all."[2] But given that the universe isn't an illusion, can it just *be*? Doesn't its existence demand an explanation?

The cosmological argument (Greek　*kosmos* = "world, universe") moves from a series of causes to some ultimate cause or sufficient reason for the existence of the world. This argument presupposes the validity of the principle of sufficient reason (PSR)—namely, for everything that exists, there is a sufficient reason for its existence.

In Russellian fashion, atheist Michael Martin challenges the PSR, saying, "this beginning [of the universe] may be uncaused." In fact, such theories from uncausedness are "being taken seriously by scientists."[3] Ironically, many such philosophers *appeal to* "science" or "nature" to argue against God's existence or his miraculous engagement of the world; but when it comes to the universe's beginning, they must appeal to notions that can *nowhere* be supported by "science"—we have no instance of something popping into existence out of nothing. Opting for this something-from-nothing scenario when science assumes something-from-something in all other instances isn't only inconsistent; this is grasping at a desperately thin reed. The cosmological argument offers a more plausible alternative.

The cosmological argument has three basic versions. The *Thomistic* version argues to a Sustainer (sustaining Ground) of the universe's existence. The *kalam* argument plausibly argues for a personal Creator (Cause) of the universe's beginning since the series of past events can't be infinite—an argument we can't discuss here.[4]

We'll focus on the *Leibnizian* version, which claims God is the answer to "Why is there something rather than nothing?" The finite existence of anything in the universe can't ultimately be explained by a string of intermediate or contingent explanations. Some *ultimate* explanation is required. For example, I write a check to cover a debt and then another check to cover the first and so on. This string of checks will be insufficient if I have no money in the bank. When it comes to the cause of the universe, we're not just looking for the explanation for each event in a series (an *intermediate* explanation)—why an oak tree happens to be growing right now in this spot, for example. We want to explain the *whole* series (an *ultimate* explanation).

We could look at it another way: the world has two kinds of beings or entities—necessary and contingent. Therefore, anything that exists must be explained either by virtue of its own nature (necessary) or by something outside itself (contingent). Now, God exists, but not by virtue of something external to him; rather, he exists by definition or by his very nature. God's existence is self-sufficient and self-explanatory. He serves as the adequate grounding for the entire series of contingent events—and for the universe's very existence.

David Hume once asked why the universe couldn't simply be a necessary being. One problem: nothing about the universe renders it necessary by definition. In fact, we have very good reason for thinking that the universe *isn't* eternal (and therefore not necessary), but finite and contingent (dependent on something else for its existence). It began to exist, and its concentration of energy is spreading out (the universe is winding down). If *every part* of the universe is contingent, we have excellent reason to conclude that the universe *as a whole* would be contingent rather than necessary. The universe's contingency implies a noncontingent (self-sustaining, necessary) cause external to it.

The world's necessary existence just isn't intuitively obvious. Nothing about the properties of matter renders it necessarily existent. The material universe could very well not have existed. In fact, cosmological models such as the "steady state," "oscillating," "vacuum fluctuation," or "quantum gravity" (among others) are flawed precisely because they neglect the universe's obvious contingency. On the other hand, God, by definition, cannot *not* exist. To suggest that a necessarily existing Being is contingent and so may not exist in some possible world conflicts with the very definition of God.

Philosopher Charles Peirce said that universes aren't as numerous as blackberries. So, some allege, we can't be confident that the PSR applies to the universe *as a whole*, even if it applies to the particulars *within* the universe. So why can't an uncaused universe simply exist, without needing a sufficient reason for existing? Does the believer in God simply assume what he wants to prove—namely, that only God can exist necessarily and self-sufficiently? Not at all! Let's consider a few things about the PSR and God's existence. *First, many scientists themselves are seeking for that naturalistic holy grail—a "theory of everything" or a "grand unified theory"—a comprehensive and sufficient explanation for everything.* Their pursuit assumes the legitimacy of the PSR, and that it can be comprehensive.[5] *Second, we assume the PSR in everyday life—a basic intuition.* We tend to reject "just because" responses to our "why" questions. We want to "get behind" such questions to arrive at sufficient explanations. Further reinforcement for assuming the PSR is the fact that we don't live in constant fear that grizzly bears could pop into existence uncaused out of nothing. If we cross paths with them, there's a sufficient reason for their presence.

Now the atheist might say that while the PSR is true in regard to particular things or events in everyday life, the universe as a whole itself could be uncaused.[6] But this brings us to our third point: *it is still a meaningful fact about the universe that none of its members is necessary*. This fact, as Stephen Davis argues, "strongly suggests that there is *no* telling reason to consider the universe a necessary being."[7] What's more, all the physical evidence points to a universe that is temporally finite. Nothing is absurd or strange about the suggestion that the universe, unlike God, isn't a necessary being if that being is by definition self-existent, self-sufficient, and self-explanatory. Nothing about the universe suggests it is a necessary being. Indeed, nothing is absurd or unintelligible in the idea of there being no universe at all. The PSR doesn't beg the question—that is, assume what it wants to prove (in this case, God's existence). The defender of the cosmological argument can utilize the PSR without invoking or presupposing God. At least the PSR is a principle that atheists can appreciate and understand.[8] Though they may *reject* the PSR, presumably they will give some *sufficient reason* why this is so!

The question of why there is something rather than nothing is not only relevant for atheists and agnostics, but also for adherents to nontheistic religions. Noted British Buddhism scholar Paul Williams became a Christian after thirty years' devotion to Buddhism because it couldn't answer this fundamental question: Why *does* the contingent universe exist at all? He concluded that only a *necessary* being—something classical Buddhism rejects—could serve as an adequate explanation to that question: "I have come to believe that there is a gap in the Buddhist explanation of things which for me can only be filled by God, the sort of God spoken of in a Christian tradition such as that of St. Thomas Aquinas."[9] Williams kept on bumping up against implications of this question, which would worry him, eventually prodding him to a different understanding. Williams came to see that the existence of God answers key *why* questions.

The Teleological Argument: A Designed World

He counts the number of the stars; He gives names to all of them.
(Ps. 147:4)

In *Jane Eyre*, Charlotte Brontë writes of Jane's walking out into the night to pray for Mr. Rochester and reflecting:

> We know that God is everywhere; but certainly we feel His presence most when His works are on the grandest scale spread before us; and it is in the unclouded night-sky, where His worlds wheel their silent course, that we read clearest His infinitude, His omnipotence, His omnipresence....Looking up, I, with tear-dimmed eyes, saw the mighty Milky-way. Remembering what it was—what countless systems there swept space like a soft trace of light—I felt the might and strength of God.[10]

In his work *On Providence,* Stoic philosopher Seneca, who died by Nero's order (65 C.E.), spoke of the structure of the universe and the movements of its heavenly bodies—that they do "not persist without some caretaker."

Early modern scientists believed the universe to be God's artifact. And in addition to "the moral law within," the philosopher Kant was struck by "the starry heavens above" as pointers to God.

A more contemporary example of belief in design is biology professor Dean Kenyon. Having attempted a strictly naturalistic account of life's emergence from non-life (*Biochemical Predestination*), he later concluded that nature by itself couldn't have produced life. That requires intelligent planning. This retraction brought intense pressure and criticism from his colleagues, who didn't like the inference Kenyon had drawn.[11] We've also noted former atheist Antony Flew, who concluded that a divine designer must be responsible for the interrelated or integrated complexity he sees in the universe. Even if we may disagree with Darwinian evolution, Darwin himself, in the last pages of *The Origin of Species* (1859), indicated that God was necessary for evolution to get going. Indeed, he uses the word *creation* over one hundred times throughout his book. He even quotes Sir Francis Bacon's *Advancement of Learning* in the book's inscription: "To conclude, therefore, let no man…think or maintain that a man can search too far or be too well studied in the book of God's word, or in the book of God's works; divinity or philosophy; but rather let men endeavor an endless progress or proficience in both." Darwin didn't see God and evolution as inherently contradictory.

The teleological argument (Greek *telos* = "goal, end") points to features in the universe that are *specifically*, *complexly*, and *interrelatedly* arranged or ordered in such a way that suggests some personal directing intelligence or mind behind these arrangements. Human minds can grasp many such deep, specific patterns.[12] This *nature-mind* correlation produces a mind-pleasingness that we should not take for granted. We'll see how the scientist's appreciation for the beauty and elegance of basic physical laws not only indicates their truth or rightness, but also suggests design.

We're able to detect design at the *macro-level*: A beautiful and complexly arranged universe exists that is life-permitting, life-producing, and life-sustaining. We can detect design at the *micro-level*–for example, the human brain and eye or the body's various interworking systems (nervous, circulatory, reproductive, and so on). At *both* levels, we witness an intelligence or wisdom directed toward certain purposes–balanced cosmic conditions for biological life and eyes for seeing or hearts for pumping blood.

The universe is a razor's edge of delicately balanced life-permitting conditions:

- Unlike other planets, the Earth is located precisely the correct distance away from the correct-sized sun to sustain carbon-based life. It's "not too hot," "not too cold," but "just right." Indeed, this and similar conditions are called the "Goldilocks effect"!

- A star's surface temperature must be warm enough to allow construction of new chemicals (through, say, photosynthesis) but cool enough to limit potentially destructive ultraviolet light.[13]
- If gravity's force were just slightly stronger, all stars would be blue giants, which burn too quickly for life to develop. If slightly weaker, all stars would be red dwarfs, which are too cold to support life-bearing planets.[14]
- A .01 percent increase during the Big Bang's early stages would have yielded a "present-day expansion thousands of times faster than what we find. An equivalent decrease would have led to recollapse when the cosmos was a millionth its present size."[15]
- If the Big Bang's gravitational pull were to *increase* just 2 percent in strength, hydrogen atoms couldn't exist, making life impossible; all hydrogen would become helium. A 5 percent *decrease* would be equally devastating, producing a universe of only hydrogen.[16]
- The four balanced forces of nature—gravity, strong and weak nuclear force, and electromagnetism—wouldn't allow for life if even slightly out of proportion.

No wonder astronomers John Barrow and Joseph Silk describe the universe as "a surprisingly complex place," "unexpectedly hospitable to life," and in many respects "tailor-made for life." They even admit our universe resembles the "traditional metaphysical picture of creation out of nothing."[17] This fits a design hypothesis quite nicely. The alternatives to design seem to be only two—*chance* or *necessity*. Let's explore these.

Why expect such a universe if left up to *chance*? Unlike a lottery, *the actual universe is not just as probable as any other possibilities.* Cambridge physicist Stephen Hawking mentions just one fragile scenario: "If the rate of the [universe's] expansion had been smaller by even one part in a hundred thousand million million, the universe would have recollapsed before it ever reached its present size."[18] Noted theoretical physicist Roger Penrose calculates the odds of a precisely-tuned universe like ours being actualized to be one part in $10^{10(123)}$, offering this scenario to help us better grasp his point: "Even if I were to write a '0' on each separate proton and on each neutron in the entire universe—and we could throw in all the other particles for good measure—we should fall short of writing down the figure needed."[19] Of course, *chance* isn't some power; it doesn't actually *do* or *cause* anything; it's simply a prediction about statistical probabilities. Chance as a *possible* explanation of a randomly caused, life-permitting universe is *unlikely* in the extreme. Wise persons won't take such an outrageous gamble; they'll seek *more probable* explanations for specified, interrelated complexity.

The other alternative is that such order can be explained by *necessity*—the inevitable outworking of natural laws and the Big Bang's initial conditions. Physicist Paul Davies reminds us, though, that nature's laws are "contingent":

"it seems, then, that the physical universe does not have to be the way it is: it could have been otherwise."[20] And quite a lot could have "gone wrong" throughout the lengthy history of the universe.

Chance and necessity don't adequately explain the universe's apparent design. Rather than simply shrugging off these specified, balanced, complex unlikelihoods, we should react with surprise, shock, or curiosity. Whatever our questions or contentions, *design* seems the preferable option given its greater explanatory power. If God exists, a delicately balanced universe *isn't* surprising at all. If God doesn't exist, shock is appropriate.

Some suggest that ours is just one of a vast number of universes that exist—the Many Worlds Hypothesis (MWH) or World Ensemble Hypothesis (WEH), which allows for universes to split off from others; luckily, our particular universe just happens to be life-permitting. How do we respond to such scenarios?

- They *still* don't exclude the God-hypothesis, who could have created many distinct universes. God turns out be the *simpler* explanation, though: *many* worlds vs. *one* God.
- Though naturalists insist on *evidence* when challenging theists, no actual evidence exists for such universes.
- No known mechanism exists for *generating* these universes. That *itself* would require impressive design; philosopher John Earman calls such world-splitting a "miracle": "Not only is there no hint as to what causal mechanism would produce such a splitting, there is not even a characterization of when and where it takes place."[21]
- We're still left with the problem of these worlds emerging *from nothing.*
- There's no reason *coordinated, widespread* order should exist—as opposed to *patches* of order scattered here and there throughout the universe.
- The MWH hypothesis is *metaphysical speculation* that isn't even a mere inference from the scientific evidence; rather the speculation goes far beyond any and all evidence.
- We should be highly *suspicious* of MWH scenarios because they create conditions whereby *no amount of evidence—however intricate and vast—could ever count as evidence for actual design.*

We're rightly suspicious of poker players who "happen" to get four aces every time they deal a hand. We don't think, "Well, this just happens to be the overwhelmingly unlikely, once-in-a trillion trillion succession of poker hands that luckily came together at this moment. So we shouldn't be surprised." No, some intelligent planning is the more obvious explanation.

Albert Einstein and other scientists have marveled that the basic laws of physics exhibit a high degree of beauty, elegance, harmony, and ingenuity—*and* that we can understand them seems miraculous. Physicists commonly appeal to beauty and elegance in formulating theories. Such criteria make fine sense if God designed the universe, but not if God doesn't exist.

Issues Related to Design

The design argument raises some interesting and important issues.

1. *Who designed the designer?* This is similar to the "Who made God?" objection. If the designer is an intelligent being, why does the designer need to be designed? The designer is a sufficient explanatory stopping-point. Further, to say a designer brought about the universe's specified complexity is a better explanation than appealing to "that's just the way it is."

2. *Is design opposed to science?* To a significant degree, science actually *presupposes* design: the universe is *comprehensible*; its patterns and processes can be *studied* by human minds. Physicist Paul Davies reminds us: "Science began as an outgrowth of theology, and all scientists, whether atheists or theists...accept an essentially theological worldview."[22] Kant himself affirmed that science can't get underway without certain theistic assumptions such as the world's knowability and orderliness. The world has been placed in an "artfully arranged structure," having a "determinative purpose, carried out with great wisdom," and created by a "sublime and wise cause."[23]

Indeed, SETI—the Search for Extraterrestrial Intelligence—is considered by many to be scientifically legitimate. Now what if life emerged on Earth through the intelligent planning of *Martians* rather than God? Would *this* be a scientific explanation? *If God did exactly the same thing as Martians—initiating life on this planet—based on the identical evidence, why would this, even if true, be bad science or even no science at all?*[24] Why should we exclude God from fulfilling this role?

Consider *human agents*: Nature can't by itself produce skyscrapers or computers; human agents must bridge that gap. So why can't the actions of human agents in nature serve as an analogy to God's actions in nature? And why can't we speak of a God who has designed nature's laws and processes? If nondivine agents can act in nature (humans or Martians), why not God? Divine activity could well be a legitimate inference from the observable evidence.

Even if God never supernaturally acted within the world, the structure of the universe could still be supernaturally ordered. God's involvement would still be necessary for both the universe's precision-tuning for life and for life to emerge and be sustained. If left up to unguided processes, such conditions would never produce and sustain life. So even if Darwin's thesis rejects divine action in the world once life came about, that doesn't exclude original design.[25] Another inscription in the front of Darwin's *Origin of Species* is from Joseph Butler's *Analogy of Revealed Religion,* where "natural" means only "stated, fixed, or settled": "what is natural as much requires and presupposes an intelligent agent to render it so, i.e., to effect it continually or at stated times, as what is supernatural or miraculous does to effect it for once." God is at least the universe's Artist and Architect.

3. *Even if we don't know the designer's intentions or purposes, we can still detect design.* A biology professor once told me: "If God brought about first life, I'd like to know exactly *how.*" Wouldn't we all! But even if we don't know exactly how satellites transmit photos to earth or how cell phones work, we can readily see that intelligence is behind such technology. We can even detect design in certain machines when we don't know the point of their design. Nor do we have to *observe* how something is designed—nor do we have to reproduce an artifact—to know it was designed. Why even assume all space-time events must be gradualistic and predictable?

Ironically, many who declare design to be "unscientific" readily offer "empirical evidence" or "naturalistic explanations" for *apparent design,* but that suggests *it's in principle possible to detect design empirically.* Scientists such as Richard Dawkins and Francis Crick, we'll see below, acknowledge that, say, DNA *appears* designed but can be explained naturalistically. But even if this is the result of evolutionary processes, it hardly excludes divine purposes.

4. *Why isn't this world perfect?* Some people mistakenly assume the world, if designed, should have been a perfect utopia, both biologically and morally. However, Romans 8 affirms that creation groans not only because sin is now present, but also because creation, being limited *from the start*, was moving toward a *new* creation. God didn't create us with perfect, immortal bodies from the outset, but we await "the redemption of our [resurrected] body" (8:23). God didn't give humans eagle-vision, but he endowed us with the possibility of seeing quite adequately. While God created a "very good *[tôb me'od]*" world (Gen. 1:31), it wasn't absolutely perfect—like the new heavens and earth will be. The same Hebrew phrase for "very good" is used elsewhere in *post-fall* settings. Rebekah, though "very beautiful *[tobat mar'eh me'od]*," wasn't absolutely perfect. The same phrase is used of the promised land, flowing with milk and honey: Numbers 14:7 states that, despite the fall, it is an "exceedingly good land *[tôbah ha'eretz me'od me'od]*"—even more strongly stated than Genesis 1:31! Furthermore, Psalm 104, a creation psalm, and God's description of his own creation in Job 38–41 suggest that animal death and the food chain are present *at creation*—not after the fall.[26] God's "very good" creation of heaven and earth wasn't ultimate perfection—an end in itself—but a *foreshadowing* of or *means* to something greater and enduring.[27]

So why would God make an African rhino with two horns and an Indian rhino only with one? Why is the human spine prone to problems? Why are our bodies so vulnerable to cancer? Or why would God create a species and then allow it to become extinct before human beings even emerged on the scene? Again, we aren't forced to choose between *absolute perfection* or *no design.* We have ample indications of *adequate* design. We can detect design even if things don't run as efficiently as we think they should—or even if they become extinct. The more primitive Model-T Ford and the more advanced Saleen S7 clearly exhibit design and purpose. So long as design is adequate for reasonable function, why assume design must entail perfection? And some critics have had to "eat crow" in light of further investigation. The panda's "clumsy thumb," for example, is more than adequate for scraping leaves from bamboo branches twelve hours a day; human opposable thumbs couldn't accommodate such activity without developing carpal tunnel syndrome.

5. *Why aren't things more efficient in the universe?* Some charge that if God exists, he would make organisms function as efficiently as possible. This, though, is a flawed assumption. A cursory review of Scripture reveals a God who often takes his time. He's in no hurry to grant Abraham and Sarah a promised child, to bring Israel out of Egypt, or to bring history to its climax in the new heavens and new earth (2 Pet. 3:9, 13).

Why can't God—according to his pleasure—create odd, whimsical, and even clumsy and lumbering creatures? As we read the end of the book of Job (38–41), we see that God creates flightless, winged ostriches that even abandon their own nests; he creates a food chain in which animals kill and devour other animals. Such matters aren't a problem for design, according to Scripture. If evolution is true, why couldn't God have used variation and even randomness to bring about certain results that need not be perfect? Some atheists have asked why God took billions of years before bringing human life into existence and why Earth is the only piece of cosmic real estate that is inhabited. As it turns out, creating the right conditions for life on our planet takes billions of years. Even if less time were required or if our planet alone is inhabited, so what?

6. *Many scientists utilize certain questionable theological assumptions, which are worth probing.* Einstein once wrote that when he assessed a theory, he would ask himself: "If I were God, would I have made the universe in that way?" This question, while interesting, can easily lead to idolatry. Why should we creatures presume to know better than the Creator (Rom. 9:20), condemning God that we may be justified (Job 40:8)? Demanding a maximally efficient deity who adheres to a Protestant work ethic goes against Scripture, which regularly reminds us that God does things for his pleasure without feeling time-pressure or the need for efficiency.

7. *What about the apparent cruelty of a Creator who would make viruses, tapeworms, or bacteria?* Ironically, skeptics point out that "the design argument doesn't prove that the designer is all-good," but then they slip the moral issue into the design argument to discount it. However, the moral argument addresses issues like goodness and a response to evil. Also, something can still be *designed*, though for *evil* purposes—like chemical weapons or medieval instruments of torture like racks and thumbscrews. While evilly intended, they are clearly *designed*. Also, so far as humans go, God may have morally sufficient reasons for bringing viruses and tapeworms into existence. Though protected and preserved from death and danger before the fall, humans became vulnerable to viral diseases, hurricanes,

and earthquakes once they turned away from God. We now live with regular—even harsh—reminders of life's fragility, that all isn't well in the world. These present opportunities to humbly seek God, casting ourselves on his mercy. Evil need not diminish our amazement at the world's specific order and interrelated complexity.

Again, even if evolution turns out to be true, it hardly undermines God's design, but only removes it a step. Even atheistic evolutionists speak of the apparent design in biological life (e.g., "the appearance of having been designed for a purpose"); this is hardly a negation of God's existence but rather in keeping with it.

God's self-revelation in nature, despite puzzles and questions, reveals signs of intelligent planning by God. To cite Paul Davies again:

> Some of my colleagues embrace the same scientific facts as I, but deny any deeper significance. They shrug aside the breathtaking ingenuity of the laws of physics, the extraordinary felicity of the physical world, and the surprising intelligibility of the physical world, accepting these things as a package of marvels that just happens to be. But I cannot do this.[28]

The Moral Argument: A World of Goodness

For when Gentiles who do not have the Law [of Moses] do instinctively the things of the Law, these, not having the Law, are a law to themselves, in that they show the work of the Law written in their hearts, their conscience bearing witness and their thoughts alternately accusing or else defending them. (Rom. 2:14–15)

Here Paul indicates that people *don't* need the Bible to know right from wrong. As part of God's general self-revelation, he has endowed us with the basic capacity to recognize goodness—even if some people may resist or suppress this knowledge and harden their consciences. The prophet Amos delivers severe warnings from God to surrounding *Gentile* nations because of their atrocities and crimes against humanity—ripping open pregnant women, breaking treaties, acting treacherously, stifling compassion (Am. 1–2). The Bible assumes that nations without God's special revelation *still should have known better.* C. S. Lewis's *Abolition of Man* catalogues the same moral codes from vastly different civilizations and cultures—Babylonian, Egyptian, Hebrew, Greek: *Don't murder; honor your parents; don't take what isn't yours; tell the truth.*[29]

Despite cultural distortions and biases, *we instinctively know to treat others as we want to be treated*—and that rape, torturing babies, committing adultery, and murder are wrong. Scripture assumes humans are morally responsible agents who can generally know what's good—that they ought to do good and avoid evil.

What is the basis, though, for affirming human dignity and rights? One version of the moral argument is that a good God is connected to objective moral values/obligations and human dignity and rights: we've been made in the "likeness" or "image of God" (Gen. 1:26–27; Jas. 3:9). The *good* is *what we desire for its own sake*–not as a means to an end. The intrinsically good and worship-worthy God is the *Source* of all finite goods. Though human sin has introduced pervasive, distorting, damaging evil into the world, goodness within human nature–a creation by God–still remains. But how, given naturalism, could *valueless* processes actually produce such *value*? The more likely scenario is that some intrinsically valuable Being exists: *If objective moral values exist, then (most probably) God exists. Such values do exist. Therefore God (most probably) exists.* Let's look at this.

First, moral values are properly basic. Our legal and penal systems take for granted human moral responsibility and human dignity. Unlike animals–driven by instinct and environment–humans have free will and are capable of recognizing basic moral values: don't murder, rape, commit adultery, take what doesn't belong to you, or torture babies. Our revulsion at such evils–the "Yuck factor"–is an indicator we should take seriously. If we have a decently functioning conscience, we can recognize that Jesus or Mother Teresa is morally superior to Hitler–and that basic moral values aren't *invented* but *discovered*. African Americans had rights before the Civil Rights Movement or any official declarations; countries, constitutions, or "social contracts" don't *bestow* value on humans; they simply *recognize* it. Amnesty International or the UN Declaration of Human Rights (1948)–with its language of "the inherent dignity" and "the equal and inalienable rights of all members of the human family"–take for granted such intrinsic rights.

The *credulity principle* is relevant once again: we should reasonably believe what's apparent or obvious to us unless we have overriding reasons to reject it. This notion applies to our *sense* perceptions, our *reasoning* faculty, and our *moral* intuitions or perception. We generally take for granted that these faculties or capacities are *innocent until proven guilty*. We're wise to accept their testimony as reliable *unless* we have strong reasons to doubt them. This makes good sense if we've been made in the image of a trustworthy God. Though damaged by sin, we can detect right and wrong. It's simply dysfunctional to constantly doubt these faculties. We've been designed to trust them *unless* we have good reason not to (maybe having taken strong prescription drugs or committed adultery could lead to distorted thinking). Atheist philosopher Kai Nielsen comments on the vileness of child abuse and wife-beating:

> It is more reasonable to believe such elemental things to be evil
> than to believe any skeptical theory that tells us we cannot know
> or reasonably believe any of these things to be evil….I firmly
> believe that this is bedrock and right and that anyone who does

not believe it cannot have probed deeply enough into the grounds of his moral beliefs.[30]

Again, no appeal to Scripture is necessary.

Second, it's important to distinguish between knowing and being. Even though nontheists can endorse these moral values (they often say, "You don't need God to be good"), the deeper question is, "How did we come to *be* morally responsible, rights-bearing beings?" Since all human beings are God's image-bearers, nontheists—not surprisingly—recognize the same sorts of moral values theists do. The basic issue, though, is this: Why think humans have rights and dignity if they're products of valueless, physical processes in a cause-and-effect series from the Big Bang until now? The more plausible scenario is that human value and moral responsibility come from a good God who created us as intrinsically valuable, morally responsible creatures. We function properly when living morally. We glimpse something of a personal God in the world's moral order: without a personal God, no persons would exist at all. If no persons would exist, then no moral properties would be realized in our world.

Third, the existence of an independent moral realm seems unnecessary given naturalism. Some nontheists—and even some theists—will say that "Murder is wrong" would hold true even if God didn't exist; such moral values are just "brute facts."[31] But it's hard to see how love or justice itself—or wickedness, for that matter—could exist during the Jurassic period. Without God, moral properties wouldn't be realized or actualized in this world in the form of human rights or dignity or moral duties: *no God, no moral values.* Since our personhood is rooted in a personal God's specially creating us, a deep connection exists between personhood and objective moral values.[32] Like believers, atheists can *know* what's good. Why? We're all *beings* made in God's image. Who we *are* enables us to *know* right from wrong. While nontheistic Jains believe that the soul (*jiva*) in each creature entails strict nonviolence (*ahimsa*), this value is simply a brute given. But what is the basis of *any* value in this finite world if God doesn't exist?

Furthermore, if nature is all there is, how do we move from the way things *are* (the descriptive) to the way things *ought* to be (the prescriptive)? Why bring in *moral* explanations when bare *scientific* descriptions are all that naturalism requires? Moral categories can be eliminated in the name of scientific simplicity. Rather than saying *Hitler killed millions of Jews because he was morally depraved,* perhaps we can use a nonmoral "scientific" explanation: *Hitler was bitter and angry. He falsely believed that Jews were responsible for Germany's defeat in WWI. His hatred for the Jews helped release his pent-up hostility and anger, and his moral beliefs placed no restraints on his expression of hatred.*[33] In a material universe of mindless, valueless origins, scientific explanations are all we need; moral ones are superfluous.

Another problem in assuming moral values as unexplained brute facts is this: A huge cosmic coincidence would exist between (a) these *moral facts* and (b) the eventual evolutionary and highly contingent development of *self-reflective, morally responsible beings* that can actually recognize them and are obligated to them. This connection begs for an explanation. It appears that this realm of moral facts was *anticipating* our emergence—a staggering cosmic coincidence! *Even if* a moral standard exists independently of God, the question still remains of how morally valuable and responsible beings could emerge from valueless matter. The existence of a good personal God, who created humans in his image, offers a simpler and less-contrived connection.

Fourth, many critics have recognized that God's nonexistence makes it difficult to ground moral responsibility and human rights. Derk Pereboom expresses what flows from metaphysical naturalism: "our best scientific theories indeed have the consequence that we are not morally responsible for our actions"; indeed we're "more like machines than we ordinarily suppose."[34] Beyond this, atheist philosopher J. L. Mackie remarked that objective moral values would constitute evidence for God's existence: "Moral properties constitute so odd a cluster of properties and relations that they are most unlikely to have arisen in the ordinary course of events without an all-powerful god to create them."[35] Mackie went ahead and bit the bullet, claiming humans simply invent right and wrong.

Fifth, naturalistic evolutionary explanation can't adequately account for our moral nature. If we're biologically hard-wired to form moral beliefs that contribute to our survival and reproduction, then these beliefs simply *are* what they are. We can have no confidence that they are *true. Can we trust our minds if we're merely products of naturalistic evolution trying to fight, feed, flee, and reproduce?* Darwin himself was deeply troubled by this:

> With me the horrid doubt always arises whether the convictions of man's mind, which has been developed from the mind of the lower animals, are of any value or at all trustworthy. Would any one trust in the convictions of a monkey's mind, if there are any convictions in such a mind?[36]

Naturalistic evolution is interested in *fitness* and *survival*—not *true belief.* Morality then is just a *biological adaptation*—like the polar bear's thick fur: thick fur isn't more true than thin fur; it just better enhances survival.

So not only is *objective morality* undermined if naturalism is true; so is *rational thought.* Our beliefs may help us *survive*, but there's no reason to think they're *true.* So we may firmly *believe* that human beings are intrinsically valuable or that we have moral obligations or that we have free will and our choices really matter. This cluster of beliefs may help the species *homo sapiens* survive, but they may be completely *false.* So if we're blindly hard-wired by nature to form certain beliefs because of their survival-enhancing value, then we can't have confidence about the *truth-status* of these beliefs.

Again, the existence of a good—and truthful—God offers a way out: we depend on our *rational* faculties in pursuit of truth. We trust our *sense* perceptions as basically reliable; and we tend to assume our general *moral* intuitions to be trustworthy. A biblical worldview inspires confidence that we can *know* moral and rational truths—*even if they do not contribute one whit to our survival.* But if we're naturalistically hard-wired to reproduce and survive, then we can't trust these faculties. As we've noted, the scandal of such skepticism is this: we're relying on the very cognitive faculties whose unreliability is the conclusion of my skeptical argument; that is, *I'm assuming a trustworthy reasoning process to arrive at the conclusion that I can't trust my reasoning!* A nontheistic context doesn't inspire confidence in our belief-forming mechanisms.

Sixth, the Euthyphro problem isn't an irresolvable dilemma for believers. In Plato's *Euthyphro* dialogue, Socrates asks: "Is what is holy holy because the gods approve it, or do they approve it because it is holy?" (10a). Various philosophers of religion have followed up on this dilemma: (a) God's commands are *arbitrary*—something is good *because* God commands it (he could have commanded, "You *shall* commit adultery"); *or* (b) some *independent moral standard* exists (which God consults in order to command). So is morality just whatever God arbitrarily says it is—maybe an *evil* God cruelly commanding whatever he wants and calling it "good"? *Or* does a moral standard external to God exist, in which God is an unnecessary standard of goodness?

To resolve this dilemma, we need look no further than *God's good character* as the foundation and standard for morality. As God's image-bearers, we're *moral beings* with *the ability to recognize divinely rooted values* that enable us to flourish. So morality isn't arbitrary, nor does a moral standard exist independent of God.

Some critics, though, push the dilemma further: "Is the very *character* of God good because it is God's character or is it God's character because it is good?" Here are some responses.

- *The question assumes some standard external to God must exist, but the critic can't escape a similar dilemma*—why are these moral values good, *or* is there an independent standard of goodness to which *they* conform? The critic offers no advantage over the position that God's good character sufficiently grounds goodness.
- *The critic's question seems pointless as we must eventually arrive at some self-sufficient, self-explanatory stopping point.* Why is this "independent moral standard" any less arbitrary a stopping-point than God's nature?
- *A necessarily perfect God doesn't have obligations to some moral standard outside himself; he simply acts, and it is good.* God doesn't fulfill moral duties but simply expresses the goodness of his nature.

- *That God could be evil or command evil is utterly contrary to the very definition of God*–intrinsically morally excellent, maximally great, and worship-worthy. If a merely powerful *evil* being exists, that being is not worthy of our devotion.
- *Acceptance of objective moral values assumes an ultimate goal or design plan for human beings, which makes little sense given naturalism's mindless, unguided processes.* God's existence and nature and his creating us in his image presume a design plan or ideal standard for humans.

As we've seen, even if some moral standard exists independent of God, it doesn't help show how humans–given their valueless, unguided, materialistic origins–evolved into morally valuable, rights-bearing, morally responsible persons who are duty-bound to this standard. So the Euthyphro dilemma poses no serious threat to an ethic rooted in God.

Seventh, recognizing we've fallen short of the moral standard can point us in the direction of divine assistance. How do we handle our moral deficiency, guilt, and shame? (a) Our ability to recognize basic moral values and ideals as well as (b) our morally failing to live up to these ideals reveal a "moral gap." This serves to remind us of the need for (c) divine grace to enable us to live as we ought. So rather than think that "ought implies can," as Kant suggested, we failing humans can recognize our need and cast ourselves on God's readily available mercy and grace. So a more biblical understanding prompts us to conclude: "Ought implies can–with divine assistance."[37]

Philosopher John Rist finds that there is "widely admitted to be a crisis in contemporary Western debate about ethical foundations."[38] Taking seriously a personal God and Creator, the infinite Good and source of all finite goods–including human dignity–helps provide the needed metaphysical foundation for human rights and objective moral values. Apart from such a move, it seems that the crisis will become only more pronounced. If objective moral values exist and if humans have rights and dignity, however, we have good reason for believing in God. Furthermore, a successful moral argument, while enhanced by the doctrine of the mutually loving Trinity, can point us to the need for divine grace and forgiveness through Christ; it can prompt us to ponder our moral and spiritual plight and prayerfully seek assistance through more specific revelation from God. That said, the moral argument does point us to a supreme personal moral Being (1) who is worthy of worship, (2) who has made us with dignity and worth, (3) to whom we are personally accountable, and (4) who may reasonably be called "God."

The Aesthetic Argument: A Beautiful World

One thing I have asked from the LORD, that I shall seek:
That I may dwell in the house of the LORD all the days of my life,
to behold the beauty of the LORD
and to meditate in His temple. (Ps. 27:4)

Strength and beauty are in His sanctuary. (Ps. 96:6)

The aesthetic argument suggests that God makes the best sense of the world's beauty–and our appreciation of it. Scripture connects God with beauty, splendor, and glory. His wisdom is to be desired as something of "beauty" (Prov. 4:9). He commissioned craftsmen Bezalel and Oholiab to beautify the tabernacle with their God-given artistic and creative skills (Ex. 31:1–11). Psalm 90 ends by invoking God's beauty, delightfulness, or pleasantness to rest on Israel. God is the very source of beauty, and as Augustine asserted, is Beauty itself, being infinitely perfect in every way. He expresses his beauty in the creation he has made, including the creativity he bestows on humans.

Agnostic philosopher Paul Draper acknowledges that "a beautiful universe, especially one containing beings that can appreciate that beauty, is clearly more likely on theism than on naturalism and so is evidence favoring theism over naturalism."[39] Such abundant beauty, most of which isn't connected to reproduction and survival, suggests the existence of an artistic, creative God rather than a nontheistic outlook.

Further indicators of God as the source of beauty are the remarkably creative capacities of his image-bearers to craft beautiful things through art, architecture, literature, and music. Alvin Plantinga tells of a remarkably powerful aesthetic experience while studying at Harvard in the late 1950s:

> I was coming back from the university dining hall one miserable November evening, and suddenly felt as if the heavens had lit up and opened. I heard music of the most incredible beauty and sweetness (Mozart)….There weren't any voices….[I]t just felt like a kind of confirmation of what I'd thought all along.[40]

This aesthetic experience was far more forceful than any intellectual argument he'd ever heard.

Many have connected aesthetic experience in art or music to experiencing the presence of God. Just as God can use philosophical and theological arguments (Acts 17:4) and the love of the Christian community (Jn. 13:35) to show people God's reality, the paintings of Rembrandt or the music of Johann Sebastian Bach can inspire sacred wonder, awe, and delight; the Spirit can use these as an entry point to experiencing and encountering God. In fact, many of Japan's elite have been profoundly moved by the beauty of Bach's works. These have brought them courage, comfort, and *hope*–a nonexistent word in the Japanese vocabulary. Hearing Bach's *Goldberg Variations,* Japanese theologian Masashi Masuda recounts, "prompted me to probe deeper and deeper [*sic*] into its spiritual origins"; this eventually led to his conversion and interest in theology. In light of Japan's enthusiastic reception of Bach, the rector of Japan's Lutheran seminary put it this way: "Bach is a vehicle of the Holy Spirit."[41]

Furthermore, physicists and cosmologists have observed that the basic laws of physics display a remarkable degree of beauty, elegance, ingenuity, and harmony. James Clerk Maxwell's equations for electromagnetism serve as one example of this. Beauty and elegance have typically guided scientists in their quest to grasp the workings of nature and in formulating correct laws. The same is true of mathematics. Princeton mathematician Eugene Wigner has written of the "uncanny usefulness of mathematical concepts" in the natural sciences; it "is something bordering on the mysterious" and "there is no rational explanation for it."[42] But why prize beauty, elegance, and ingenuity? Whence the instinct that an elegant or beautiful theory is more likely true and preferable to an inelegant one? Such preferences seem to reflect a correlation between deep, tight patterns in nature and mind-pleasingness. This correlation seems quite odd given atheism: *the elegant interrelatedness of natural laws somehow anticipates minds that could eventually appreciate them*—another remarkable cosmic coincidence! Atheistic physicist Steven Weinberg muses: "sometimes nature seems more beautiful than strictly necessary."[43] If a beautiful, creative God has put such laws in place, then appreciating and pursuing elegant theories are both natural and appropriate.

Despite varying tastes, disagreements, and gray areas, we can detect *objective* beauty in the world. To reduce beauty to mere subjective judgments ("beauty is in the eye of the beholder") is clearly false and counterintuitive. Consider obvious, staggering examples of beauty: New England's fall foliage, Brazil's Iguazu Falls, the Boundary Waters Canoe Area on the Minnesota-Ontario border—or, more generally, crashing ocean waves, tropical sunsets, evergreen forests, glacial lakes, rugged mountains, new-fallen snow in the countryside, starry skies, deep canyons, coral reefs. Then consider the contrasts: a pile of tennis shoes or a junkyard. Furthermore, *beautiful scientific theories aren't subjective; this is evidenced by their yielding fruitful, accurate predictions.* Additionally, art appreciators know people can be *trained* or *attuned* to detect and grasp subtle beauty and elegance—just as logic and humility are needed to grasp and appreciate philosophical and theological truths.

Philosopher-theologian Jonathan Edwards (1703–1758) claimed that the universe's beauty reflects the deeper spiritual beauty rooted in God himself. As a young Christian, he would gaze at the moon or the clouds "to behold the sweet glory of God in these things." He would watch powerful thunderstorms with the flash of "lightning's play"; this would lead him to "sweet contemplations" of his "great and glorious God."[44] Just as we are attracted to physical beauty when we're functioning properly, we are also attracted to God when we are functioning properly spiritually. In fact, the cross of Christ, though ugly and cruel from a human vantage point, powerfully displays the beauty of God's love, grace, and humility.

The argument from beauty may also be evident in a well-lived life. We can be attracted to God not only through his creation and gifted humans, but through the way Christ's followers live. Paul exhorts Christians to work with integrity for their masters so "they may adorn the doctrine of God our Savior in every respect" (Titus 2:10).

Beauty is partial and incomplete, however. While heaven and earth are full of God's glory, beauty in this world points beyond itself toward a transcendent source and toward a renewed creation. The beauties of creation (or music, art, or literature) can't be captured as objects. When we try to grasp at beauty (say, to "save" the moment with a video camera), the full experience of it eludes us. We're left longing for something more. Just as there is a "moral gap" that leaves us looking for outside assistance ("grace") to live as we should, so there is an *aesthetic* gap, by which we recognize our limited experience of beauty points us to the direct experience of God's infinite beauty. In this fallen world, our vision of God's glory is incomplete. The perfect experience of beauty can only be realized in the new heavens and earth, when God and the Lamb dwell in the midst of the redeemed community.

In light of such considerations, Christians shouldn't engage in defending the Christian faith merely because it's *true*, but also because it is *good* and *beautiful*–precisely what we encounter in the life and ministry of Jesus, the Wisdom of God.

The Argument from Religious Experience: Encountering God

"I also found an altar with this inscription, 'TO AN UNKNOWN GOD.'"
(Acts 17:23)

Many people throughout history and across cultures have claimed to have profound experiences of the transcendent.[45] In Athens, Paul noticed the "unknown God" altar–one of many dating back to the sixth-century B.C.E., when the philosopher Epimenides helped deliver the plague-oppressed city, urging the citizens to sacrifice to the unknown God. Paul reminded the Athenians that "we live and move and exist" through this God and that "we also are His offspring" (Acts 17:28).[46]

Do people genuinely experience God–*even if not savingly*? Can non-Christians have a profound sense of God's presence, glory, and holiness? If heaven and earth are saturated with God's glory (Ps. 19:1–4; Isa. 6:3), it seems that people throughout the world would at least *partly* encounter the God who isn't far from each one of them–even if these encounters or experiences aren't necessarily salvific (saving).

Across many cultures, people have had (a) *mystical* encounters–a feeling of unity with God, an ecstasy or an overpowering awareness of his love. Others have had (b) *numimous* experiences (Latin, *numem* = "God" the "wholly other," a spiritual/transcendent presence or influence). Rudolf Otto's *The Idea of the Holy* considers the *numinous* the fundamental element cutting across religious traditions.[47] This is a sense of *awe* or *dread*–a *mysterium tremendum*–in the presence of a holy power. The subject feels *unworthy*–also *astonished* and *awed*–before this penetrating presence. Isaiah, for instance, felt unclean and unworthy before the thrice-holy God (Isa. 6:5); Peter told Jesus to depart, for "I am a sinful man" (Lk. 5:8). Otto claims that encountering the transcendent *also* includes a certain fascination or irresistible attraction (*fascinans*). So these profound religious experiences are a dreadful and fascinating mystery (*mysterium tremendum et fascinans*).[48] Maybe Otto is onto something. Perhaps religious experience points us *beyond*–to a transcendent God.

The Christian has come to know God through Christ and is made aware of God's loving presence and fatherly acceptance (Rom. 5:5; 8:15; Gal. 4:6). Such genuinely saving experiences are life-transforming and self-authenticating–not officially requiring evidence or argument (1 Jn. 2:20, 27). Thoughtful Christians, though, must recognize the need to offer *public* reasons for belief to the questioning outsider. An argument from religious experience is only part of the *broader* explanatory case for our examinable faith. It can offer existential power–think of Paul's repeated testimony throughout the book of Acts–when added to the *other* reasons and arguments for believing in the biblical God. This God, concerned about our condition of alienation (from ourselves, others, and God) and our search for meaning and immortality, can be personally and directly known.

1. *Why take religious experience seriously?* If something seems clearly present to me, if I'm *profoundly aware* of it, I shouldn't simply dismiss it as wholly false but should take it seriously and explore it further. We're back to the principle of credulity, a presumption of innocence: we typically assume that if something *seems* true, then we take it as true *unless* we have good reasons to question it. In Richard Swinburne's words, "How things seem to be is good grounds for a belief about how things are."[49] Plenty of honest, morally upright people have claimed some encounter with the Divine. Even if they misinterpret their experience, should their testimony be casually dismissed? Maybe they're partly right, and perhaps there's something fundamental and basic to these experiences.

2. *What if people misinterpret religious experiences?* What about non-Christians such as Mormons, who claim to have a true, deep experience of God–a "burning in the bosom"? The Mormons' faulty apprehension of God doesn't cancel out the genuineness and power of the Christian's experience–no more than a color-blind person's perception negates my seeing the color correctly.

People may and do "over-report"–that is, infer or extrapolate beyond–what their mystical or numinous experiences seem to allow. Meister Eckhart (1260–1328) interpreted his religious experience as him being indistinct from God–a problem indeed! *Union* with God is different from *identity* with God. Over-reported interpretations don't necessarily undermine their veridicality (truth). The mystic may be *over*emphasizing God's immanence (nearness) while a person having a numinous experience might be glimpsing something of God's transcendent otherness–and *both* immanence and transcendence characterize the God of Scripture. Another point: Why think over-reporting must imply or favor the *secularist's* viewpoint? Indeed, despite conflicting interpretations, we actually have good reason to think something beyond nature exists.[50]

Now, *delusional* persons may claim to experience something "transcendent" or "divine" but could be hallucinating, confused, or projecting something from their minds that isn't real. Despite this, creation is full of God's glory and is hardly a cold, hostile, and impersonal place. People may be appropriately awed and even overwhelmed by it. We would *expect* people around the world to sense God's presence and power. But, because of their background or perspective, they may infer something *less* than personal from this experience: they may *select out* or *focus on* certain apparently "impersonal" attributes of the "Ultimate Reality"–"otherness," infinity, greatness, power, sheer existence–and *filter out* any personal qualities such as love, grace, holiness, and goodness. Despite differing cultural or religious traditions in the world, *real* numinous or mystical experiences of God that share *common features* can occur–even if not *savingly.*

3. How do we distinguish true religious experiences from false ones? Perhaps the following might help offer some guidance.[51]

- A genuine experience from God *won't serve as the basis for an immoral or self-destructive lifestyle:* Indian guru Bhagwan Shree Rajneesh claimed that permissive sexual encounters bring spiritual enlightenment. No, this *wasn't* from God!
- The consequences of the experience are *good for the person* in the long run. Presumably a true religious experience, even if initially troubling, ought not to lead to instability or mental disturbance, but to *greater wholeness.*
- The *consequences are good for others.* Does one's experience create a spirit of love and self-sacrifice–or self-absorption and aloofness?
- If "religious" experiences are *self-contradictory or self-refuting* (like a Buddhist's experiencing a non-self), then the religious object doesn't exist.
- If the Christian faith is true, then religious experiences, properly understood, would *match up with the Scriptures.*

The only true and triune God graciously allows believers to experience his loving presence in Christ in a saving way–a self-authenticating encounter. We don't need further evidence to persuade us. Whether sudden or gradual, our transforming encounter with God is *properly basic*–what Calvin called the *sensus divinitatis* (the sense of the Divine). This doesn't mean my belief is infallible; it's logically possible I could be wrong. But a basic belief is proper if (a) *conditions or circumstances are right,* providing the context for belief that God is near or has forgiven me or that I need his grace, that (b) *my faculties—rational, emotional, spiritual—are properly functioning, in the way they've been designed*; and that (c) *these beliefs are successfully directed toward the truth.* While I may not be able to come up with arguments showing that other minds exist or that the earth is older than five minutes, these beliefs are still warranted in the absence of undermining arguments. The Christian's experience of God could be properly basic in this same way.

Let's get back to the Mormons' "burning in the bosom." Simply asserting, "my experience is more legitimate than yours," won't get us very far. Here's where we must go *beyond* a properly basic, self-authenticating experience through Christ—or the occurrence of "mixed experiences of God" in non-Christian settings. We should winsomely, wisely present a *public case* for our faith; perhaps these reasons can create doubts, unsettling the Mormons' (or Buddhists', etc.) false convictions that give way to true ones. With grace and gentleness, we must appeal to reasons for the hope within us (1 Pet. 3:15).

Despite conflicting religious truth-claims, a strong case can be made for the Christian faith. We have solid reasons for believing in a personal, good, wise, and powerful God—namely, the beginning and fine-tuning of the universe, moral obligations/human rights, consciousness, rationality, beauty, and the further support of religious experience. The strong evidence for God's existence would undercut a large percentage of (non-theistic) belief systems, making the task far more manageable.

4. Where do we look for guidance about religious experience given the various conflicting religious viewpoints? Despite charlatans or well-intentioned—but partially informed—religious claimants, Jesus of Nazareth stands out as the authoritative model and touchstone over all other religious experiencers. No mere human teacher, this paragon and exemplar of religious experience testified that experiencing him meant experiencing God (Jn. 14:9); he was speaking with all authority (Mt. 28:18), revealing God's wisdom (Mt. 12:42; cp. Mt. 11:19; 13:54), and bestowing saving spiritual knowledge (Mt. 11:27–30). We are wise to contemplate Peter's insightful question of Jesus: "Lord, to whom shall we go? You have words of eternal life" (Jn. 6:68).[52]

10

God–The Best Explanation

In the beginning God created the heavens and the earth. (Gen. 1:1)

"Not Enough Evidence"?

John Searle recounts what happened at a Voltaire Society banquet at Oxford, which Bertrand Russell, then in his mid-eighties, attended. Russell was asked what he would say to God if it turned out he existed. Russell replied, "Well, I would go up to Him, and I would say, 'You didn't give us enough evidence.'"[1]

In light of God's universally accessible self-revelation, Scripture asserts that "every mouth"–including Russell's–will be "closed" and "all the world" held "accountable to God" (Rom. 3:19). Such evidence becomes all the more relevant and powerful in God's special revelation in Jesus of Nazareth (Rom. 1:16–17).

Moreover, Romans 1–3 indicates that any ignorance God condemns isn't the *innocent* kind, but the *willful* sort. We may be ignorant of the speed limit, but we're not off the hook. Why? Because *we've still failed in our duty to pay attention to traffic signs.* Similarly, many people fail to attend to God's initiating grace and his presence, even resisting his revelation in nature, reason, and conscience. Instead of gratefully acknowledging that *everything* they have they've *received* (1 Cor. 4:7), they may usurp the credit for their talents, intelligence, good looks, fortunate circumstances, or other such gifts. (By the way, Christians aren't exempt from such idolatry either!) Perhaps they rationalize their actions and resist their conscience about their wrongdoing and the need for outside assistance. They may be harder on others than on themselves, holding others to a standard they themselves don't keep. They may smugly say, "Well, I'm not as bad as

Hitler or Stalin"—rather than compare themselves to fine moral exemplars like Jesus or Mother Teresa. They may simply refuse to pay attention to the available clues. The casual shoulder-shrug and cavalier dismissal of "I don't know if God exists" reflects a willful ignorance.

We've looked briefly at certain arguments for God's nature and existence. Let's step back now and look at *the broad range of the universe's features and of human experience* to see why the biblical understanding of God offers the *best explanation* and thus the *more natural context to make sense* of them. Rather than appealing to the necessary conclusions of *deduction* or the probabilities of *induction,* we can use the tools of *abduction;* that is, we can pursue the *best explanation* for the widest range of phenomena—a convergence of divine indicators. God's existence and nature furnish us with a *more powerful, wide-ranging, less-contrived* (non-ad hoc), and far *more natural or plausible setting* to explain certain important phenomena than the alternatives—rather than naturalism or nontheistic "religious" alternatives like Buddhism, Jainism, Shintoism, and certain versions of Hinduism.

Skeptics may tell us, "Despite its complexities, the universe *could be* the product of mindless, unguided processes. *Even if* the chances are remote—one in billions of billions of billions—so what? We just happened to get lucky; if not, we wouldn't be here talking about it!" This is a common, but faulty, assumption: *If an explanation is remotely logically possible, then it's just as reasonable as any other.* In everyday life, however, we typically do—and should—prefer explanations that are *more likely or probable,* not whatever's merely *logically possible.* Does the skeptic's outlook do a *better* job of explaining things than the Jewish-Christian one? We're wiser to accept a more robust, wider-ranging, less-contrived explanation—since it's more likely to be true—than rely on *it-could-have-happened-this-way* scenarios and other thin reeds.

Alvin Plantinga correctly observes that God's existence and nature offer "suggestions for answers to a wide range of otherwise intractable questions."[2] Not only will the biblical God yield the best available explanation given the range of relevant considerations, but many naturalists themselves admit they're hard-pressed to explain certain fundamental features of the universe and human experience. These tend to be the very features that God's existence and supreme nature can easily accommodate.

To see this more clearly, below is a chart comparing theism and naturalism—which maintains that (a) nature is all there is (no God, miracles) and (b) science is the best—or only—means of knowing. Charts have their limits, but hopefully these summaries are fair representations. We could also make such comparisons with *other* worldviews, but we're just picking on naturalism here! For the record, however, Eastern philosophy and Asian religion scholar Ninian Smart noted that in addition to the fact that the "Western [i.e., theistic] concept of the importance of the historical process is largely foreign to these faiths"; he adds that "the notion of a personal

God is altogether less prominent."[3] The context of God provides a very natural setting and explanation for the phenomena listed below—not so for naturalism *and* other nontheistic views.

God vs. Naturalism		
Phenomena We Recognize/Observe/ Tend to Assume	**Theistic Context**	**Naturalistic Context**
(Self-)consciousness exists.	God is *supremely self-aware/self-conscious.*	The universe was produced by *mindless, nonconscious* processes.
Personal beings exist.	God is a *personal* Being.	The universe was produced by *impersonal* processes.
We believe we make *free personal decisions/ choices.* We assume humans are *accountable* for their actions.	God is *spirit* and *a free Being,* who can freely choose to act (e.g., to create or not).	We have emerged from *material, deterministic processes* beyond our control.
We *trust our senses and rational faculties* as generally reliable for producing true beliefs.	A God of *truth and rationality* exists.	Because of our impulse to survive and reproduce, *our beliefs would only help us survive, but a number of these could be completely false.*
Human beings have *intrinsic value/dignity* and *rights.*	God is the *supremely valuable* Being.	Human beings were produced by *valueless* processes.
Objective *moral* values exist.	God's character is the source of *goodness/ moral values.*	The universe was produced by *nonmoral* processes.
The *universe began to exist* a finite time ago.	A *powerful, previously existing* God brought the universe into being without any preexisting material. (Here, *something* comes from *something.*)	The universe came into existence *from nothing by nothing*—or was, perhaps, self-caused. (Here, *something* comes from *nothing.*)
First *life* emerged.	God is a *living, active Being and the cause of all life.*	Life somehow emerged from *nonliving matter.*
The universe is *finely tuned for human life*— "the Goldilocks effect": the universe is "just right" for life.	God is a *wise, intelligent Designer.*	All the cosmic constants *just happened to be right;* given enough time and/ or many possible worlds, such a world would eventually emerge.

Beauty exists not only in landscapes and sunsets, but in "elegant" or "beautiful" scientific theories.	God is **beautiful** (Ps. 27:4) and **capable of creating beautiful things** according to his pleasure.	Beauty in the natural world is **superabundant** and in many cases **superfluous (often not linked to survival).**
Many virtuous, honest people have claimed to have awesome, life-altering **religious experiences,** encountering the transcendent (numinous) realm.	God's **presence** fills the heavens and the earth (Ps. 19:1; Isa. 6:3). He is **not far from** any one of us (Acts 17:23).	These are purely **psychological** experiences, perhaps the result of wish fulfillment or even delusions.
We (tend to) believe that life has **purpose** and **meaning.** For most of us, life is worth living.	God has created/ designed us for certain **purposes** (to love him, others, etc.); when we live them out, our lives find **meaning/enrichment.**	There is **no cosmic purpose,** blueprint, or goal for human existence.
Real evils–both moral and natural–occur in the world.	Evil's definition assumes a **design plan** (how things *ought* to be, but are not) or **standard of goodness** (a corruption or absence of goodness), by which we judge something to be evil. **God is a good Designer;** his existence supplies the crucial moral context to make sense of evil.	Atrocities, pain, and suffering **just happen.** This is just **how things are**–with no "plan" or standard of goodness to which things *ought* to conform.

Getting Help from Egypt and Babylon

"Moses was educated in all the learning of the Egyptians, and he was a man of power in words and deeds." (Acts 7:22)

…youths…showing intelligence in every branch of wisdom, endowed with understanding and discerning knowledge and who had ability for serving in the king's court; and he ordered [Ashpenaz] to teach them the literature and language of the Chaldeans. (Dan. 1:4)

Moses and Daniel with his three friends–Hebrews in foreign lands– benefited from the learning offered by their host countries, Egypt and Babylon. They became better equipped for carrying out God's purposes for their lives. Likewise, we can benefit from unbelieving scholars in the academy whose insights actually *help reinforce* the Christian message and *enhance* our communication of the gospel. With God's aid, we can defend belief in God, getting by with a little help from our naturalistic friends.

Now, if God doesn't exist, if nature is all there is, the implications are enormous. Naturalism is "imperialistic," affirms philosopher and naturalist Jaegwon Kim, exacting a "terribly high" price.[4] Harvard biologist E. O. Wilson declares that "all tangible phenomena, from the birth of the stars to the workings of social institutions, are based on material processes that are ultimately reducible, however long and torturous the sequences, to the laws of physics."[5] Naturalism's implications are monumental.

In addition to the usefulness of the chart above, we have another helpful tool as we consider the best explanation for the range of features in the universe and human experience—namely, naturalists who find naturalistic explanations *un*natural. This doesn't mean Christians have complete, airtight answers and no mystery or puzzles to deal with. However, the biblical God helps us make the best *overall* sense of crucial phenomena (although we can't cover the *all* the phenomena on the chart). Unless otherwise noted, we'll quote *only* naturalistic philosophers and scientists (in italics). As it turns out, they actually help reinforce the need for the biblical God as the better explanation.

Consciousness

Our first of several philosophers of mind, *Ned Block,* confesses that we have no idea how consciousness could have emerged from nonconscious matter: "we have nothing—*zilch*—worthy of being called a research programme.... Researchers are stumped."[6] Berkeley's *John Searle* says this is a "leading problem in the biological sciences."[7] *Jaegwon Kim* notes our "inability" to understand consciousness in an "essentially physical" world.[8] *Colin McGinn* observes that consciousness seems like "a radical novelty in the universe";[9] he wonders how our "technicolour" awareness could "arise from soggy grey matter."[10] *David Papineau* wonders *why* consciousness emerges: "to this question physicalists' 'theories of consciousness' seem to provide no answer."[11]

If, however, we have been made by a supremely self-aware Being, then the existence of consciousness has a plausible context.

Free Will, Personal Responsibility, and Truth-seeking

Despite genetic, family, or cultural influences, we typically take free will and personal responsibility for granted: our choices make a difference, and we're accountable for our actions. Our judicial system assumes that genes and environment don't excuse criminal behavior. But if all we do and believe is determined by genes and culture, why think we're morally responsible for our actions? *Thomas Nagel* sees this: "There is no room for agency in a world of neural impulses, chemical reactions, and bone and muscle movements." Naturalism implies that we're "helpless" and "not responsible" for our actions.[12] Zoologist *Jane Goodall* sees moral responsibility and free will as distinctly human—in contrast to chimps and other animals: "only humans, I believe, are capable of *deliberate* cruelty acting with the intention of causing pain and suffering."[13]

John Searle acknowledges that our intuition that "we could have done something else" is "just a fact of experience." But rather than taking this intuition seriously, he rejects free will because it allegedly interferes with the "scientific" idea of "the causal order of nature."[14] Nobel Prize winner *Francis Crick*'s "astonishing hypothesis" is that our joys and sorrows, our sense of identity and free will "are in fact no more than the behavior of a vast assembly of nerve cells and their associated molecules."[15] But then Crick's *own* beliefs "are in fact no more than the behavior of a vast assembly of nerve cells and their associated molecules." Crick's beliefs aren't more rational than anyone else's; if Crick is correct, it's just *by accident.* No wonder philosopher *Richard Rorty* considers the desire for "Truth" to be utterly "un-Darwinian."[16] We saw earlier that if we're just biological organisms, we can hold beliefs that help our species survive—"humans have rights and dignity," or, "I have certain moral obligations"—but they would be utterly *false.* Even the atheist's own rejection of God is a by-product of his survival instinct—as is the theist's belief in God. Indeed, *all* our beliefs are ultimately beyond our rational control, having been "pumped into" us through our genes and environment.

However, if we do have free will, if we are morally responsible for our actions, and if we can freely pursue truth (rather than simply being biologically programmed for survival), these all make excellent sense if we have been made in the image of a free, rational, and truthful Being. If God exists, we have good reason to think we can rise above our genes and our environment; that our choices make a difference; that we can seek the truth and find it—rather than believing that forces beyond our control dictate to our minds.

God's existence provides a much more suitable context for these features of our existence.

Objective Moral Values and Human Rights

Like the UN Declaration on Human Rights (1948), the *Humanist Manifesto III* (2003) asserts the "inherent worth and dignity" of humans. The post-WWII Nuremberg trials assumed a moral law above any country's laws; the line "but I was just following orders" was no excuse. Philosopher *Simon Blackburn* confesses a preference for dignity over humiliation, but finds that nature offers no grounds for affirming human dignity or objective moral values: "Nature has no concern for good or bad, right or wrong....We cannot get behind ethics."[17] No wonder: if we are the products of mindless and valueless processes, it's hard to see how value could emerge. *From valuelessness comes valuelessness.* Human rights and dignity or moral duties are difficult to justify if God doesn't exist.

Of course, many naturalists *reduce* ethics to biological drives and social forces. *Bertrand Russell* asserts that "the whole subject of ethics arises from the pressure of the community on the individual."[18] *Derk Pereboom* affirms that "our best scientific theories indeed have the consequence that we are not morally responsible for our actions," that we're "more like machines than we ordinarily suppose."[19] *E. O. Wilson* thinks morality is rooted in "the hypothalamus and the limbic system"; this moral sense is a "device of survival in social organisms."[20] Similarly, *James Rachels* rejects the claim that we live according to some noble moral ideal: our behavior is "comprised of tendencies which natural selection has favoured."[21] As we just saw, however, why trust *any* of our beliefs since we have no control over what is pumped into us?

If, however, a good God exists in whose image humans have been made, then we have a readily available basis for affirming objective moral values, human dignity and rights, and moral obligations. To quote *J. L. Mackie:* "Moral properties constitute so odd a cluster of properties and relations that they are most unlikely to have arisen in the ordinary course of events without an all-powerful god to create them."[22]

Objective moral values and human dignity and worth point us to God.

The Origin of the Universe a Finite Time Ago

The universe began to exist a finite time ago, and in physicist *Stephen Hawking*'s words, "Almost everyone now believes that the universe, and *time itself,* had a beginning at the Big Bang."[23] Nobel Prize-winning physicist *Steven Weinberg* acknowledges his dislike of this fact: "[The now-rejected] steady state theory [which views the universe as eternally existent] is philosophically the most attractive theory because it *least* resembles the account given in Genesis."[24] Indeed, the Big Bang gives us very good reason for thinking that something independent of the universe brought it into existence. Astrophysicists *John Barrow* and *Joseph Silk* point out: "Our new picture is more akin to the traditional metaphysical picture of creation out of nothing, for it predicts a definite beginning to events in time, indeed a definite beginning to time itself." They ask: "what preceded the event called the 'big bang'?": The "answer to our question is simple: nothing."[25] Agnostic *Anthony Kenny* notes, "A proponent of the big bang theory, at least if he is an atheist, must believe that matter came from nothing and by nothing."[26]

Does this cosmic "free lunch" make sense? No, our universe couldn't be uncaused or self-caused. Philosopher *Kai Nielsen* puts it this way: "Suppose you hear a loud bang…and you ask me, 'What made that bang?' and I reply, 'Nothing, it just happened. You would not accept that. In fact you would find my reply quite unintelligible."[27] If nothing can begin to exist without a cause when it comes to little bangs, why not the Big Bang?

So if a powerful God exists, then we have good reason for thinking that the world began to exist by his activity. Being comes from being, not from nonbeing. Something can't come from nothing since there's no *potential* for anything to begin existing.

The Emergence of First Life

The emergence of life from nonlife is a huge issue. In 2005, Harvard University launched an initiative to discover how life began; it includes biologists, astronomers, chemists, and scientists from other fields. For the naturalist, this is a difficulty indeed. *Francis Crick* has acknowledged: "The origin of life itself appears…to be almost a miracle, so many are the conditions which would have to be satisfied to get it going."[28] *Jacques Monod* notes that the origin of self-replicating, information-transferring cells from a "primordial soup" poses "Herculean problems." This is a "riddle," and how this came to be "is exceedingly difficult to imagine."[29] Indeed, *how could inert, lifeless matter produce life?*

Despite scientists' attempts to conjure up life from nonlife, such theories have thus far failed.[30] Additionally, *even if* they could produce life from nonlife by strictly natural processes, this would further support our claim that *it takes a lot of intelligent planning to do so!* The believer has no such difficulties: *If a living and active God exists, then we have a plausible context for the existence of living beings.*

The Universe's Delicately Balanced Conditions for Life (and the Existence of Remarkably Complex Organisms)

If an intelligent God exists, then a delicately balanced life-permitting universe wouldn't be surprising. We could reasonably expect a universe that involves wise planning. Given naturalism, though, the chances of a life-prohibiting universe are vastly greater than a life-permitting one. The odds are staggering enough that (a) a life-*permitting* universe exists; these are compounded exponentially to account for (b) a life-*producing* universe: just because a universe *permits* life doesn't guarantee it will *produce* life. The odds become even more remote, as our universe is also (c) a life-*sustaining* one: even if life began by itself, nature's many harsh forces could have easily snuffed it out.

While life's emergence and sustenance, despite vast improbabilities, is remotely logically possible, we should consider what's most *plausible.* No wonder one physicist describes the earth's history as "a gigantic lottery" involving "millions of fortuitous steps" that "would surely never happen the second time around, even in broad outline."[31] We've noted astrophysicists' recognition that scores and scores of exact conditions are necessary for life to exist. *Bernard Carr and Martin Rees* speak of nature's "remarkable coincidences" that "warrant some explanation."[32] Astronomer *Fred Hoyle* admits the same: "Such properties seem to run through the fabric of the natural world like a thread of happy coincidences. But there are so many odd coincidences essential to life that some explanation seems required to account for them."[33]

So remarkable is this "integrated complexity" that former atheist philosopher Antony Flew has come to believe that an intelligent God explains this.[34] Physicist *John Wheeler* summarizes his own thinking: "When I first started studying, I saw the world as composed of particles. Looking more deeply I discovered waves. Now after a lifetime of study, it appears that all existence is the expression of information."[35] Even two outspoken atheists admit the world shows every indication of design and purpose, but they add this qualification: it only *looks* that way. Again, *Richard Dawkins* says biology is "the study of complicated things that give the appearance of having been designed for a purpose."[36] *Francis Crick* advises biologists to "constantly keep in mind that what they see was not designed, but rather evolved."[37]

Despite Dawkins' claim that Darwin made it possible to be an "intellectually fulfilled atheist,"[38] we've seen that Darwinism didn't do away with design. Darwin's *Origin of Species* assumes a Creator got the evolutionary ball rolling: "To my mind, it accords better with what we know of the laws impressed on matter by the Creator, that the production and extinction of the past and present inhabitants of the world should have been due to secondary causes." Again, "There is a grandeur in this view of life, with its several powers, having been originally breathed by the Creator into a few forms or into one....[F]rom so simple a beginning endless forms most beautiful and most wonderful have been, and are being evolved."[39] If anything, Darwin made design appear less immediate. So let's grant evolution and then ask: "What if God utilized the evolutionary process to bring about his purposes?" In the end, the issue isn't so much "creation vs. evolution" but "God vs. no God." If evolution is true, then it's a great argument for God's existence!

Contrary to Dawkins, the "evolution-did-it-all" blanket explanation for the existence of various animal and plant species is inadequate. It involves huge assumptions. That is, *before* the evolutionary process can get going, certain crucial conditions must be in place:

a. the universe *came into existence* (out of nothing)
b. it is *precisely tuned* for life
c. it actually *produces* life
d. life continues to be *sustained* despite harsh conditions.

These items must *first* be in place for evolution to have any chance of success—and they happen to point us in the direction of *God.*

When it comes to organisms, we readily think of the complex human brain or the human body with all of its remarkable inter-working systems—circulatory, muscular, nervous, digestive, reproductive, respiratory, excretory, skeletal, endocrine, lymphatic. We're not surprised when the psalmist says we're "fearfully and wonderfully made" (Ps. 139:14).

If a remarkably wise God exists, then the delicate balance of the universe and amazing complexity of organisms can be readily anticipated.

Beauty

As I write this, I'm in eastern Connecticut's "quiet corner," where my siblings and I are celebrating the 100th birthday of "Tante Vody"—my great aunt, Evodia Maximovitsch. My family and I are enchanted by New England's cold streams and lakes, dark hemlocks and dazzling white birches, massive boulders, and spectacular autumn colors. (In addition, its stone walls, winding roads, and town greens have a beauty and charm all their own!) Such impressive natural beauty is in no way linked to survival. So why think this overwhelming beauty should exist given naturalism? Why isn't everything functional, monotonously textured, and a battleship-gray color? And why should (human) creatures exist who can admire and appreciate the world's loveliness and majesty? And why do scientists prefer elegant or beautiful theories, often without observational support? To cite *Paul Draper* more fully here: "Theism is supported by the fact that the universe contains an abundance of beauty." He adds: "A beautiful universe, especially one containing beings that can appreciate that beauty, is clearly more likely on theism than on naturalism and so is evidence favoring theism over naturalism."[40] Naturalism seems to offer little help in resolving the emergence of such beauty.

When it comes to science and mathematics, *Paul Dirac* goes so far as to say: "it is more important to have beauty in one's equations than to have them fit an experiment."[41] *Bertrand Russell* wrote of the "supreme beauty of mathematics…like that of a sculpture"; it is "sublimely pure" and, like poetry, inspires the "true spirit of delight" and "exaltation" within us.[42]

If, however, an imaginative, beautiful God exists, then such magnificent beauty should not surprise us. God provides a suitable context for it.

We could go on to discuss other phenomena in defense of theism's greater explanatory power, which is indeed remarkable. When skeptics dismiss God by appealing to less-plausible, though *logically possible* scenarios as to how consciousness or first life emerged, we can respond, "Yes, that's *possible*, but I'm offering very good—and I think, superior—contextual reasons for taking God seriously." Hopefully these features will suffice to show that the nature and existence of God does exhibit a more natural, suitable context to establish and explain all these features.

11

Science, Nature, and the
Possibility of Miracles

The earth is the LORD's, and all it contains,
The world, and those who dwell in it. (Ps. 24:1–2)

"How great are His signs
And how mighty are His wonders!" (Dan. 4:3)

The triune God has created a world that humans–his priestly and kingly image-bearers–could study with sweet pleasure and with humble gratitude toward their Maker. We're able to understand many of creation's marvelous workings: "Great are the works of the LORD; they are studied by all who delight in them" (Ps. 111:2). Since God created the world and how it operates, he isn't bound or limited by nature, as though its processes were necessary and inviolable.

In this chapter, we'll look, first, at the God-science question and then, in light of this, at miracles. We'll see that the biblical worldview has a place for *both* "science and wonders"–for the scientific disciplines *and* the miraculous.

God and Science

How great are Your works, O LORD!
Your thoughts are very deep. (Ps. 92:5)

People such as Richard Dawkins think *God* and *science* are contradictory terms: "Scientific beliefs are supported by evidence, and they get results. Myths and faiths are not and do not."[1] Harvard biologist Richard Lewontin believes science alone can give us knowledge: the "social and intellectual apparatus, Science, [is] the only begetter of truth."[2] However, such assertions aren't really *science* but *scientism.*

How do these two differ? Although *science* is notoriously difficult to define, we could suggest this simple working definition: *science* is the attempted objective study of the natural world/natural phenomena whose theories and explanations do not normally depart from the natural realm.[3] Not everyone will agree with the inclusion of "whose theories and explanations do not normally depart from the natural realm," but we'll see that this is warranted in light of available scientific pointers to God's existence.

Scientism, though, comes in two basic flavors. The *strong* version of scientism declares that *only* science can give us knowledge. The *weak* version sees science as the *best* path to knowledge. Scientism tends to assume that (a) *nature is all the reality there is* and (b) *science is the (only) means of obtaining knowledge.*

Though often called "science," scientism assumes *naturalism* and *materialism*: nature is all there is, and it's composed of matter. But from the beginning it was not so. The roots of modern science—the work of founding fathers such as Newton, Copernicus, Boyle, Maxwell, Faraday, and others—took seriously biblical authority, divine creation, miracles, and design. Indeed, their worldview created an environment for significant scientific progress.[4] Simply glancing at recent scientific history should serve as a warning against excluding God to explain important features of nature. Indeed, two chief twentieth-century discoveries—the universe's *beginning* (the Big Bang) and *delicate fine-tuning*—are best supported by the existence of a powerful, intelligent God. Indeed, it is a scientific *fact* that the universe began to exist and is finely tuned for life. (This fact isn't itself "miraculous.") The relevant—and revealing question—is: Which *interpretation* or *explanation*—a naturalistic/materialistic one or a supernaturalistic/theistic one—makes the best sense of these phenomena?

Another reason to reject scientism—especially its strong version—is that it's (a) *arbitrary* and (b) *self-refuting.* It's *arbitrary* because we have no reason to think *all* truth-claims have to be scientifically or empirically verifiable. Philosopher John Post proclaims that the origin of the universe can't have a cause since "by definition the universe contains everything there is or ever was or will be."[5] But *if God really created and designed the universe,* Post's methodology actually obstructs us from considering God's relevance for the universe's beginning or fine-tuning. What kind of open-minded pursuit of explanations is *that*? Besides this, why think the physical universe is *all* the reality there is? Post's stance arbitrarily excludes not just God, but objective ethics, free will, the soul's existence, life's meaning. Post's view implies that naturalistic explanations of things—perhaps even silly ones—should always be preferred over supernaturalistic ones, no matter how simple and plausible. But isn't the goal to pursue the *best* explanation, not the best *naturalistic* explanation. We should be cautious about knee-jerk preferences for all things naturalistic or materialistic, which is itself a philosophical preference or bias.

Scientism is *self-refuting* in that *we can't scientifically prove that everything must be scientifically provable.* The challenge, "Prove that scientifically!" shows us that our challenger believes he's an exception to his own rule—the rule that everything must be scientifically provable, which itself can't be scientifically proven. No wonder: it's a *philosophical* claim (a statement *about* science), not a *scientific* one (a statement *of* science—that is, the result of scientific investigation). But doesn't science deal with *verification, falsification, testability, observability,* or *repeatability?* While these are helpful *guidelines* for scientists, they shouldn't be absolutized, lest they become self-refuting: the Big Bang can't be *repeated;* sub-atomic particles (quarks, neutrinos) can't be *observed.*

The danger here is what philosopher Alfred North Whitehead called "the fallacy of misplaced concreteness"—absolutizing *one* legitimate discipline or avenue of knowledge, making it the *only* one. What's worse, many scientists don't realize just how many scientifically unprovable *philosophical* assumptions they make:

- A physical, mind-independent world exists. Some Eastern philosophical schools deny its existence.
- Certain laws of logic are inescapable, universal, and necessary. Without them, thought would be impossible. This assumption isn't the result of mere fact-inspection.
- The human mind can understand the natural world.
- There are important criteria for a decent hypothesis (elegance, simplicity).
- Nature is, generally speaking, uniform and thus capable of observation and study.
- What we observe in nature can provide clues and indicators of unobservable processes and patterns (subatomic particles, gravitation).
- We trust our reason and sensory abilities, believing they don't regularly deceive us.
- Scientists often place great personal trust in others' research as reliable.

The late Carl Sagan famously pontificated, "The Cosmos is all that is or ever was or ever will be."[6] Many scientists assume this, and they believe science rules out God's existence. But *which* particular scientific discipline rules out God's existence? Some might suggest *biology,* but Darwin and others have considered God necessary to get evolution going. What about *chemistry, physics, geology,* or *astronomy?* As it turns out, *none* of these rules out God's existence (indeed, they lend support to God's existence). If so, *why think that putting all these disciplines together can rule God out?* Philosophical presuppositions, not scientific disciplines, rule God out.

The popular myth that science and God are inherently at odds is actually a relatively recent historical *invention*–from the late 1800s; serious historians of science now recognize this fact.[7] Early modern science was spearheaded by *theists*. The "Galileo affair" is instructive: it was largely due to conflicting *philosophical* differences between the Aristotle-opposing Galileo and the pro-Aquinas/-Aristotle church hierarchy. Galileo himself wrote the Grand Duchess Kristina (1615): "Scripture can never lie, as long as its true meaning has been grasped."[8]

Those believing this God-vs.-science warfare motif are too late; the "damage" has already been done! Earlier we noted that, according Paul Davies, theology produced and shaped the modern scientific worldview–and that science, Kant said, presupposes design. That modern science takes for granted the world's knowability and orderliness is due to theism's profound influence. What's more, the existence of an intelligent, rational, creative Being opens up the door for interesting, fruitful directions in science, not to mention providing a structure and various guidelines for doing science. For example:

- God's creating the universe out of nothing suggests that matter isn't eternal. So cosmological models assuming eternally preexistent matter won't succeed.
- God's rationality and creativity suggests that nature will generally be uniform and understandable to human minds and that our best scientific explanations will be beautiful or elegant.
- God's agency and design suggest simplicity of explanation. Although some scientists claim that a huge–even infinite–number of mindlessly directed universes explains how ours happens to be life-permitting, the God hypothesis is less contrived and far simpler, requiring only one universe!

Finally, we have the *God-of-the-gaps* charge: the more we study the world, the less relevant God is for explaining its operations and for plugging the holes (gaps) of our ignorance. The believer should remember that (a) *this charge assumes a Deistic approach to nature, ignoring God's/Christ's continual sustenance of creation in its very being* (Col. 1:16; Heb. 1:3) and being present *within* creation. The cosmos *can't* get along just fine without God. God doesn't "intervene" so much as "act within" creation. (b) *Believers shouldn't insert "God did it" explanations for whatever they don't understand in nature* ("God must have caused that chemical reaction"), but only when we have *good theological or philosophical reasons* for such "gaps" in nature. Solid, noncontrived theological justification for God's direct, free action within the world would include the initial creation and its design, the emergence of first life, and the in-breaking of God's kingdom through Christ's teaching, miracles, death, and resurrection. (c) *The explanatory power of God's existence and action in the world could lead to more fruitful lines of scientific research and actually save time and money.* If God created and designed the universe, then many naturalistic scientific explanations or scenarios will ultimately prove futile; the "God hypothesis" will prove the more fruitful.[9] (d) As we've pointed out, *two of the twentieth century's greatest scientific discoveries—the universe's beginning (Big Bang) and delicately balanced cosmic constants—actually invite God to fill the explanatory gap.* (e) *Many naturalists complaining about the God-of-the-gaps are guilty of an opposite and equal reaction—a naturalism-of-the-gaps!* They assume: "One day (naturalistic) science will give us the answer to our questions." Ironically, many naturalists tell believers who find evidences for God's existence in nature, "Science is always changing; we have to be careful about drawing positive theological conclusions from it." But their naturalism-of-the-gaps implies so great a confidence in scientism that ultimately no evidence for God can ever emerge.

We have good reasons—biblically, philosophically, and empirically—for taking seriously the intersecting of God and science. If the self-revealing, creating, designing triune God exists, then integration of theology and science isn't only possible; it's essential.

Miracles

"Why is it considered incredible among you people if God does raise the dead?" (Acts 26:8)

President Thomas Jefferson, a Deist who believed Jesus to be merely a powerful moral teacher of reason, cut up and pasted together portions of the four gospels that reinforced his belief in a naturalized, nonmiraculous, nonauthoritative Jesus. The result was the severely edited *Life and Morals of Jesus of Nazareth Extracted Textually from the Gospels*—or, *The Jefferson Bible.* He believed he could easily extract the "lustre" of the real Jesus "from the dross of his biographers, and as separate from that as the diamond from the dung hill." Jefferson believed Jesus was "a man, of illegitimate birth, of a benevolent heart, [and an] enthusiastic mind, who set out without pretensions of divinity, ended in believing them, and was punished capitally for sedition by being gibbeted [i.e., crucified] according to Roman law."[10] Jefferson edits Luke 2:40, "And [Jesus] grew, and waxed strong in spirit, filled with wisdom," omitting, "and the grace of God was upon him." This "Bible" ends with an un-resurrected Jesus: "There they laid Jesus, and rolled a great stone to the door of the sepulchre, and departed." The end!

Deism's chief motivation for rejecting miracles—along with special revelation—was that they suggested an inept God: He didn't get everything right at the outset; so he needed to tinker with the world, adjusting it as necessary. The biblical picture of miracles, though, shows them to be an indication of a ruling God's care for and involvement in the world—indeed, his concern for human salvation. In fact, many in modern times have witnessed specific indicators of direct divine action and answers to prayer.[11]

The Christian faith stands or falls on God's miraculous activity, particularly in Jesus' resurrection (1 Cor. 15). Scripture readily acknowledges the possibility of miracles in nonbiblical religious settings. Some may be demonically inspired,[12] but we shouldn't rule out God's gracious, miraculous actions even in pagan settings—say, the "unknown" God's response to prayers to avert a plague in Athens. However, we'll note below that, unlike many divinely wrought miracles in Scripture, miracle claims in other religions are incidental—not foundational—to the pagan religion's existence.

In earlier chapters, we've looked at plausible reasons for thinking a good, powerful, wise personal God exists. He's not some generic deity, but a covenant-making, initiative-taking God who responds to the human situation of sin, misery, alienation, suffering, and evil. Discussions of God's existence and nature typically fail to ask, "If God exists, has he done anything to address this profound problem?" The Christian story emphatically answers, "Yes!" God's existence and his concern for humanity go hand-in-hand; he gets his feet dirty and hands bloody in Jesus, bringing creation and redemption together. His ministry and the salvation-event signaled a new exodus and a new creation. His miraculous resurrection from the dead in particular guarantees hope and restoration, and this cornerstone event is accompanied by many publicly accessible reasons—historical, theological, and philosophical.[13]

Divine miracles don't *guarantee* belief, though: "If they do not listen to Moses and the Prophets, they will not be persuaded even if someone rises from the dead" (Lk. 16:31). Miracles can be rationalized away (Jn. 12:29) or even suppressed by people who don't want to believe anyway, such as Jesus' enemies seeking to kill miraculous evidence—the resuscitated Lazarus (Jn. 12:1, 10)! Miracles don't compel belief, but, for those willing to receive them, they do serve as sufficient indications of God's activity and revelation. John calls them "signs" that point beyond themselves to Jesus' significance: Jesus miraculously feeds bread to a crowd of over 5,000 and then declares, "I am the bread of life" (Jn. 6); he says, "I am the light of the world," illustrating it by healing a man born blind (Jn. 8–9); he affirms, "I am the resurrection and the life" and shows it by raising Lazarus (Jn. 11). No wonder Jesus says, "Believe Me that I am in the Father and the Father is in Me; otherwise believe because of the works themselves" (Jn. 14:11). His miracles, revealing God's in-breaking reality, are available for public scrutiny.

As we think about miracles, *what are they, first of all?* Definitions may include terms like "suspension of," "exception to," or "nonrepeatable counterinstance to" nature's order and laws. Simply put, they're *direct acts of a personal God that can't be predicted or explained by merely natural causes;* they wouldn't take place if left up to nature. Naturally, dead people don't live again; however, Jesus' bodily resurrection—impossible according to natural processes—is possible because God exists. God's involvement in the world, however, may even be tied to apparently natural events but reveal their supernatural quality by their remarkable *timing*–say, an earthquake causing Jericho to fall at the precisely predicted moment. (These are part of God's "extraordinary providence"–in distinction from his "ordinary providence" of sending sunshine and rain and fruitful seasons [Mt. 5:45; Acts 14:17].) True blue *miracles,* in contrast to these two workings of divine providence, simply cannot be accounted for–they can't happen–by any natural processes.

Second, "natural law" or "natural order" describes how the world generally operates, but it doesn't control *what happens in it.* Now, Hume called miracles "violations" of natural laws; since natural laws can't be violated, he reasoned, miracles can't happen! (Richard Dawkins refers to miracles as "a violation of the normal running of the natural world."[14]) This argumentation, though, is another example of question-begging (assuming what one wants to prove); it takes for granted that a world-engaging God doesn't exist. But as C. S. Lewis said, if we admit God into the picture, then we have no security against miracles! The universe isn't "closed" but open to God's involvement within it.

Consider this irony. (a) Hume notably posed the "problem of induction": the past's unvaried, repeated sequence of, say, sunrise and sunset offers no guarantee the sun will rise tomorrow–even if it's prudent to believe that it will. Yet with miracles, (b) Hume's assumption of nature's fixed, unbreakable laws disallows miracles. But what if, as with the sunrise, these "laws" will be "violated" tomorrow? Hume can't have it both ways.

If all knowledge comes through our senses, as Hume insists, then we'll draw conclusions about what has taken place in nature, not that things couldn't be otherwise. If science describes how the natural world operates, we shouldn't presume to know how things will look in advance of the evidence or experience. Science is *descriptive* (how things *do* work), not *prescriptive* (how they *must* work). Canceling a university class doesn't exactly "violate" the class schedule! In fact, the criterion that all things must conform to prior experience would make scientific progress impossible. If, for instance, the universe came into existence from nothing, that certainly couldn't be predicted by natural laws.

"Natural laws" could just be a description of nature's workings; they're a framework or pattern, but they *do* nothing and set nothing into motion. A "law of nature" simply describes what happens when no agent (divine, human, angelic) is acting or interfering with the causal order.[15] In a sense, human activity in the world is a type of "miracle." So natural laws aren't "violated"; they're not even necessary–especially if God is the one who puts nature's laws into place.

Third, God's existence provides the necessary religious context or "background information" to affirm the possibility of miracles. Typically, people don't reject miracles like Jesus' resurrection because of lack of good evidence but rather because of philosophical assumptions that overwhelm the evidence. ("No matter what the evidence looks like, dead people don't come back to life—period!") One's openness to the supernatural makes a huge difference, and Scripture regularly illustrates that, despite signs and wonders, unbelief persists.

Radical theologian Rudolf Bultmann boldly claimed that since "the forces and the laws of nature have been discovered," we can't believe in good or evil spirits or miraculous cures from sickness and disease: "It is impossible to use electric light and the wireless and to avail ourselves of modern medical and surgical discoveries, and at the same time to believe in the New Testament world of spirits and miracles."[16] When people claim miracles just can't happen, they're implying a Creator can't exist: if a God exists who can create a universe from nothing, resurrection and healings are at least possible. But a miracle-denying worldview simply won't be open to whatever evidence there is, since experience by itself is insufficient; it can always be explained away. As C. S. Lewis points out: "If anything extraordinary seems to have happened, we can always say that we have been the victims of an illusion. If we hold a philosophy which excludes the supernatural, this is what we always shall say."[17] If the context of God's existence and possible working in human history are granted, however, why think it impossible that God should raise the dead? Sure, dead people don't *naturally* come to life. *Both* the believer and the skeptic can agree here! *Unless* God acts, dead people stay dead.

That said, too often philosophical considerations overwhelm the historical evidence, no matter how strong. Miracles are probable (or not) relative to the background information or context. Of course, miracles are "initially improbable" or "highly improbable" if God doesn't exist. Yes, naturalistically speaking, miracles defy all probability. However, a miracle's probability greatly increases if "God's existence" is part of the relevant background information, making miracles a live option. We shouldn't decide in advance that miracles are impossible, particularly if (a) God exists and creates and has revealed himself in history, and, given this context, (b) there is good historical evidence to support such a miracle-claim.

Against Hume, miracles aren't "violations" of nature; they become quite plausible given the triune God's saving intentions. So, given the appropriate, spiritually significant religious context, we shouldn't prefer naturalistic explanations—which may be inferior or even ridiculous—but rather supernaturalistic ones with far greater explanatory power. Hume got things terribly wrong. No wonder the prominent agnostic philosopher John Earman wrote *Hume's Abject Failure*[18] to make this very point.

So should we be "open" to reports of John Lennon or Elvis "sightings"? The background information here is crucial: Does the Lennon scenario occur randomly, out of the blue? And how was he raised—by God? To what purpose? Why is Lennon so significant? By contrast, Jesus' resurrection involves a historical and theological context–God's workings in Israel, Scriptures that anticipate a new creation, Jesus' own predictions–to make sense of that event. If this self-revealing God exists, miracles like Jesus' resurrection–and supernatural explanations in general–become a live option, but not just for *any* miraculous claim.

Fourth, the Christian faith's most theologically significant miracle is Jesus' resurrection–a historically well-supported event. Though history yields only probable–not absolute–knowledge, we don't have to be mired in historical skepticism. We can still have a good degree of confidence in our historical knowledge as we consider evidence for Jesus' resurrection. The chief facts surrounding this miracle are

1. Jesus' burial in Joseph of Arimathea's tomb;
2. the discovery of Jesus' empty tomb;
3. the postmortem appearances;
4. the origin of the earliest disciples' belief in Jesus' resurrection.

These are well-established historical facts accepted by the majority of critical biblical scholars–including the most skeptical who reject Jesus' bodily resurrection.[19] For instance, some scholars may believe the "appearances" were hallucinaions or psychological/guilt projections, but they acknowledge that something triggered the disciples' belief in Jesus' postmortem appearances.

In themselves, these four lines of evidence *aren't* "miraculous facts" that are somehow beyond historical research; *they're available to all historians.* The point at issue is: Which *interpretation* or *explanation*–natural or supernatural–makes the best sense of these facts?

In addition to the ready explanation of God's raising Jesus from the dead, consider also the very low historical probability of available naturalistic explanations of the first Easter–the disciples stole the body; the women went to the wrong tomb; Jesus' followers suffered massive and widespread hallucinations; Jesus didn't really die but swooned, and the cool tomb revived him; the common, but virtually universally rejected view[20] that the resurrection is just another pagan or "mystery religion" legend. The inadequacy of these naturalistic explanations further reinforces the plausibility of the miraculous explanation.

While historical *facts* themselves are not miraculous, an *explanation* certainly may be; and, if God exists, such an explanation is legitimate and theologically warranted. Historian N. T. Wright, quite judicious and not given to overstatement, concludes that the combined historical probability of (a) the empty tomb–something Jesus' enemies assumed (Mt. 28:12–15)– and (b) the postmortem appearances is "virtually certain," being on the level of Caesar Augustus's death in 14 C.E. or the fall of Jerusalem in 70 C.E.[21] To have one without the other wouldn't do: just an empty tomb would have been merely a puzzle or a tragedy, and Jesus' postmortem appearances alone could have been chalked up to hallucinations. But taken together, these two matters give the origin of the early church its powerful impetus. Jesus' resurrection isn't "beyond history."

The biblical testimony of (a) *many*, (b) *independent*, (c) *credible* and *sincere* eyewitnesses should be taken seriously. First Corinthians 15 reports that Jesus appeared to over 500, to Peter, to the unbelieving James (Jesus' half-brother), and, though in visionary form, to the hostile persecutor, Paul. John 20 tells us that Jesus showed himself to the skeptic Thomas. Women were the first witnesses, whose testimony wouldn't have been taken seriously in first-century Palestine. The basic facts surrounding Jesus' resurrection are consistent in an array of sources—the gospels, the early Christian sermons in Acts, Paul's epistles, and the very early Jerusalem tradition mentioned in 1 Corinthians 15, which dates to less then two years after Jesus' death.[22]

Furthermore, the Jews of Jesus' day (second-temple Judaism) believed that "resurrection" entailed an empty tomb; a resurrection couldn't take place without a thoroughly dead body being made gloriously alive again. Naturalistic attempts to explain away the first Easter (hallucination theory, wrong-tomb theory, disciples-stole-the-body theory, swoon theory, and the like) are inadequate and without sufficient explanatory power. The far more probable conclusion for Jesus' empty tomb and for postmortem appearances of an alive-and-well Jesus is that God raised Jesus from the dead.

Commonly Asked Questions about Miracles

1. Do extraordinary claims require extraordinary evidence? Hume ("Of Miracles") claimed no testimony is sufficient to establish a miracle unless that testimony's falsehood would be even more miraculous than the claim it's trying to establish: extraordinary claims demand extraordinary evidence. It initially sounds plausible: we shouldn't be gullible about all miracle claims we hear. However, it's simply false that Christians have an unusually heavy burden to bear. Earman calls it "nonsensical."[23] He's right: (a) *If God exists and we have an explanatory theological-religious context to make sense of a particular miracle, then we have the relevant background information to render that miracle plausible.* (b) *All we need to show for, say, the resurrection is that, given this context, a supernatural explanation makes better sense of the historical facts than a naturalistic one.*

2. Do only gullible and uncivilized people believe in miracles, as Hume claimed? Besides the fact that modern science was established by Bible-centered thinkers, plenty of well-informed believers today hold to the miraculous. Yet even in Jesus' day, *his own disciples*—especially Thomas—refused to believe initial reports that Jesus was raised. They hadn't expected an *individual's* resurrection before the final "day of the Lord." Or, *Joseph*, who knew where babies come from, didn't take the virgin Mary's word for it, but an angelic messenger's instead. From *Abraham* to *Zacharias,* Scripture portrays plenty of miracle-doubters in all their skeptical colors.

If we push Hume's logic, we can draw parallels between his view both on miracles and on white racial supremacy. For Hume, "ignorant and barbarous" peoples (who believed miracle-claims) were basically *non-whites*–people he believed to be of "naturally inferior" intelligence. The implication? Despite having heard reports of exceptions, Hume's experience would have found the existence of an intelligent black person to be just as unreasonable as expecting a miracle. His "reasonable" presumption is always against intelligent non-whites. The point here is simply this: if someone has made up his mind about what is uniform–whether white superiority or miracles–he'll always dismiss any counter-examples (of intelligent blacks or well-attested miracle-claims) as going against probability.[24]

3. Must testimonies to miracles be evaluated in light of our own experience? German theologian Ernst Troeltsch claimed that we should evaluate any testimony to miracles in light of our own experience; some *analogy* must exist between what we've experienced and the miracle-claim itself. In response: (a) What if you witnessed an authentic miracle? Given Troeltsch's standard, *you'd have to reject it because you hadn't seen anything like it before.* In fact, you'd have to reject a *whole string* of miracles since you'd *never* have a starting point for declaring something miraculous. (b) What of unique miracles like the Incarnation or resurrection? No first miracle could occur since nothing previous compares to it. (c) *All events are in some sense unique.* No one sunrise is exactly like another, C. S. Lewis wrote–how much more miraculous events!

Philosopher John Locke once recounted the story of the king of Siam. This ruler thought it preposterous that in some parts of the world, water could freeze so thickly that even elephants could walk on it. Why? He'd had no previous experience with ice. Ultimately, Troeltsch's standard is simply arbitrary.

4. Should we demand how miracles are performed before we believe them? Atheist Bede Rundle says that virgin births and miraculous cures from diseases "are of no assistance at the point that concerns us; they do not advance our understanding of *how* things could come about in the way claimed. To claim that God said, 'Let there be light,' leaves us not one jot wiser as to how light came about."[25] Not so. We *are* the wiser in at least this sense–that creation's beginning can't be *naturalistically* explained. Also, knowing *that* God created doesn't guarantee knowing *how* God did it. Why expect that we *should?* We're talking about *miracles* here, not combining vinegar and baking soda.

5. What of miraculous claims in other religions–or even secular contexts? Hume believed that miraculous claims in other religions would cancel each other out. However, whatever the source of miracle claims in other religions or "secular" claims that John Lennon or Elvis are alive, we should take them on a *case-by-case basis* rather lumping them all together. It's unfair to say that conflicting miracle-claims *must* cancel each other out. After all, *anyone* can *make* a claim, but what's the *evidence* for it?

Consider the "miracle" of Osiris. His body is cut up into fourteen pieces that float down the Nile. His wife/sister (?) Isis gathers up thirteen of the pieces and eventually resuscitates him. Isn't this just another ancient (mythical) resurrection claim? The myth's point, though, is actually Osiris' death and Isis' mourning, *not* resuscitation. Additionally, such myths tend to be part of a cyclical view of history—with no datable event for this story—but this lack of historicity doesn't really matter anyway. None of these gods and goddesses is a historical person.[26] A lot of alleged ancient resurrection parallels turn out to be quite unlike Jesus' resurrection.

Here are some further concerns: (a) *Miraculous claims in other religions tend to be incidental and not crucial to the religion's validity.* Muhammad's translation from Mecca to Jerusalem and back in one evening is hardly foundational to Islam—unlike the exodus, Jesus' exorcisms, and the resurrection. (b) Historian-philosopher Gary Habermas has investigated purported miracle-claims from the *ancient* world such as the resuscitation ("resurrection") or translation into heaven of great personages. He concludes that *the sources are generally late in their "recounting," put forth questionable or contradictory accounts, and are not open to any sort of verification.*[27] (c) *Nontheistic or pantheistic ("God is everything") worldviews have no conceptual room for miracles.* Miracles associated with Buddha or Confucius just don't "fit," given their worldview. (d) *Biblical miracles are both theologically plausible and historically/archaeologically supportable.* The places and historical events surrounding these miracles are quite unlike, say, the *Book of Mormon*'s claims of the Nephite civilization in North America and a massive battle in New York.[28] Not surprisingly, the Smithsonian Institution's 1996 statement rejects the *Book of Mormon* as "a scientific guide" and "has never used it in archaeological research."[29] Ironically, many skeptics tend to take more seriously the bizarre and ultimately insignificant miracle claims in other religions than they do the sane, sincere, reliable resurrection reports of the New Testament.

So not all miracle-claims are created equal. Conflicting miracle-claims between religions don't imply that all are false or that one religion's claims can't be true. If the triune self-revealing Creator exists, then there's no reason he can't override the natural order he has put in place. He is *God,* after all.

Part III

FALL

...in Adam all die. (1 Cor. 15:22)

12

The Problem(s) of Evil

"...unless you repent, you will all likewise perish" (Lk. 13:3, 5).

It is good for me that I was afflicted,
That I may learn Your statutes. (Ps. 119:71)

Introductory Comments

God created all things "very good." His priest-kingly image-bearers were made to worship and enjoy God and to rule creation with him. Then, following a cosmic rebellion of angelic creatures who "abandoned their proper abode" (Jude 6; cp. 2 Pet. 2:4), human sin entered the world, and with it, human death (Rom. 5:12–14). God warned the first humans: "You will surely die" (Gen. 2:17). Sure enough, the genealogies in Genesis 5 repeat the somber line: "And he died...and he died." Physical human death reflects a deeper, spiritual death–separation from God–symbolized in Genesis 3 by eviction from paradise.

In their primal sin, humans foolishly abused their freedom, resorting to *stealing* what wasn't theirs. Though unaware of the profound ramifications of their choice, they should have trusted God's reliable character instead of an imposter. The consequences were momentous. God's co-ruling, worshiping image-bearers, despite their dignity, entered into exile–alienation–from their *God and Maker*. They became estranged from their *fellow human beings*. They were now at odds with *nature,* vulnerable to its dangers and powerful forces with their work being toilsome and laborious rather than perfectly joyful.

They experienced alienation *within themselves.* Instead of being naturally directed toward God, their deeply disordered or mal-aligned souls–will, emotions, intellect, reason, imagination, and spirit–directed them away from God and became curved in on themselves. This self-directed existence now pervades the human condition; it involves proneness to pride, rationalization, and self-deception; the tendency to be harder on others than on self; the inclination to consider oneself "good" and opponents "evil," failing to recognize the depths of evil anyone is capable of; the pursuit of self-preservation and living in fear of death (Heb. 2:14–15).

A further element is the damaging activity of *dehumanizing evil spiritual agents and the demonically inspired oppressive power structures in the world's societies.* The result is genocide, concentration camps, gulags, tyranny, persecution, institutionalized racism, corporate scandals, demonization–the list goes on.

The world's history includes inexpressible and miserable suffering, sadness, and despair. Evil touches each of us, but rocks and devastates many. Scripture doesn't diminish its force, extent, depth, mystery, or messiness. Against Leibniz, the German philosopher, this *isn't* the best of all possible worlds. Evil isn't something we easily "explain" or "deal with"–let alone "solve." Yet, as opposed to its theological and philosophical competitors, the good news of the gospel offers not only the most adequate explanatory context for responding to evil, but presents the best hope for fully and finally overcoming it.[1]

Responding to Evil

Each worldview–not just the Christian story–must come to grips with horrendous evils: Which perspective or philosophy of life has the spiritual, intellectual, and emotional resources to help us more adequately navigate these difficult waters? Richard Dawkins takes a stab at it by denying its existence entirely: a universe of "blind physical forces and genetic replication" results in some people getting hurt, others getting lucky.[2] Some Eastern religions pass off evil as illusory. But are these appropriate responses?

The universe is ultimately a personal place created by the tri-personal God; he reveals himself within it for the sake of enabling humans to enjoy his presence in the company of fellow worshipers. So, in the face of evil, a fruitful question that will help move us in the right direction is: What if the existence of evil reflects our exile or alienation from God–a departure from God's intended designs? What if evil can actually serve as a means of alerting us to this estrangement?

Despite the worn-out philosophical claim that God and evil can't coexist, Scripture's realism grapples with the troubling presence of evil; it hardly implies God's nonexistence. Indeed, the horrific ravages of evil can potentially move us nearer to God. In Scripture, we read that God had sent wayward national Israel huge chunks of trouble–famine, drought, scorching wind, mildew, a scourge of caterpillars, warfare, and death–all kinds of plagues. After each affliction, God laments, "Yet you have not returned to me" (Am. 4:6–21). During the time of the judges, a five-fold cycle continually recurs: sin-judgment-call for help-deliverance-rest. When

God's people forsake Yahweh's loving covenant with them, he threatens their national security to rouse them to love and obedience. Elsewhere, the psalmist sees God's goodness through affliction, drawing him nearer to God: "It is good for me that I was afflicted, that I may learn Your statutes" (Ps. 119:71). The Old Testament prophets consistently point to *both* God's blessings and disasters—in hopes of alerting God's people to their exile and alienation from God.

When quizzed about certain Galilean worshipers "whose blood Pilate had mixed with their sacrifices" (Lk. 13:1), Jesus tells his questioners that these Galileans weren't worse sinners than the rest. Unlike certain pop-Christian spokespersons today, Jesus isn't necessarily in the business of telling *why* specific evils take place ("This is God's judgment for x"); rather, he reminds Israel of her need to be reconciled to God: "unless you repent, you will all likewise perish" (13:3, 5; cp. Jn. 9:3). Likewise, Paul's sufferings for Christ, rather than turning him from God, prompted him to set his hope on God: "we were burdened excessively, beyond our strength, so that we despaired even of life; indeed, we had the sentence of death within ourselves so that we would not trust in ourselves, but in God who raises the dead" (2 Cor. 1:8–9). Scripture repeatedly shows that the existence of evil, when rightly understood and received, can be used to get us back on track with God. Evil is hardly impersonal and abstract; it has profoundly personal implications.

The Philosophical and Emotional Dimensions of Evil

Various problems of evil confront us, not just one, and appropriate responses often correspond to those particular problems. Books about evil or suffering may claim to deal with *the* problem of evil, but this is a multifaceted task. In his preface to *The Problem of Pain,* C.S. Lewis aptly wrote that the *sole* purpose for writing was to address "the intellectual problem raised by suffering":

> For the far higher task of teaching fortitude and patience I was never fool enough to suppose myself qualified, nor have I anything to offer my readers except my conviction that when pain is to be borne, a little courage helps more than much knowledge, a little human sympathy more than much courage, and the least tincture of the love of God more than all.[3]

Here we have two broad aspects to the problem of evil—the *philosophical* and the *emotional/practical.* These problems often overlap, but we may find that attending to these facets of evil will often require very different approaches.[4] The emotional problem most importantly calls for pastoral counseling, personal relationship, and a caring presence. Those having suffered sexual abuse or having just lost a loved one may not—at least immediately—need philosophical answers to their deep emotional upheaval. Yet, by God's grace, intellectual answers and arguments may still help them gain better footing or properly focus their minds when in the throes of the emotional ravages of evil.

Defining Evil

Every philosophy of life must grapple with evil. Claiming it doesn't exist or that it's illusory seems profoundly unsatisfying–a denial of the obvious. Horrendous evils do exist, and, unless we're suppressing the truth and hardening our hearts, we can readily recognize massive disorders in the world.

What *is* evil? While Scripture regularly contrasts "good" and "evil" (e.g., Gen. 3:22; 50:20; Deut. 1:39; Ps. 34:14; Prov. 11:27; Mt. 12:35; 3 Jn. 11), technically, they're not quite opposite. Contrary to a common assumption, *goodness doesn't require that evil exist so that we can know what goodness is.* We intuitively grasp that goodness is more basic than evil: evil states of affairs are *abnormal* and ought to be different, and the good should triumph, not evil. The Christian story shows this to be true: the triune God existed in perfect harmony, joy, and goodness *before* the abuse of creaturely freedom and the entrance of evil on the scene.

Rightly understood, evil surprisingly points us *to* a good God rather than away from him, to a confidence that goodness *must* exist, to hope rather than despair. We can't properly understand evil without an awareness of goodness. Goodness is that which is intrinsically valuable, to be desired in and of itself rather than a means to something else. Ironically, rather than eliminating God, evil actually directs us to God as the solution. The fact that theists, not atheists, are more likely to define evil reinforces the greater explanatory power of the "God hypothesis."[5] Below are two mutually reinforcing definitions.

a. Evil is the absence, lack, or corruption of what is good. While God creates good conditions, the potential exists for misuse by free creatures. Sex in marriage is a gift from God but becomes evil and twisted when it moves outside these bounds–say, in adultery or sexual abuse of children. Similarly, chaos presupposes order, and darkness light. We know blindness by understanding sight: "If there were no light in the universe and therefore no creatures with eyes, we should never know it was dark. *Dark* would be without meaning," Lewis wrote.[6] The critic wielding the argument from evil has two problems to address–the problem of evil *and* the problem of goodness: In a cosmos of matter, chance, and time, where does goodness come from? Evil's existence actually points us to a standard of goodness– namely, God's character–and thus to a resolution.

So evil's existence can serve as an argument for God's existence:

1. If objective moral values exist, then God (most likely) exists.
2. Evil (a negative moral value) exists.
3. Therefore God (most likely) exists.

b. Evil is a profound departure from the way things ought to be, from a design plan. An even more basic definition of evil assumes that a lot isn't right in the world. We intuitively recognize at a deep level–not at the level of mismatched clothes or making a mistake on a test–that things *ought* to be different. Children should be loved, not abused; relationships ought to be loving and trusting, not dysfunctional. So if the critic assumes that much in the world *should* be different, we must ask *why* this is so: If God doesn't exist, why *expect* nature to be configured a certain way rather than another? Why be disappointed when it's not? Isn't that just tough luck? Assuming a pattern to which things *should* conform suggests a design-plan, which in turn implies a *Designer*.

Evil and Logic

Following in Hume's steps, atheist J. L. Mackie confidently asserted that the following statements are logically inconsistent: (a) *God is all-powerful*; (b) *God is wholly good*; (c) *evil exists*. The theologian, it seems, "at once *must* adhere and *cannot consistently* adhere to all three."[7] This is the *logical* or *deductive* problem of evil.

Mackie assumed an all-good, all-powerful being must eliminate evil insofar as he can, but why think this? God *could* eliminate lots of evils, but doing so might undercut certain *goods* like human freedom, causing a far worse state of affairs. "Eliminating" migraines, for example, by taking mind-altering drugs would render the last state worse than the first. God created self-determining agents whose free choices make a difference, bringing about one state of affairs rather than another. Like Mother Teresa, we can bring about great good, or, like Hitler or Pol Pot, great harm. Scripture assumes human responsibility is a good worth having, which shouldn't be undermined, even by God. Having only the power to help others but being blocked from harming them *wouldn't be a deep or meaningful sort of responsibility*.[8] Ours is no superficial world, but one in which we deeply influence others–for good or ill. From a biblical vantage point, a creaturely freedom that can never (a) negatively affect others or (b) choose separation from God isn't a freedom worth having.

We've already seen that God, the source of reason and goodness, can't do what's *logically* and *morally* impossible. He won't override important goods like genuine human freedom and the opportunity to respond to his gracious initiative. A world in which we freely do good all the time, while *theoretically possible*, may not be *feasible* for God to create since it's up to humans to do the choosing. Perhaps this world has the balance of the *greatest* amount of good and the *least* amount of evil.

Furthermore, the alleged logical contradiction of an all-good, all-powerful God's coexistence with evil fails to consider *God's intentions*. *What if he has morally justifiable reasons for permitting the evils he does?* If he has such reasons, though we may not *know* them, any contradiction evaporates. So a good being will try to prevent evil as far as he can *unless sufficient reasons justify his permitting it*.[9]

Indeed, a consensus among theistic and nontheistic philosophers has emerged that the logical problem of evil *isn't* really a problem after all. Christian philosopher Peter van Inwagen puts it this way: "It used to be widely held that evil…was incompatible with the existence of God; that no possible world contained both God and evil. *So far as I am able to tell, this thesis is no longer defended.*"[10] Atheist philosopher William Rowe agrees: "Some philosophers have contended that the existence of evil is *logically inconsistent* with the existence of the theistic God. No one, I think, has succeeded in establishing such an extravagant claim."[11]

Evil and the Likelihood of God

Though the logical problem of evil is a relic of the past, contemporary critics put forward the *evidential*–the *inductive* or *probabilistic*–problem from evil.[12] Acknowledging that God and evil could *possibly* coexist, this argument claims it's highly *improbable* given the vast amounts of evil in the world: AIDS in Africa, the torture of innocents for entertainment, child abductions and kidnappings, civil wars, ethnic hatreds, oppression of women and racial minorities, tyrannical dictatorships, deaths by natural disasters. Besides this, many evils go unreported in the news: child abuse and wife-beating, adulterous relationships, gambling addictions and debts, political and corporate corruption, black-market crime. Add to this the fact that deep, heart-breaking, and mystifying evils have been going on for many millennia of human history.

We're left wondering what possible reason could account for all sorts of evils. At the heart of the evidential problem from evil is the assumption that no morally justifiable reason for such evils exists. Does evil render God's existence *improbable*?

In response, *we should first consider whether we're in the best position to assess whether evil excludes God.* I can confidently say that no elephant is in my office, and I'm in an excellent position to make this assessment. On the other hand, what if I'm looking (with the naked eye) at the New York City skyline from Liberty Island, claiming that no pigeons are atop the Empire State Building? You'd rightly question whether I'm in the best position to make that assessment. I've made the *noseeum inference*– if I can't see 'em, they must not be there!

Similarly, when the critic tells us that the world is full of unnecessary evils that render God's existence improbable, we should question whether he's properly positioned to assess this. Scripture indicates that he's not. God's ways and thoughts are beyond ours (Isa. 55:8–9; cp. Rom. 11:33). So we should distinguish between (a) *gratuitous* evil (unnecessary evil, no morally justifiable reason for it) and (b) *inscrutable* evil (evil whose justification we simply can't discern). To confuse these creates a problem: An *inscrutable* evil (one we can't figure out) doesn't mean it's *gratuitous* (purposeless or morally unjustifiable). While evils may *appear* gratuitous, this doesn't mean they truly *are*. Lots of people may not be able to figure out Newton's or Einstein's writings, but that doesn't imply that their scientific ideas are meaningless nonsense. What's more, *even if God fully explained his purposes to us, there's no guarantee we'd comprehend them.*

The triune God frequently thwarts our expectations: the first are last, the humble are exalted, and the wisdom of the cross appears foolish. God rebukes human presumption about what a wise and good God "should" do. Job's encounter with God illustrates the *relational* component in grappling with evil. Despite his afflictions, profound personal tragedy, and *still-unanswered* questions (42:1–6), Job realized that he could *trust the character* of the wise, powerful, and good Creator (Job 38–41). Although Job didn't get his demanded answers, what he got was *God* himself—and that was enough.

Second, the evil and suffering, rightly received, can help us see our need for God and for a deepening trust in him. While I was visiting Moscow, a Christian asked, "What do I tell my friend who says she doesn't need God? Everything's going just fine for her." I replied, "Just watch. When life disappoints her, she'll probably complain, 'How could a good God allow this to happen to me?'" *God can't win either way!* Hardship can make us bitter—or prompt us to pursue God. No matter what the conditions, however, some people won't turn to God.

The prodigal son (Lk. 15) left home with his share of the inheritance to live self-indulgently. Only when he hit rock bottom were his eyes opened. Then he repented and was reconciled to his father (Lk. 15:11–32). Now what if the father tried to cushion his son from the consequences of his folly (e.g., sending more money)? He would be shielding his son from his desperate moral condition. Similarly, what if God always intervened to prevent our seeing the havoc wrought by sin and separation from God? *We'd live a life of illusion,* thinking we're *doing just fine in our state of sin and separation from God.* Nothing would prompt us to move in a Godward direction because we'd *never be dissatisfied in our alienation from God.* In other words, *for God to deliver us from sin and separation from him, he must make us aware of the problem.*[13] So God allows us to make this connection by allowing sin's natural consequences to be visible; then we can see our exile and our desperate plight. Finding ourselves terribly maladjusted to God, hopefully this realization will move us back to God. Pain is *God's megaphone* to rouse a dulled world, as Lewis put it. Yes, life's enjoyments and beauties can point us toward God's reality and our deep need for him (Ps. 19:1–20; Acts 14:15–17): God "whispers to us in our pleasures" and "speaks to us in our conscience," but suffering has a way of getting our attention: God "shouts to us in our pain."[14]

Third, while we don't know why God allows this *or that particular evil, we can say that God* generally *allows evil to reveal to humans their deep need for God and to awaken trust in him.* Jesus himself didn't offer specific reasons for worshipers massacred by Pilate or the Galileans' accidental death. Instead Jesus urged his hearers to consider where they stood with God (Lk. 13:1–5). Likewise, we often won't be able to discern what's behind specific evil events, but evil generally can remind people that all is not well, that we are exiled from God morally and spiritually, and that we must respond to God's promptings by casting ourselves on his grace. (Perhaps a further mistaken assumption is that we should have the capability to divine why specific evils take place.)

Some may wonder: "What of infants who die at birth and so aren't able to grasp their need for God?" This question assumes that *each person* should be able to learn important lessons from an awareness of evil. However, God's permitting evils goes beyond what benefit this or that individual may receive through suffering; it is a more general condition that sends the ringing message that something is desperately wrong and that we don't have the resources in ourselves to handle this. And the very fact that things *ought not* be this way can generally help point us in the proper direction.

Fourth, natural forces—tornadoes, hurricanes, earthquakes—are actually necessary for human earthly existence, even if resulting in natural evils at times. Planetary scientists have observed that certain natural processes—though they can be deadly—bring overall benefit to humankind. They help the earth maintain its delicate atmospheric balance and other environmental conditions necessary for our survival. Tornadoes and hurricanes help equalize global temperatures. Tectonic plate-shifting, which produces earthquakes, actually helps replenish the soil so that it isn't all washed away. The list goes on. However, because of our alienation from God, our once-protected status in Eden gave way to vulnerability to these destructive natural forces. Although we can't argue for it here,[15] perhaps Daniel Howard-Snyder is correct when he suggests:

> The potentially destructive forces of nature became [our first ancestors'] foe since a consequence of separating themselves from God was the loss of special intellectual powers to predict where and when natural disasters would occur and to protect themselves from disease and wild beasts, powers dependent upon their union with God. The result is natural evil.[16]

These apparently impersonal forces of nature still have a personal aspect to them: they help expose our helplessness and, by God's help, may prompt us to call out trustingly to the Maker of heaven and earth.

Fifth, while focusing solely on evil may make God's existence seem less likely, we must consider the full scope of evidence. When we look through a telescope on a clear night, we may be wholly absorbed in looking at the moon's surface, Jupiter's "red spot," or a certain constellation; we may completely forget that another ten billion trillion stars exist. Similarly, focusing on evil alone may unfairly distort or obscure our perspective so that we neglect important, relevant indications of God's nature and existence in creation, conscience, and reason—not to mention his self-revelation in Christ.

The argument from evil assumes the existence of the universe, of moral and rational human beings, and of a standard of goodness; these factors, among others, imply that evil is *secondary* to more basic features of the universe that point us in the direction of God's existence.

Principalities and Powers

For our struggle is not against flesh and blood, but against...the spiritual forces of wickedness in the heavenly places. (Eph. 6:12)

"Principalities," "rulers," and "powers" exist whether we realize it or not (Rom. 8:38; Eph. 6:12; cp. 1 Cor. 15:24; Eph. 1:21; Col. 2:10). Unfortunately, Christian philosophers tend to overlook this aspect of the problem of evil–a crucial biblical theme.

The versatile Lewis reminds us of two opposite and equal dangers: (a) seeing demons behind every bush and under every stone (the "magical" view) and (b) not believing they exist (the "materialist" view). Psychiatrist Scott Peck, who at one time didn't believe in a devil, has written a couple of books detailing his own unexpected encounters with the demonic. Two patients, Jersey and Beccah, displayed certain characteristics that Peck couldn't clinically explain away: snakelike facial expressions and weaving patterns; violent outbursts; near-superhuman strength; being a "walking textbook of heresies"–which suggested another, sinister power at work.[17]

Scripture tells precious little about a heavenly rebellion. Once part of God's good creation (Col. 1:15–20), these certain personal angelic powers (Satan/the devil and his angels) "abandoned their proper abode" (Jude 6). These dark forces aren't merely oppressive, dehumanizing "power structures" in economics, politics, society, and global affairs. They're evil agents attempting to subvert God's purposes in the world, to destroy human beings, and undermine the created order. Though humans are morally responsible agents, they can be influenced not only by "this world" but also by "the prince of the power of the air" (Eph. 2:2), who beguiles and leads astray.

Naturalism or materialism would lead us to consider multiple murderers like the Columbine killers or Jeffrey Dahmer necessarily and always as "mentally ill" or "statistical abnormalities." But such categories seem wholly inadequate and hollow. The laughter or pleasure of these murderers while committing such horrific acts brings us face-to-face with Satan. The perversity and depth of certain evils simply can't be explained by naturalism. Redemption, not therapy, is required for such profoundly evil, demonically inspired actions.[18] As it turns out, even Dahmer himself found redemption through Christ while in prison–providing amazing, even disturbing and shocking, testimony to hope and grace for even the worst of us.[19]

Jesus came to overthrow the prince of darkness, announcing before his death: "now the ruler of this world will be cast out" (Jn. 12:31) and, "the ruler of this world has been judged" (16:11). Indeed, he appeared to "destroy the works of the devil" (1 Jn. 3:8). Revelation anticipates Satan's ultimate overthrow, which was signaled at the crucifixion (Col. 2:15; Rev. 5:5; 12:11). He knows his time is short and that he's inevitably doomed. Still Satan lashes out, doing whatever damage he can.

Omitting the demonic from discussions about evil will skew our perspective.

Evil and the Cross of Christ

Rather than placing confidence in "rational solutions" or optimistic social engineering projects to address evil, we can trust in the triune God who speaks and acts. The ultimate resolution to evil is (a) rooted in the *past*–in the cross-work of Christ, who stripped "rulers and authorities" of their power, triumphing over them (Col. 2:15); but (b) its hope will be fully manifested in the *future* in the new heavens and new earth (Rev. 21–22). Jesus, the true Israel and new Adam, comes to rescue not only a *covenant people*, but to extend the benefits of his death to *all humans* willing to receive them.

The implications of Christ's work are, in fact, *cosmic*: reversing the curse of sin, death, and exile (alienation) by establishing a new creation, in which God and his people joyously dwell together; removing Satan and his hosts from doing any further damage; judging those who refuse to enjoy God's grand, everlasting celebration. Thinking rightly about evil must incorporate considerations about *past* and *future* combined with *personal trust in God's good character and purposes* as we consider these final points.

First, this-worldly oriented discussions about evil will be shortsighted and misleading. To speak about evil without considering that God will one day overcome it gives evil a greater place than it deserves. God will one day bring about his righteous reign, judging the unrepentant and establishing those who love him within the transformed creation. Those wondering where God is in the midst of the world's evil and suffering must consider future punishment and reward and the vindication of God's purposes.

The believer, moreover, has a hopeful perspective: Paul considers persecutions, afflictions, perplexities, and carrying about "the dying of Jesus" in his body (2 Cor. 4:8–16) to be but "momentary, light affliction" in contrast to the "eternal weight of glory far beyond all comparison" (v. 17). The Christian's earthly life *flows into a glorious afterlife.* Because we have "the victory through our Lord Jesus Christ," evil won't have the last word. So we can remain "steadfast, immovable, always abounding in the work of the Lord" (1 Cor. 15:58). God's love in Christ, through whom we "overwhelmingly conquer" (Rom. 8:35–39) enables us to endure "tribulation," "persecution," "peril," and "sword": "In the world you have tribulation," Jesus tells his disciples: "But take courage; I have conquered the world" (Jn. 16:33).

Second, our ultimate goal isn't simply earthly comfort or utopian ease, but rather the knowledge and love of God, which may be deepened and strengthened through evil and suffering. We're misguided if we think God owes us a pain-free existence or that this is the best of all possible worlds. As he weaves together the tapestry of history, God can redemptively utilize evil to alert us to our alienation from God and to foster perseverance, courage, and dependence on him. He magnificently takes evil acts and brings about good through them (Gen. 50:20; Rom. 8:28). The North African theologian Tertullian (c. 155 C.E.–c. 220) wrote: "The blood of the martyrs is the seed [of the church]" (*Apology* 1). By this he meant that the church often grows dramatically amidst fierce opposition.

Third, knowing and trusting in God's good character enables us to endure harsh circumstances. God's trustworthiness can override the demand for explanations. "Many are the afflictions of the righteous" (Ps. 34:19), but having tasted and seen God's goodness enables us to take confident refuge in him (v. 8) in the most desperate circumstances.

Fourth, God's facing evil head-on may help us overcome certain emotional reactions to evil. Hardly aloof or coolly distant, God suffers and sufferingly identifies with his people in Christ. We've seen how the "high and exalted" God identifies with the "contrite" and "lowly" (Isa. 57:15). God's climactic moment, his glorification (Jn. 12:23; 17:1), is when the Suffering Servant (Isa. 52:13) is physically "lifted up" in a humiliating death of nakedness, shame, and curse on a Roman cross (Jn. 3:14–15; 8:28; 12:32–34). John emphasizes how the crucifixion is the "high point" of the divine theodrama: God's greatness is evidenced by how low he is willing to go to rescue us from our sin to restore and reconcile us to himself.[20] *Jesus manifests the very presence and power of God precisely when God seems most absent and unable to help.* Plantinga remarks: "As the Christian sees things, God does not stand idly by, cooling observing the suffering of his creatures. He enters into and shares our suffering. He endures the anguish of seeing his Son, the second Person of the Trinity, consigned to the bitterly cruel and shameful death of the cross."[21] No wonder the crucifixion distinguishes the gospel from the mythologies of all other peoples.[22]

Fifth, God's past work in Christ and our future hope should prompt us to overcome evil in the present. As Jesus preaches the gospel, heals the afflicted, frees the oppressed, comforts those who mourn, and brings peace (Lk. 4:17–21), he fulfills his messianic task (Isa. 61). As the true Son who fulfills Israel's calling, he calls his oppression-relieving, comforting, peacemaking, rejoicing "new Israelite" community to share in this messianic role (Lk. 6:18–21 // Mt. 5:3–12) in fulfillment of Isaiah 61.

Responding to evil isn't merely *past* and *future*; it involves an empowered, vibrant, loving Christian community as we name and address *present* evils while simultaneously recognizing the need for God's grace to deal with our own evil hearts.

13

The Hiddenness of God

"I praise You, Father, Lord of heaven and earth, that You have hidden these things from the wise and intelligent and have revealed them to infants." (Mt. 11:25)

To Friedrich Nietzsche's mind, God isn't a very clear communicator: How could an all-knowing and all-powerful God be *good* if he doesn't make clear his intentions to his creatures but leaves them tormented by doubts and questions?[1] Another atheist, N. R. Hanson, has claimed he could be convinced to believe in God if suddenly the world's inhabitants were knocked to their knees by a "shattering thunderclap," followed by swirling snow, blowing leaves, heaving earth, toppling buildings, and a Zeus-like figure declaring convincingly with a thundering voice, "I most certainly do exist."[2] Then there's Russell's complaint of God, "You didn't give us enough evidence."[3]

Now the mere *acknowledgment* of God's existence is a start, but even demons believe that much (Jas. 2:19). The relating triune God desires that we earnestly seek him and his wisdom as "for hidden treasures" (Prov. 2:4)–with all our heart. He not only *reveals* and *performs signs*, but also *woos* and *hides.*

But is it right that God hides? While it would be unjustifiable to be held accountable when we're absolutely clueless, various indicators of God's presence and echoes of his voice are available to all people–whether of great intelligence or not. However, God honors human responsibility so greatly that he has configured his self-revelation to be *accessible* but *noncoercive*: he doesn't *compel* or *force* belief in himself. For whole-hearted seekers, God gives ample signposts of his grace and presence, but sufficient ambiguity for the half-hearted or the hard-hearted. He provides ample breathing room to allow us to distance ourselves from God and resist his grace if we choose. The demands of Nietzsche and Hanson miss the point.

First, plenty of evidence won't inevitably lead to seeking God and repentance; an arsenal of reasons doesn't guarantee a loving Father-child relationship. Socrates and Plato believed that knowing the truth means acting in accordance with it. But think about this: We know a steady diet of cheeseburgers and fries is unhealthy; cigarette cartons plainly warn of smoking's negative effects. Yet knowing this doesn't prevent many from "junking out" or chain-smoking.

When it comes to God, plenty of evidence doesn't necessarily result in repentance and loving God deeply. One's will and mind-set may resist or suppress evidence or seek loopholes. Scripture abundantly illustrates this. For example, God caused the ground to swallow up the defiant ringleader Korah and his followers (Num. 16)—just the kind of the display Nietzsche and Hanson call for! Regrettably, the Israelites weren't convinced and humbled. They didn't resolve to love and obey God. The *very next day* "all the congregation of the sons of Israel grumbled against Moses and Aaron, saying, 'You are the ones who have caused the death of the LORD's people'" (16:41). All along the way, God had miraculously supplied Israel with daily manna. His presence was ever visible in their midst—a column of cloud by day and fire by night (Num. 14:14). Despite all this, God's people routinely grumbled, complained, and rebelled against God. God's ongoing blessings to Israel yielded dismal returns on his investment; he wonders what more he could have done (Isa. 5:4).

The self-indulgent, Lazarus-ignoring rich man, condemned in Hades, asks Abraham in paradise to send Lazarus back from the dead to warn his brothers: surely, they'll believe! Abraham isn't optimistic: If they don't listen to Moses and the Prophets, he replies, they won't be persuaded even if someone rises from the dead (Lk. 16:31). This is precisely what happened with Jesus' friend, the *other* Lazarus: Jesus raised him from the dead, and the religious leaders, suppressing the evidence, attempted to put Lazarus back into his tomb (Jn. 12:10–11).

Doesn't Jesus pronounce judgment, though, on Chorazin, Bethsaida, and Capernaum, where he performed miracles yet the people remained unresponsive (Mt. 11:21–24)? Doesn't he affirm that the incinerated city of Sodom would have "remained to this day" had he performed miracles there? The answer—in light of Lk. 16:31—is that Jesus speaks *hyperbolically*: miracles—even rising from the dead—won't persuade the proud and hard-hearted. Jesus holds his contemporaries to a *higher* standard than Sodom since they refuse the clear revelation in God's Son, who brings God's just reign to Israel.

Demons, we've seen, are hardly evidentially challenged. They believe that one God exists (Jas. 2:19), but this hardly prevents their mad attempts to sabotage God's work.

Second, the more evidence one has of God, the more resentful one might become toward him. Evidence often seems beside the point. Atheist Thomas Nagel confesses to a "cosmic authority problem"—he doesn't *want* there to be a God.[4] In her poem "Mastery," Sara Teasdale (1884–1933) announced she wouldn't want a god to come in to her life; indeed, she would rather be lost than have her soul vaguely slip from her own control. She wanted mastery—however feeble—over her own spirit.[5] Those refusing *any* moral authority over their lives may well *know* God exists, but also *hate* him.[6] A self-protective spirit might be increasingly hardened to God's presence—despite God's good intentions for us. So instead of demanding that God play our Simon-says games by "proving" himself according to our criteria, we should ask, *What does God demand of me?*

Third, the question of God calls for a humble, grateful spirit, not a demanding one. Shouldn't we be humble as we approach God, grateful for whatever breakthroughs and glimmers of light he gives? Are we willing to live with unanswered questions and mystery as well? "If anyone is willing to do His will," Jesus affirmed, "he will know of the teaching, whether it is of God or whether I speak from Myself" (Jn. 7:17). We're not observers in a spectator sport, sitting back and watching God jump through our hoops and wait for our approval. God isn't content with our having justified true belief that he exists. We don't become lovingly related to God as his children by having *all* questions answered with *mounds* of evidence. Again, the appropriate stance for the seeker is not to *demand of God,* but to ask what God, if he exists, *demands of me.*

Fourth, what would an absolutely certain, irrefutable divine manifestation look like? What if Hanson's Zeus-like figure appeared? Couldn't we always second-guess or explain away such "manifestations"? How do we become absolutely sure this remarkable figure isn't an extra-terrestrial *pretending* to be divine? And what if the Advaita Vedantan Hindu is right—that any such manifestation is ultimately illusory? If we put our mind to it, we can, like Descartes, doubt the majority of our most basic beliefs. What if God did perform something spectacular for someone, but then, afterward, his child is diagnosed with cancer or his spouse is killed in an auto accident? Would God's spectacular manifestation be nullified?

God will make himself known to those responding to his initiating grace, humbly seeking him (Heb. 11:6), and gratefully accepting whatever he reveals. For those demanding irrefutable proofs of God, he becomes more elusive. There's enough *light* for those who humbly seek and enough *murkiness* for those who don't. As the brilliant French mathematician-philosopher Blaise Pascal wrote:

> Willing to appear openly to those who seek Him with all their heart, and to be hidden from those who flee from Him with all their heart, [God] so regulates the knowledge of Himself that He has given signs of Himself, visible to those who seek Him, and

not to those who seek Him not. There is enough light for those who only desire to see, and enough obscurity for those who have a contrary disposition.[7]

Humans don't need Ph.D.s to know God exists and to put their trust in him. From the least of them to the greatest, God's presence and grace can be known. Those determined to resist or ignore God, on the other hand, can still find loopholes for nonbelief.[8] Again, the evidence is *ample*, not *coercive*.

Fifth, God will make his presence obscure for various reasons. God is more concerned with humble hearts than shrewd minds. He resists the proud, but gives grace to the humble (Jas. 4:6). Indeed, he hides himself from the self-sufficiently smart. "You have hidden these things from the wise and intelligent and have revealed them to infants" (Mt. 11:25). God may even hide himself from *believers* at certain times for various reasons—to give us a deeper appreciation for God, to teach us to trust him when things look black, to foster a greater sense of dependency on God and a renewed determination to obey, to teach us to yearn for relationship with God, to encourage gratitude, or to humble us in our pride.[9] Furthermore, even though God desires that *all* acknowledge his existence, he might also value the human realization of sin's disastrously negative consequences (Rom. 1)—*even if* this involves some obscuring of God's reality. The absence of miracles or God's not acting as speedily or efficiently as we'd like may be for our good. As with ancient Israel, the constant, obvious divine manifestations don't necessarily inspire freely offered loving commitment to God. The idea of universally available evidence for God *doesn't conflict* with divine hiddenness. Again, Pascal gives insight into how the will can shape how we filter the evidence:

> The will, which prefers one aspect to another, turns away the mind from considering the qualities of all that it does not like to see; and thus the mind, moving in accord with the will, stops to consider the aspect which it likes, and so judges by what it sees.[10]

God doesn't want us to come to know him apart from knowing him as loving Lord and Father—personally embracing and committing ourselves to him. Purely intellectual knowledge of God's existence is inadequate; God doesn't want us to treat him as just another object of knowledge—like memorizing lines from Shakespeare or having figured out how a computer program works. He desires *personal, loving knowledge.*

So instead of being *passively "open,"* we must be *morally serious* toward God who makes momentous demands of us. And we can't be morally serious seekers if we say we'll believe in God if and only if we have firsthand miraculous signs from him. We also must be *humble* and *undemanding* seekers, grateful for indicators or pointers to the God who hides, seeks, and graciously reveals. God, by his Spirit, will not disappoint (Rom. 5:5).

14

Original Sin

...through one man sin entered into the world. (Rom. 5:12)

Our first ancestors have passed on a spiritual infection to the human race—what Christian theologians call "original sin": "Therefore, just as through one man sin entered the world, and death through sin, and so death spread to all men, because all sinned" (Rom. 5:12). The old Puritan *New England Primer* declares, "In Adam's fall / We sinned all."

Exactly how we've been affected—and infected—remains the subject of much debate. Critics claim it's unfair to be held responsible for and strapped with the consequences of an act committed by (1) *someone else,* (2) *in completely different circumstances,* (3) *ages ago.*[1] One thinker asserts that no Christian doctrine "is received with greater reserve and hesitation, even to the point of outright denial" than original sin.[2]

Our primal ancestors' sin brought momentous—indeed cosmic—consequences. Rather than ruling as kings over the slithering serpent by following God's wisdom, they submitted to the snake's suggestion. Instead of loving and trusting God in worship and service as priests in Eden's sanctuary, they sought to usurp God's place. The downward spiral began, subjecting humans to misery, oppression, calamity, disease, and death ever since.

How are we to understand "original sin" and address the charge of divine injustice? First, some context: as God's image-bearers, we were made to rule creation with him and to worship him. Though Christ came as the successful King and Priest to fulfill—and restore—our kingship and priesthood, this divine image, though diminished, hadn't been obliterated (Jas. 3:9). Christians are mistaken if they believe that humans are "nothing but worthless, depraved sinners." No, we're first of all God's "very good" creation; human nature is therefore good. Sin is *foreign* to God's creation. Theologian Colin Gunton has rightly observed: "It is necessary to conclude that evil…is not intrinsic to the creation, but some corruption of, or invasion into, that which is essentially good."[3] Indeed, Genesis 3 comes *after* Genesis 1–2!

Despite sin's universality and pervasiveness, like poison mixed into wine, this fact doesn't obliterate goodness in God's creation: human creativity, reason, moral responsibility, the capacity for deep relationships–including a relationship with God. We've been made "a little lower than God"–crowned "with glory and majesty" (Ps. 8:5). In other words, we're good by nature–even if marred by the fall.

What then is the exact connection between Adam's sin and us? Some theologians make a very tight connection, asserting that the guilt of Adam, our "federal head," has been imputed to us–charged to our account. Scripture leaves us with considerable wiggle room on the matter, however, and we shouldn't load Romans 5:12 with too much theological freight.[4] Having surveyed various approaches to the Adam-us connection, theologian James Leo Garrett notes the *consensus* about the *lack* of consensus: "To affirm the universality of sin is easy and to affirm the universality of depravity is not difficult, but to settle on the relationship of the sin of Adam and Eve to our sin is indeed difficult."[5] While there is human solidarity with Adam, Paul just hasn't given us enough information to tell us exactly what the connection is.[6]

Damage or Guilt?

For as in Adam all die. (1 Cor. 15:22)

Our deeply sinful condition should be understood as the *damage* or *consequences* of Adam's fall, not his *guilt.* This position seems both biblically accurate and much less morally problematic. *Being in sin*–a given condition from birth, indeed, from conception–is different from *sinning,* for which we're responsible and which renders us guilty and blameworthy.[7] We're born with an original corruption, a self-centered orientation that permeates all we do. But simply *being born* or conceived in sin (Ps. 51:5) doesn't render a human guilty before God. While we can accept original *sin* (the "damage" view), original *guilt* seems morally troublesome.

In addition, we don't sin *necessarily*–that is, it's not assured that we *must* commit this or that particular sin; we do sin *inevitably,* though–that is, in addition to our inclination to sin, given the vast array of opportunities to sin, we eventually do sin.[8]

What is the status of those dying in infancy or the mentally retarded? As biblical scholar Douglas Moo notes, Paul in Romans 5 "does not seem even to be considering in these verses the special issues created for the doctrine of universal sin and judgment by mentally restricted human beings."[9] The mentally handicapped or those dying in infancy, though not guilty before God, still need Christ's gracious atoning death to remove any residue of sin's damaging consequences affecting both soul and body. From conception onward, each of us has inherited a certain deformity (not guilt) of *soul*–a mal-alignment of will, desires, emotions, and reason, which results in a self-centered inclination. What's more, our fragile *bodies*, often racked by handicaps and diseases, eventually die–all of which have come to us through the fall.[10] Christ's conquering death and resurrection will bring perfect wholeness in the re-creation.

Thus, Adam's sin *didn't impute or strap his guilt to us.* We're judged according to deeds done "in the body" (2 Cor. 5:10; cp. Rom. 2:6; Col. 3:25), and infants and the severely mentally handicapped don't *do* anything morally blameworthy. Indeed, the "soul who sins will die" (Ezek. 18:4; cp. 18:20). Under Israel's civic law, only the guilty party is to be punished: "everyone shall be put to death for his own sin" (Deut. 24:16).

However, the *consequences* of Adam's sin profoundly *affected* or *damaged* the priest-kingly image of God in us. Consider how *one's individual actions can have a powerful effect on others*–AIDS and crack babies or children caught in the crossfire of divorce or alcoholic parents. While our earthly freedom can produce great goods like hospitals or hospice care or endowments for art museums, it can also bring great harm such as concentration camps or gulags or tyrannies. Such freedom means our choices make a real difference in others' lives, for good or ill. The biblical text illustrates how one's actions powerfully affect others who have no say in the matter. For instance, after David had arrogantly demanded that a census be taken in Israel, he confessed to the Lord: "I am the one who has sinned and have done wrong. These are but sheep. What have they done? Let your hand fall on me and my family" (2 Sam. 24:17, NIV).

Despite our inborn self-centered tendency, the corruptibility of our bodies, and even the fallenness of human societies (all *consequences* of Adam's sin), Adam's transgression *doesn't* confer *his guilt* on us by virtue of our being conceived! Guilt comes when we responsibly sin, whether in thought, word, or deed. Our guilt is *conditional,* not unconditional: *when we side with our sinful condition against the purposes of God, we become morally blameworthy.*[11] Though we're *damaged* by corporate solidarity with Adam, *guilt* comes with the abuse of each individual's personal responsibility and moral accountability before God.

Original Sin and the Grace of God

Behold, the LORD's arm is not so short
*   That it cannot save…*
But your iniquities have made a separation between you and your God.
(Isa. 59:1–2)

Is it fair that we're strapped with the consequences of Adam's sin? Admittedly, we're dealing with some mysteries and puzzles here, and we may have more of a worm's-eye view than a God's-eye view on these deep questions. However, we'll see that the doctrine of original sin, though perplexing, is still more plausible and presents a far richer explanation of the human condition than secular or nontheistic alternatives.

First, real evils—not simply "abnormalities"—obviously exist in the world; this serves to support the Christian faith as opposed to various philosophical alternatives. G. K. Chesterton famously declared: "Certain new theologians dispute original sin, which is the only part of Christian theology which can really be proved." In fact, the "ancient masters of religion" began with the fact of sin—"a fact as practical as potatoes."[12] We can readily observe sin's embeddedness in the fabric of human existence. Scripture's realistic dual emphasis of (a) human goodness and (b) pervasive sin better explains our human disposition, behavior, and relationships than optimistic or neutral secular approaches—or Eastern approaches that consider evil illusory (*maya*). Naturalistic philosopher of science Michael Ruse observes the explanatory power of original sin:

> I think Christianity is spot on about original sin—how could one think otherwise, when the world's most civilized and advanced people (the people of Beethoven, Goethe, Kant) embraced that slime-ball Hitler and participated in the Holocaust? I think Saint Paul and the great Christian philosophers had real insights into sin and freedom and responsibility, and I want to build on this rather than turn from it.[13]

The existence of *evil* is evident to our most basic and reliable intuitions. While many may wonder how a morally respectable God could allow human beings to get *this* bad, the *more basic* question is: Without the context of God as a standard of goodness and humans are morally accountable to him, why think humans really *are* evil? Aren't they just *abnormal, maladjusted, dysfunctional, statistically deviant,* or *highly individualistic*? Therapeutic or psychoanalytic categories are simply insufficient to account for the deep evils that exist. Various Eastern views are similarly inept. For example, Arthur Koestler tells of one Zen Buddhist scholar calling Hitler's gas chambers "very silly," claiming that evil is "relative" and merely "a Christian concept."[14] The very clear existence of *evil*, we've noted, suggests a standard of goodness or design plan: evil is a *deviation* from or *corruption* of this standard and a *departure* from what ought to be. To say that the actions of Hitler, Stalin, Pol Pot, Mao Tse Tung, or even the Columbine killers were simply "abnormal" or "maladjusted," not *evil*, is not only hollow, but grotesquely distorted.[15]

Second, to focus only on damage brought on by Adam's sin presents an incomplete picture. To better understand evil's depth and significance, we must consider the fuller context of the grace, redemption, and hope in Christ, the second Adam. The most optimistic secular therapeutic alternatives are short on genuine hope. What do we advise those facing a fatal illness or the pain of broken relationships—"go actualize yourself in creative activity"? Such a response is an insult. As psychologist Paul Vitz states, "It is exactly suffering, however, which is at the center of the meaning and hope of the religious life."[16] Psychologist Hobart Mowrer observed that denying sin's reality means cutting ourselves off from the possibility of radical redemption and restoration.[17]

Without the language of sin, salvation makes no sense. Relativism's denial of any moral standard implies no need for forgiveness or redemption, and modernity's therapeutic quest for pain-free self-actualization has become more important than being rightly related to God. Theologian Vernon Grounds has said that an "individual, quite completely free from tension, anxiety, and conflict may be only a well-adjusted sinner who is dangerously maladjusted to God; and it is infinitely better to be a neurotic saint than a healthy-minded sinner." A certain healthy-mindedness—"having it all together"—may actually be spiritually hazardous, blocking a person from turning to God since he senses no need for God.[18]

Third, the meaning of Adam's primal sin can't be isolated from the broader framework of the new creation brought about through Christ.[19] The consequences of Adam's sin aren't self-contained; we make sense of them through the second Adam's redemption and restoration (Rom. 5:12–21; 1 Cor. 15:21–28). Instead of caving in to hopelessness and despair because of our moral failings, we can let God's Spirit point us to the larger picture of God's gracious, available salvation through Christ. Sin need not be the total picture in anyone's biography.[20]

Our earlier mention of the "moral gap" is relevant here. The chasm between God's character and our own moral failure should prompt us to cast ourselves on his mercy and call out for his grace since he is "not far from each one of us" (Acts 17:27). Our failure—the "moral gap"—points toward the solution:[21] (a) *a moral ideal or standard*; (b) *our inability to live up to that standard*; therefore (c) *the need for divine assistance or grace to bridge this gap.* Original sin is a kind of grace God may use to remind us not only of our moral failure (Rom. 2:14–15), but also of our need for gracious redemption. Again, Kant's dictum "*ought* implies *can*"—having an *obligation* ("ought") entails the *ability* to do it ("can")—should be modified to "*ought* implies *can—with God's available grace.*"

Despite the proud claim that each human should stand or fall on her own merits rather than on God's aid, the fact is this: Our only real alternative is to acknowledge our deep failure, cast ourselves on God's mercy, and ask for help to live as we ought, which he richly provides in the cross of Christ and the gift of his Spirit.[22] We can either *tarnish* and *diminish* the divine image, or, with God's help, *develop* and *increase* it until Christ, God's very image, is more fully formed in us (Gal. 4:19).

Fourth, if God, by his Spirit, gives sufficient grace and opportunity to all people, even if most may reject it, then he isn't being unjust or unloving in allowing us to be damaged by the consequences of Adam's sin. Most humans, Scripture indicates, don't appropriate God's revelation and salvation, though they're available to all (Rom. 1:17–32). We haven't been thrown into this world without available divine resources. God furnishes us all–to varying degrees–with sufficient divine resources to awaken us to our need and enable us to respond (Rom. 2:5–7). This comes through his prevenient–"preceding" or "initiating"–grace that is near to us all (Acts 17:27; Jn. 16:8). Given (a) God's desire that all persons be saved and come to know the truth (1 Tim. 2:4; 2 Pet. 3:9) and (b) his demand that all people everywhere repent and obey him (Acts 17:30), God would deploy the needed grace for all to do so. His Spirit's initiating influence can be quenched or stifled, however. Human freedom allows for the possibility of "always resisting the Holy Spirit" (Acts 7:51).

No one, then, can blame God for his own condemnation. ("But I was born with original sin.") This inherited original corruption by itself doesn't condemn us. By resisting God's grace, humans *separate themselves* from him and seal their fate. God condemns no one without the cooperation of his will. Scripture stresses that the *direction* or *disposition* of one's heart and will condemns a person rather than individual *acts* of wrongdoing.[23]

Fifth, despite the charge of unfairness that Adam ruined things for everyone else, it could well be that God knew that any *of us human beings would have freely disobeyed in the garden.* Many have wondered, "Why should Adam be our representative head? He fouled things up for everyone else, and now we're paying for it." An unarticulated–perhaps even arrogant–presumption stands behind this complaint: "If I had been in Adam's place, I would have obeyed God's simple command not to take fruit from the tree. I could have prevented the disastrous fallout from the first disobedience." However, what if every human being God created would also have committed the primal sin, just as Adam did? Had any of us been in Adam's place, perhaps we would have–without exception–freely chosen to disobey. While human sinlessness is theoretically possible, God knew that any created human being still would have freely chosen the same course, resulting in the same curse. Selecting another person would have produced no different outcome.

This last point *doesn't* address the questions of the exact connection between Adam and the rest of the human race and how corruption is transmitted. It does, however, relate to the inappropriateness of blaming Adam, whether expressly or implicitly: *God, I thank you that I am not like Adam.*[24] This deflates the charge of divine injustice since *God knows the rest of us would have freely acted in the very same Adamic way in the same circumstance.*

The spirit of the age denies sin and humankind's fall, which obscures personal responsibility, our alienation from God, and the need for repentance. The doctrine of original sin makes the best sense of human experience; alternative suggestions–abnormality, neurosis, illusion–fail to capture the depth of the human condition. Our drastic situation in Adam can point us to God's grace in light of the "moral gap" each of us experiences. *Original sin isn't the full picture*; our failure directs us to the larger context of redemption and hope to explain our status. Even though the mystery of *un*godliness is great, the mystery of godliness is far greater and more powerful (1 Tim. 3:16). While we can't fully grasp or answer the problems of evil and human sinfulness, they point to the solution—the conquering love of God and his redemption in Christ.

Given the lengths to which the triune God has gone to go secure our reconciliation with him, we can surely leave in God's hands such difficult questions as original sin.

15

Hell

...away from the presence of the Lord. (2 Thess. 1:9)

Isaiah 5, we've noted, portrays God as a vineyard owner who had busied himself with the task of "planting" his people Israel–"the choicest vine"–on a fertile hill, digging all around it, removing its stones. Despite the legitimate expectation of Israel's bearing "good" fruit after all he had done, God is exasperated at Israel's "worthless" yield: "What more was there to do for My vineyard that I have not done in it?" (5:4). Jeremiah similarly writes of God's planting Israel as a "choice vine" and "faithful seed," but Israel rejected God (Jer. 2:21). Centuries later, Jesus lamented over Jerusalem, having longed to gather her to himself, but "you were unwilling" (Mt. 23:37). Her religious leaders had "rejected God's purpose for themselves" (Lk. 7:30). The commandment-keeping rich man for whom Jesus "felt a love" desired to "inherit eternal life," but more greatly desired his idol of wealth over following Christ. He "went away grieving" because he didn't want to let go of what would keep him from entering God's kingdom (Mk. 10:17–25). There are those who would rather avoid God's presence and blessing than turn to him and submit to his authority. And God won't forgive them without their permission. Regarding the Thyatiran false prophetess "Jezebel," Jesus warns, "I gave her time to repent; and she does not want to repent of her immorality" (Rev. 2:21).

Though many will reject God's love and holy presence, he nevertheless desires that none perish, but that all repent (1 Tim. 2:4; 2 Pet. 3:9). After all, Christ died for the sins of "the whole world [*holou tou kosmou*]" (1 Jn. 2:2)–the *same* "whole world" that lies in the hands of the evil one (1 Jn. 5:19), and that Satan leads astray (Rev. 12:9). Despite God's global love, people will still "deny the Master who bought them" (2 Pet. 2:1). Scripture strongly suggests that *the only obstacle to universal salvation is human free will and its resistance to God's loving initiative.*[1] Refusing to honor God and give him thanks (Rom. 1:21) is a sub-par life (cp. Jn. 10:10), indeed the beginning of hell itself, as C. S. Lewis' *The Great Divorce* suggests.   The Christian life, on the other hand, is meant to be "a foretaste of glory divine."[2]

We approach the troubling, sobering doctrine of hell with seriousness. Although Christians and non-Christians alike have grappled with it, we must remember that the wise and morally attuned Jesus of Nazareth spoke of hell more than anyone else in Scripture.

What Is Hell?

"And then I will declare to them, 'I never knew you; depart from Me, you who practice lawlessness'" (Mt. 7:23)

Just as Narnia isn't "just behind the wardrobe," hell isn't spatially located (e.g., below the earth's crust or 2.37 light years from Andromeda). It is a *different realm* of existence—being "away from the presence of the Lord and from the glory of His power" (2 Thess. 1:9). Scripture suggests it's both (a) *punishment* and (b) the *logical outcome* of a life of God-avoidance: "The punishment fits the crime because the punishment *is* the crime. Saying no to God means no God."[3] Hell is the withdrawal of God's presence and blessing for those refusing to receive them.[4] In the end, Lewis states, there are only two kinds of people: those who say *to God,* "Thy will be done," and *those to whom God says,* "*Thy* will be done."[5] According to Scottish author George MacDonald, "The one principle of hell is: I am my own."[6]

Scripture subtly suggests that hell *isn't* a place of *high thermal output;* rather, it describes hell *figuratively* to reveal *the terrible tragedy of life apart from God.* If we took its imagery of *darkness* and *flames* literally, they'd *cancel each other out:* "Outer darkness" or "black darkness" (Mt. 8:12; 22:13; 2 Pet. 2:17) and "eternal fire" (Mt. 18:8; 25:41) would be mutually exclusive. Extrabiblical Jewish literature also assumes this picture, linking, say, "black fire" with "cold ice" (2 Enoch 10:2). Hell's "fire" need not be taken literally—any more than should hell's undying "worm" (Isa. 66:24).

That these are figurative is reinforced by the fact that hell has been prepared for *spirit beings* without physical nerve endings—the devil and his angels (Mt. 25:41).[7] Scripture's references to fire often symbolize the severity of divine holiness or judgment: God is a "consuming fire" (Deut. 4:24), judging with "unquenchable fire" (Lk. 3:17), and whose throne is "flaming with fire" with a "river of fire" issuing from beneath it (Dan. 7:9–10, NIV). Hell's agony is primarily spiritual, mental, and emotional—utter hopelessness, restlessness, and joylessness where selfishness and rebellion continue to reign. In hell one is deprived of intimate union with God, the source of life and hope—*the greatest loss possible,* which thus brings the greatest pain—pain of soul.

It probably doesn't hurt to mention that reformers John Calvin and Martin Luther viewed hell's "fire" figuratively. Theologian J. I. Packer advises us not to try to imagine what it's like to be in hell: "The mistake is to take such pictures as physical descriptions, when in fact they are imagery, symbolizing realities...far worse than the symbols themselves."[8] We're not diminishing the significance and severity of hell, but stressing the anguish of soul produced by God's absence. Now some notable evangelicals have offered good arguments for "conditional immortality"–or the eventual annihilation of unbelievers–as an alternative to a more traditional understanding of hell.[9] Though the discussion continues, it seems they have more work to do..

Whether in "heaven"/"paradise" (Lk. 23:43)–an intermediate state–or in "the new heavens and the new earth" (2 Pet. 3:13; Rev. 21:2, 9), the redeemed will experience the opposite of hell–God's *presence*, unmediated access to him whose "face" they'll enjoy (Rev. 22:4): "the tabernacle of God is among men, and He will dwell among them, and they shall be His people, and God Himself will be among them" (Rev. 21:3).

Objections and Clarifications

Critics tend to raise certain questions about hell; we'll examine the common ones.

Objection 1: *Isn't God unjust to punish infinitely or everlastingly for sins committed during a finite period of time on earth?* The "proportionality problem" claims the punishment is extreme given the crime. In actuality, hell is the *logical outcome* of living one's life and devoting one's energies away from God. Scripture's primary focus isn't on *discrete, individual sinful acts* but on *a mind-set or direction of life away from God*. Being away from God–or present with him–isn't ultimately a surprise outcome. Final separation from God naturally flows from an earthly life lived in detachment from God and his purposes (Mt. 7:21–23; Lk. 16:22–31). Furthermore, while the condemned don't *enjoy* this separated state, this doesn't mean that they'd *rather* be in God's holy presence. Just as the new heaven and earth will be a perfect harmony and union between God and the redeemed, final separation from God is like one's finally getting a *divorce from God*. Again, the punishment fits the crime–*those who want no God get no God*. So the orthodox Christian need not hold that *every* sin merits hell or has hell as its consequence; rather hell is the final consequence (and even just punishment) for those who irrevocably refuse to seek and accept God's forgiveness of their sins. By refusing God's forgiveness they freely separate themselves from God forever.[10]

In Romans 1, God isn't condemning individual acts of sin, but a general disposition that refuses to honor God as God and give him thanks.[11] Hell is both *punishment* and the *natural consequence* of one's rejection of God–just as the new heavens and earth would be the natural outcome for those who love God. To force heaven on someone who hates God's presence would be hell for him.[12]

Objection 2: *Isn't the possibility of an everlasting destiny away from God too great a burden for humans to bear?* Is the weight of hell's horrors a terribly unfair burden for God to place on anyone, since no one can know the full ramifications of rejecting God? We *do,* however, make many momentous, life-changing decisions—a marriage commitment or having children—but that doesn't mean they're too great a weight to bear. A couple can earnestly and responsibly vow to love and be faithful "for richer, for poorer" and "in sickness and in health" without realizing the full implications. Similarly, God assumes we have enough knowledge to set our spiritual course. Conversely, we can't fully comprehend the everlasting bliss and joy of God's company (1 Cor. 2:9), but this doesn't mean responding to God's grace and finding eternal life with him is too heavy a responsibility for us. We needn't understand the *full* consequences of hell—or God's presence—to choose responsibly between them.[13]

God hasn't left human beings to make this weighty choice on their own, though. In his own way, according to his purposes, he offers his prevenient or initiating grace through his wooing, convicting Spirit (Jn. 16:8) that *all* may repent and find life (Acts 17:30). He is ready to equip anyone for salvation.[14] The problem isn't that people like Aristotle or Gandhi are *uninformed* about Jesus or aren't *completely aware* of the *full* gravity of earthly choices. Rather, the issue is that people resist the Spirit's influence and do not lovingly respond to God's kind initiative.

Objection 3: *How can God condemn those who have committed a finite set of sins to be forever separated from God?* We've noted that the "finite number" of sins persons commit—in contrast to the "eternal punishment" they receive—*isn't* the major issue. More fundamental is a *mind-set* or *disposition* against God, which *continues in the afterlife.* Those who've drawn near to God in worship and in service to others on earth continue to enjoy his presence in the afterlife; those who've resisted him on earth, thus diminishing the clarity of the divine image, continue in their hard-heartedness in hell.

Yet even more basic is this distinction: those in hell have committed the *infinite* or *ultimate* sin, not simply *a string of finite sins.* They've rejected a relationship with the gracious, self-giving God—the gravest of sins. Instead of focusing on (a) *individual* sins or even (b) a *lifetime* of sins, we should focus on *Whom* the unbeliever is rejecting.

Objection 4: *Wouldn't those who have experienced hell want to repent to be in God's presence?* Why continue to punish if they would certainly relent and repent? Lewis' *Great Divorce* idea is implied in Scripture: despite hell's miseries, the condemned wouldn't prefer God's presence; resistance continues in hell. The more they would be exposed to God, the more they would come to hate him. Hell is having one's way without God.

D. A. Carson reminds us that the Bible gives no hint of repentance in hell.[15] Even the rich man who lived so selfishly in his earthly life, now crying out in agony from Hades (Lk. 16), doesn't necessarily prefer a God-centered existence; he just wants relief. Like Judas, having betrayed Jesus, he feels remorseful—not repentant.[16] While people in hell are quite conscious of their loss, they still don't desire to change. Such a desire can't be coerced. They, not God, are responsible for their loss. Though intellectually recognizing how badly off they are in that condition, they still choose to remain in it, becoming even more hateful and bitter toward God. Just as true conversion can't be coerced by sword-point, neither can it be wrought through mere imposed psychological misery.

The drug addict who does not recover knows he has a serious problem but refuses to relinquish his habit. Perhaps we should think of hell as a place where "people continue to rebel, continue to insist on their own way, continue societal structures of prejudice and hate, continue to defy the living God. And as they continue to defy God, so he continues to punish them. And the cycle goes on and on and on."[17] Indeed, some have suggested that people in hell in principle could repent, but they remain in hell *so long as they continue to resist and rebel against God.*[18] As it turns out, the rebellion never ceases.

The probing question isn't *Would you rather be in heaven or in hell?* but *Are you willing to submit to God and his claim on your life?* Will you *diminish* the divine image or *enhance* it? Satan and his co-rebelling angels preferred their own way to God's, as Satan of Milton's *Paradise Lost* (Bk. 1) states, "Better to reign in Hell, than serve in Heav'n."

Incidentally, the punishment of separation from God won't be equally severe, but will be *degreed.* In one of Jesus' parables (Lk. 12:47–48), the master metes out different punishments—"many lashes" or "few"—depending on the slaves' degree of awareness in their disobedience.

Objection 5: *Isn't universalism—that no one will be lost but all will be saved through Christ—a biblical option?* Universalists, citing Romans 5:12–21, believe that "all" in Adam are identical to "all" in Christ; therefore all will be saved. However, the "all" in Adam are a much larger category (those affected by Adam's transgression) and so *aren't* the same as the "all" in Christ (those savingly affected by Christ's act of righteousness).

Furthermore, Jesus speaks of an "eternal sin" that can *never* be forgiven (Mk. 3:29). If possible, Paul is willing to be condemned for the sake of his fellow Jews who reject Jesus (Rom. 9:3). Some universalists claim that free choice about one's destiny means (a) *being fully informed* and (b) *never regretting one's decision.* Anyone knowing what hell is like would unquestionably want to be with God. Let's assume that's correct. The problem is that one can't be fully informed without directly experiencing God's loving presence *first;* otherwise, one won't realize the misery of separation from God. But this is precisely the problem—an overwhelming exposure to God's love that guaranteed a person wouldn't want to be away from God is the kind of compulsion God wants to avoid.[19] As Lewis wrote:

> I would pay any price to be able to say truthfully "All will be saved." But my reason retorts, "Without their will, or with it?" If I say, "Without their will" I at once perceive a contradiction; how can the supreme voluntary act of self-surrender be involuntary? If I say, "With their will," my reason replies "How if they *will not* give in?"[20]

Objection 6: *Why didn't God make us without being capable of sin, always choosing good—just like the final state of the redeemed?* If God can guarantee a sin-free existence for believers in the afterlife, why not do so from the start? In reply, our earthly freedom to choose between God and no God, to embrace God's grace or resist it, sets the stage for the afterlife. These choices shape our character, spiritual condition, and, ultimately, our destiny; we set our spiritual compass to head in one direction or another. Whether we decide as a child or late in life, like the criminal on the cross (Lk. 23:39–43), the freedom to move toward God or away from him is an earthly prerequisite to our final outcome, which is the ultimate fulfillment and realization of our desires.

(a) Some hold that this *freedom is sealed in the afterlife*: once we've set our course to embrace or reject God's grace, this freely made earthly decision is made permanent, and we get the desire of our heart—either with God or away from him.[21] (b) Or perhaps *God simply foreknows* that no redeemed saint enjoying his immediate and unshielded presence will ever freely decide to turn away from him, though theoretically possible (as happened with rebellious angels). God's foreknowledge guarantees this ongoing sinlessness. These suggestive alternatives are only tentative, which is only fitting since, "It has not appeared as yet what we shall be. We know that, when He appears, we shall be like Him, because we shall see Him just as He is" (1 Jn. 3:2).

Objection 7: *Why did God create a world knowing that multitudes of its inhabitants would end up rejecting God forever?* Though many fault God for hell's existence, all who go there have freely resisted his initiating grace and wouldn't want to draw near to God in love and worship. What if there happens to be *no* world that would yield persons who end up freely choosing to always do good? What if certain persons would *never* freely embrace God, no matter what world God placed them in? Some of these "transworldly depraved" persons may have come very close in this world, perhaps even having apostatized from Christianity, but ultimately decide against God.

So should God not create at all just because many repeatedly resist his free offer of grace? Why should God deprive the grace-responsive of the joy of belonging to God just because others refuse? He isn't going to let resisters and rebels slam the door shut on his free offer to let many people become part of his family—the greatest good possible.

Objection 8: *Isn't it morally contradictory for the redeemed to enjoy God's presence in the new heavens and earth while the unredeemed and unrepentant are forever separated from him?* Are the two final states—bliss and anguish—utterly incompatible? It's helpful to consider Jesus' prodigal son parable (Lk. 15:25-32). The older brother refuses to come in to celebrate, but the party shouldn't stop simply because some refuse to enter the banquet hall. Likewise, God isn't going to be held captive by party-poopers, spoil-sports, and grouches who haven't abandoned their pride and received God's gracious forgiveness yet think the partying should stop because they're not participating. But if God has done all he can to offer genuine forgiveness to all, then what more can God do for those who refuse to come in? We have a right to sit out, but not to hold up the party that celebrates God's redeeming us from captivity to sin and Satan. God will honor the significant, lasting choices we make in this life—whether this means being with God or away from him.[22]

No, God doesn't send people to hell; rather, they freely choose to ignore and resist God's initiating grace, condemning themselves. Hell exists for those who refuse to acknowledge their guilt and so can't receive forgiveness.[23] God withdraws his blessed presence from those refusing to receive it.[24] Ultimately, those forever separated are fully successful in their rebellion;[25] they lock the gates of hell from within and further diminish their own humanity. Human free will is the only obstacle to universal salvation.

While demonic beings tremblingly acknowledge one God exists (Jas. 2:19), everyone will have to acknowledge that Jesus is the victorious Lord over all (Phil. 2:9-11)—whether gladly or grudgingly. Now, during this day of salvation, is the acceptable time to humbly and willingly acknowledge this.

PART IV

REDEMPTION

In Him we have redemption through His blood, the forgiveness of our trespasses, according to the riches of His grace which He lavished on us. (Eph. 1:7–8a)

16

The Incarnation

God Becomes Man

The Word became flesh, and dwelt among us. (Jn. 1:14)

The self-existent triune God creates, humans turn away, and the consequences are dramatic. But God won't allow exile and alienation to have the last word. In this new creation and new exodus, God decisively steps into the human mire with both feet; in doing so, he rescues us, restoring our vocation as a new humanity and a chosen people through Christ, the second Adam and the true Israel, God's beloved Son. God becomes human—a first-century Jew—to restore his people—indeed, all humanity.

Taking their lead from Scripture, orthodox Christians have held that *two natures*—divine and human—exist in the person of Jesus of Nazareth—"perfect God, perfect man subsisting of a reasoning soul and human flesh" (Athanasian Creed).

Muslims, Unitarians, and Jehovah's Witnesses claim that this God-in-flesh doctrine is contradictory: unlike the all-knowing, all-powerful, all-good God, humans are ignorant, frail, and flawed. John Hick thinks Jesus was just a traveling preacher who was "intensely conscious of God's holy and loving presence," though "wholly human." Eventually, the "Jesus cult" developed into the "cult of the risen Christ, transfigured and deified."[1] Jesus scholar Marcus Borg maintains that Jesus *couldn't* have said, "I am the way, the truth, and the life" (Jn. 14:6), or, "I am the light of the world" (Jn. 8:12); psychologically sane people don't say such things.[2] Of course, the question remains: If early Christians put these words into Jesus' mouth, why would they make up an embarrassing, psychologically challenged Jesus?

Is it absurd to affirm the Incarnation–that the "Word" who is God (Jn. 1:1) became human (1:14)? This doctrine, along with the other great things of the gospel, is glorious and not reducible to logical formulas. But this hardly implies the doctrine is illogical. For one thing, Scriptures affirm he was *human* (1 Cor. 15:21, 47–49; 1 Tim. 2:5; 3:16), but *divine* as well:

- He *forgives sin,* not only displacing the temple, but assuming God's authoritative domain (Mk. 2:5, 7).
- He's the *judge* of the world (Mt. 25:31–46; cp. 2 Cor. 5:10).
- He is *prayed to* (Acts 7:59–60; 1 Cor. 16:22; 2 Cor. 12:9)
- He is *explicitly called "God"* (Jn 1:1, 18; 20:28; Acts 20:28; Rom. 9:5; Tit. 2:13; Heb. 1:8; 2 Pet. 1:1; 1 Jn. 5:20).
- Important Old Testament references to Yahweh ("the LORD") are used to refer to Jesus "the Lord" in the New Testament: to call on the name of *Yahweh* brings salvation (Joel 2:31–32; cp. *Jesus* in Acts 2:20–21; Rom. 10:13); every knee will bow to *Yahweh* (Isa. 45:23; *Jesus* in Phil. 2:10); a forerunner prepares the way for *Yahweh* (Isa. 40:3; *Jesus* in Mt. 3:3); *Yahweh* is my shepherd (Ps. 23:1; *Jesus* in Jn. 10:11); Isaiah sees *Yahweh's* glory (Isa. 6:1–5, 10; *Jesus'* in Jn. 12:41); *Yahweh* is the first and the last (Isa. 44:6; 48:12; 51:12; *Jesus* in Rev. 1:17; 2:8; 22:13).

Various miracle-denying New Testament critics, even theologians, have considered the Incarnation to be a myth or legend, a human fabrication. A leading literary expert in distinguishing legend from history was C. S. Lewis. He said of these critical scholars: "I distrust them as critics. They seem to me to lack literary judgment, to be imperceptive about the very quality of the texts they are reading." Though studying the New Testament from their youth up, they lack the needed literary experience and so miss "the obvious things" about these texts: "If he tells me that something in a Gospel is legend or romance, I want to know how many legends and romances he has read, how well his palate is trained in detecting them by flavour; not how many years he has spent on that Gospel."[3] As Lewis affirms, Jesus' miracles and authoritative identity-claims in the Gospels are reliably recorded history.

Furthermore, while disputes had broken out in the earliest Christian communities over circumcision, spiritual gifts, or the place of the Mosaic Law, *no* disagreement exists in the New Testament writings regarding Jesus' lofty status as Lord of all. James (45 C.E.) refers to "our glorious Lord Jesus Christ," and Paul in Galatians (48–49 C.E.) calls Jesus the "Son of God" three times (Gal. 1:16; 2:20; 4:4). Both these Jewish writers were fiercely monotheistic. Paul, writing an early Christian creed (early 50s C.E.), Christianizes the *Shema* ("Hear, O Israel") of Deuteronomy 6:4–6, declaring Jesus is the one "Lord" of Israel and the Creator of all–"by whom are all things, and we exist through Him" (1 Cor. 8:6). Jesus shares in the divine identity. The Hebrew Bible anticipates that Yahweh will come to Zion, defeat evil, and restore his people, gathering the scattered exiles into a new, redeemed community, and the early Christians affirm that Yahweh comes in Christ.[4]

Below is a fruitful, reasonable, and biblical model that attempts to make sense of God's becoming man—not to eliminate the Incarnation's mystery, but to argue that it isn't illogical. This model is quite helpful both for discussion with Muslims or Jehovah's Witnesses and for more-thoughtful worship of the triune God.

Three Important Distinctions

1. *Distinguishing between "nature" and "person."* A thing's *nature* or *essence* makes it what it is; it wouldn't exist if it lacked these features. We have human-making features—the capacity to choose or act, to be conscious, to communicate—even if we aren't presently using those capacities, say, when we're asleep or comatose. God, likewise, has characteristics that make him God. By *person,* we mean *a center of (self-) consciousness, activity, and responsibility.* These include human and angelic persons as well as the maximally great divine Persons within the Trinity—Father, Son, and Spirit.

What's the *relation* between *person* and *nature*? A person *has* a nature; you and I *possess* something that makes us what we are—the very same human *nature.* Jesus of Nazareth, though *one* person, is fully God and fully human. He uniquely possesses *two* natures—one identical to *our human nature* and the other nature *divine.*

2. *Distinguishing between being "fully" (essentially) human and what is "merely" (commonly) human.* Humans commonly have arms, legs, hair, and eyes, but even without these we can still be fully human. Humans commonly—even universally—commit moral wrongs, but, despite Alexander Pope's statement, "To err is human," sinning isn't essential to being human: Adam and Eve were created sinless; Jesus was sinless. Death, too, though common, doesn't define human beings. Enoch (Genesis 5:24) and Elijah (2 Kings 2:11) didn't die—even though death has touched all other human beings. You get the idea.

This *essentially/fully* human and *commonly/merely* human distinction reminds us that certain human features we assume to be *essential* often aren't; they may just be *common.* This can help us see that a divine-human incarnation is possible: *what is essential to human nature doesn't exclude the possibility of being fully divine.* The *image of God* figures into our discussion at this point: human beings were made "a little lower than *God*" (Ps. 8:5) to rule and commune with him (Gen. 1:26–27). Christ himself, the new Adam, *is* the very image of God (2 Cor. 4:4; Col. 1:15) who fulfills and graciously helps us live as God's image-bearers should.

In *limited form,* we share in certain attributes or properties with God—personality, relationality, rationality, morality, freedom, creativity—that enable us to fulfill our vocation. Certain essential human characteristics are derived from divine characteristics: *human nature is thus a sub-category of the divine.*

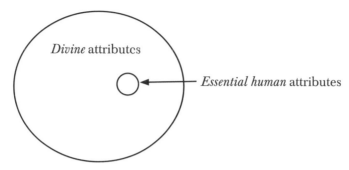

So the divine-human union in Jesus of Nazareth is possible. Biblical scholar F. F. Bruce puts it well: "It is because man in the creative order bears the image of his Creator that it was possible for the Son of God to become incarnate as man and in His humanity to display the glory of the invisible God."[5] According to one theologian, "If human beings are made in the image and likeness of God (Gen. 1:26–27), there must be something divine about every human being. If, and this is our case, the divine Logos could assume a humanity, there must be something human about God."[6] Even though the essentially human and the divine are poles apart in terms of greatness, *they aren't necessarily mutually exclusive.* Though *limited* or *finite* in ourselves, finitude *doesn't define us as* human: Jesus aside, this *common/universal* human characteristic isn't a *necessary* one.[7]

3. *Distinguishing between Jesus' two consciousnesses or levels of awareness–his developing, first-century, Jewish, human consciousness and the eternal, divine consciousness.* Imagine a spy on a dangerous mission, carrying in his mind top-secret information valuable to the enemy. To avoid divulging answers in case he's caught and tortured, he takes along a limited-amnesia producing pill–with an antidote for later use. The spy would still possess the vital information in his mind, but temporarily and voluntarily wouldn't access it.

Similarly, during Jesus' mission to earth, he *still possessed* the full, undiminished capacities of divine knowledge and power, and he had access to those capacities as necessary for his mission. But before the foundation of the world, Father, Son, and Spirit freely determined together that the Son would limit or restrain the use of those powers to accomplish his overall mission (Jn. 17:5, 22–26). So (a) Jesus gave up access to knowing, say, the time of his return (Mt. 24:36) and, as we'll see, knowing it was impossible for him to sin or to be vulnerable to temptation (cp. Jas. 1:13). However, (b) he didn't *lose* certain divine attributes; rather, he *voluntarily, temporarily suppressed* or *gave up access to* certain divine capacities and powers he possessed all along. Like a father holding back the full force of his powers while playing soccer or baseball with his kids, so the Son of God before coming to earth determined to *restrain* his divine capacities.[8]

To illustrate how we can coherently talk about two levels of awareness, consider what it's like to come out of a dream in which we're *simultaneously* still dreaming *but also* conscious that it's a dream—at once "within" the dream and "outside" it. Or take self-deception: a person knows what's right but convinces himself to suppress his conscience. These examples of two levels of awareness working together or overlapping in one person—not two egos or selves, however—give an idea of the workings of the incarnate Christ's mind.

We can usefully compare Jesus' *two levels of awareness* ("minds") with *our* two levels of awareness—the *subconscious* and *conscious.* Jesus' *human* awareness can be likened to our *conscious,* his *divine* awareness to our *subconscious.* When God the Son took on human form, *his fully-aware eternal, divine consciousness and (comm)union with Father and Spirit and sustaining of the universe didn't cease but continued uninterrupted.* Yet in his limited, developing human consciousness, Jesus grew and developed with an earthly, first-century, Aramaic-speaking Jewish awareness of things. Reading the Scriptures, he saw with increasing clarity his messianic status. He struggled, experienced the range of human emotions, and deepened in obedience and submission to his Father's will (cp. Luke 2:52; Heb. 2:18; 5:8).[9]

Jesus' human consciousness *significantly interacted* with his divine consciousness and wasn't cut off from certain heavenly illuminations—like the glow of divine light that streams through a cloth curtain.[10] Jesus, however, *didn't regularly rely on his divine consciousness* while on earth but primarily operated in his human consciousness—just like us—with the added depth of divine awareness. And being fully human, Jesus freely and fully depended on the Spirit's power as he sought to carry out his Father's purpose.

These three distinctions, then, provide a helpful framework for addressing questions such as: (a) If Jesus was God, who was running the universe when he was a baby or on the cross? (b) How could God die? (c) If God "so loved the world," why did he send his Son rather than come himself? This two-levels-of-awareness incarnational model helps us see that Jesus experienced the ongoing mutually indwelling Trinitarian life—still governing the universe as a baby and while dying on the cross. And he died as a mere—not essentially—human being; the divine nature wasn't crucified, but the divine person, who is also human.[11] The mutual life of the Trinity suggests that each divine person experienced pain at the crucifixion; Jesus didn't suffer alone: "God was in Christ reconciling the world to Himself" (2 Cor. 5:19).

If Jesus Was God, How Could He Be Tempted?

For we do not have a high priest who cannot sympathize with our weaknesses, but One who has been tempted in all things as we are, yet without sin. (Heb. 4:15)

The natural follow-up question to our discussion is: *If Jesus was God, how could he be tempted?* Because of God's intrinsic goodness (Jas. 1:18), he can't be led into sin or overpowered by an outside force: "Let no one say when he is tempted, 'I am being tempted by God'; for God cannot be tempted by evil, and He Himself does not tempt anyone" (Jas. 1:13). But wasn't the incarnate Christ tempted to depart from his Father's will, to take the easy way out (Matt. 4:1–11)? Doesn't his temptation mean he can "come to the aid of those who are tempted" (Heb. 2:18)? But doesn't this imply Jesus *could have* sinned? And if *not*, then wasn't his temptation simply play-acting? As we'll see, the Bible portrays Jesus' temptations as a genuine anguished struggle—hardly play-acting. Let's explore further.

First, the "merely/commonly" vs. "fully/essentially" human distinction reminds us that the ability to sin isn't part of the definition of "human." The impossibility of humans' sinning in the new heaven and earth won't diminish their full humanity. Though common among human beings, the ability to sin isn't essential to our humanity. For Jesus to be fully human, he didn't need to have the ability to sin.

Second, for his redemptive mission on earth, the Son of God voluntarily set aside having access to knowing certain things; one such item was the awareness that he couldn't sin. The gospels portray Jesus' supernatural knowledge of people's thoughts and details about future events (e.g., Lk. 22:10–13; Jn. 1:47–50). But Jesus is also ignorant of certain things—such as his return (*parousia,* literally "presence"): "But of that day and hour no one knows, not even the angels of heaven, nor the Son, but the Father alone" (Mt. 24:36). We could also add Jesus' ignorance about the fig tree (Mk. 11:13) and the hemorrhaging woman who touched him (Mk. 5:30–33) or his amazement at a Gentile centurion's faith (Mt. 8:10).

Likewise, Jesus' mission included intentionally surrendering the knowledge that *he, being divine, couldn't ultimately deviate from his Father's will.* In Gethsemane he prayed, "My Father, if it is possible, let this cup pass from Me; yet not as I will, but as You will" (Mt. 26:39). Theologian Gerald O'Collins asserts that Jesus' growth in self-knowledge and self-identity and in struggling in prayer "supports the conclusion that the divine reality was not fully and comprehensively present to the [human] mind of Jesus."[12]

For temptation to be meaningful, Jesus, unable to sin, must have been unaware that sinning was impossible. *Jesus was unaware of the time of his own return—so why not of the impossibility of sinning?* In his pre-incarnate state, the Son of God (with Father and Spirit) determined to give up access temporarily to knowing *both* of these things as part of his mission. He voluntarily limited access to expressing certain divine attributes (in being weak, hungry, and tired)—as well as having access to his divine knowledge (ignorance of his second coming and his invulnerability to sin), though he at any time could have chosen to be aware of them. Jesus thus identifies with us by experiencing *real* temptations and limitations. If Jesus' human awareness saw the divine reality in all its clarity, being obedient, struggling in prayer, being tempted couldn't have taken place.[13]

The incarnate Son's temptations *were* real; acting on them seemed a genuine possibility to him. Though *unique,* his situation is *conceivable*: Imagine entering a room and closing the door behind you. Unbeknownst to you, the door has an automatic two-hour time lock. You consider leaving once or twice, but you freely decide to read for the full two hours, after which you leave the room. Would you have been able to leave earlier? No. But why did you *stay* in and *not try* to go out? Because you *freely decided* to. Similarly, Christ freely chose, in submission to the Spirit, to resist temptation; his divine awareness didn't not overwhelm or impose itself on his human awareness.[14]

> Jesus could be truly tempted and tested, provided that he did not know that he could not sin. If he had known that he could not sin, it would be difficult, if not impossible, to make sense of genuine temptations; they would be reduced to make-believe, a performance put on for the edification of others. It was quite a different situation to be incapable of sin and not to know that.[15]

But if Jesus knew he stood in God's place as the great "I am" (John's gospel) or the final judge (Mt. 7:23), how could he *not* know sinning was impossible? The simple answer is that, though standing in God's place, he, as part of his mission, *was* ignorant about his return—*and* other matters.

Rather than play-acting, Christ suffered real temptation because he didn't know he couldn't sin. Through moment-by-moment submission to his Father's will and his being "led around by the Spirit" (Lk. 4:1), he also sets an example for us to be "led by the Spirit" (Rom. 8:14). Some Christians think, "Of course, Jesus didn't sin; he was God!" Yet his overcoming temptation wasn't automatic because he was divine, but because he steadfastly committed himself to his Father's will and relied on the empowering Spirit.

Though an amazing *mystery,* the doctrine of the Incarnation isn't a *contradiction.* In this mystery, a fully divine, fully human Jesus possesses a certain dual awareness. In one, he is fully knowing; in another he is voluntarily limited in his knowledge so that he could *truly* endure temptation, identifying with us in every way—except without sin.

17

The Cross of Christ

I have been crucified with Christ; and it is no longer I who live, but Christ lives in me; and the life which I now live in the flesh I live by faith in the Son of God, who loved me and gave Himself up for me. (Gal. 2:20)

The "word of the cross" is *madness* (*moria*) to those without God's Spirit (1 Cor. 1:18). A crucified messiah was offensive to *Jews*; those hanging on a tree were cursed by God (Deut. 21:23; Gal. 3:13). Cultured *Romans* wouldn't speak of crucifixion in polite company; its victims faced a punishment of indignity and humiliation–flogging, carrying the cross-beam to a public place of execution (crossroads or high hill), being nailed naked to the cross, and then being left there for birds of prey to devour. So the unlikelihood that a story about a crucified messiah could get off the ground is very high. As historian John Meier observes, "Such an embarrassing event created a major obstacle to converting Jews and Gentiles alike"–one "that the Church struggled to overcome."[1]

What was Jesus' death intended to accomplish? Various theologians have offered their theories of the atonement. Peter Abelard viewed Jesus' death only as a moral example that inspires love and self-sacrifice in us. Though quite true (Phil. 2:3–8; 1 Jn. 3:16), this aspect isn't a *primary* one. In 1 Pet. 2:21–25, Christ's death does serve as "an example" to follow, but Jesus also suffered "for you," and, "He Himself bore our sins in His body on the cross." His death not only stirs up something *within* us (*subjectively*), but also accomplishes something *for* us (*objectively*).

Anselm attempted to explain the atonement *philosophically* in *Why God Became Man.* Jesus satisfied the debt humans owed God but couldn't pay. God, who alone can pay it, becomes man since humans must pay but are unable. God both *demands* the debt be paid, but also *provides satisfaction* for that debt. Anselm has a point: God is, as Paul says, the "just" and the "justifier" of those who trust in him (Rom. 3:26). The atonement has profound and wide-ranging and multifaceted significance.

First, the atonement is primarily a corporate *rather than an individual achievement.* The Son of God, Paul writes, "loved me and gave Himself up for [*hyper*] me" (Gal. 2:20). Yet to see more clearly what Christ's death accomplished, we must move beyond the atonement's benefits to the *individual* believer (the Reformers tended to stop here), and place it within a broader *cosmic* and *corporate* framework—namely, the *narrative* of God's work of *creation* and *covenant-making* with Israel. *Jesus' death wasn't ahistoric and abstract.* Jesus was a first-century Jewish prophet and messiah ("anointed one") who was crucified on a Roman cross to remove *Israel's* curse and, by extension, *humanity's.* In his death, the second *Adam* creates a new humanity and restores creation; as the true (new) *Israel*—the beloved Son that national Israel was not—he restores God's covenant community, enabling them to carry out their role as priest-kings. In Christ God brings about a new creation and a new exodus. We're no longer "in Adam" (our participation in the fallen race of our "old man"), Romans 5 indicates; we're "in Christ" and have put on "the new man"—that is, corporately identified with Christ as head of a new community and operating in a new sphere.

Our union with Christ helps us better appreciate Scripture's atonement language. We are members of Christ's body (1 Cor. 12; Eph. 4:1–13). He takes on our failings and weaknesses as his own and graciously transforms them. Like the *king* in Jesus' parable who forgives a massive debt (Mt. 18:21–35), Jesus absorbs the brunt of our debt, making it his own. In a *family,* parents take on the responsibility of damages caused by children under their roof—breaking a window or a teen's totaling a car during driver's training. Large *corporations* buy up smaller, troubled companies, assuming their debts and liabilities as part of the transaction. Similarly, Christ's atonement has a *corporate* aspect.

Second, Christ's atonement is also a cosmic *achievement.* This view of the atonement emphasizes how Christ's death *defeats Satan and his hosts* (Jn. 12:25; 16:11; 1 Jn. 3:8), disarming these evil powers (Col. 2:15). Jews of Jesus' day mistakenly believed the dominant Roman Empire was the ultimate enemy. It was actually *Satan.* Jesus' exorcisms, even within Israel's own synagogues (e.g., Mk. 1:21–27), signified God's advancing reign, foreshadowing Satan's defeat at the cross and his ultimate demise. Christ's death signals the victory over all *evil political powers* and *oppressive, dehumanizing social and religious structures:* "The kingdom of the world has become the kingdom of our Lord and of His Christ; and He will reign forever and ever" (Rev. 11:15). If Jesus is *Lord* (*kyrios*), then Caesar *isn't.*

Jesus' conquest in death extends from *Israel* and her calling (the covenant community) to *humanity* (in Adam) to the *cosmic* dimension of Satan and his hosts: "Jesus suffers the full consequences of evil, evil from the political, social, cultural, personal, moral, religious, and spiritual angles all rolled into one, evil in the downward spiral hurtling towards the pit of destruction and despair."[2] He suffers and endures shame (Heb. 12:1–3; 13:13), even to the point of desolation and feeling forsaken (Mk. 15:34).

Third, Jesus' death is substitutionary, judicial, *and* penal. Christ died *for* us, having become a sin offering "for [*hyper*] us"–on our behalf (2 Cor. 5:21)–and "for many [*anti pollon*]" (Mk. 10:45). Jesus is the atoning sacrifice for [*peri*] the sins of the whole world (1 Jn. 2:2). In his life and death, Jesus, the very image of God, fulfills the human vocation, achieving what those in Adam couldn't. As true Israel, he fulfills her vocation as light of the world (Is. 42:6; 49:6; Jn. 8:12) and blessing to the nations, bearing the curse of disobedience to God's law (Deut. 30; cp. Lev. 26; Deut. 28).

Jesus is a substitute, a *representative* for Israel and for humanity. He takes our place, bearing sin's just penalty to rescue us from the curse of exile that sin and evil bring. Romans 8:3–4 brings these themes together:

> For what the Law could not do, weak as it was through the flesh, God did: sending His own Son in the likeness of sinful flesh and as an offering for sin, He condemned sin in the flesh, so that the requirement of the Law might be fulfilled in us, who do not walk according to the flesh but according to the Spirit.

This verse asserts Jesus' death was *substitutionary* ("God did"; "an offering for sin"), *judicial* ("the requirement of the Law...fulfilled in us"), and *penal* ("condemned sin").[3]

Why doesn't God just forgive us? Isn't that his job? To assume that he should actually diminishes *human responsibility,* the *gravity of sin,* and *the holiness of God.* The issue isn't why God finds it *difficult* to forgive, but how he finds it *possible* to do so at all.[4]

Fourth, Jesus' bearing the penalty for our sin isn't contrary to justice. While punishment is a legitimate response to human sin, why should Jesus be punished or pay our debt when *we* are the guilty ones? Why should our debt be transferred to him? What is the connection between the cross and our forgiveness?

1. Important goods or benefits come to us by Jesus' taking our punishment. Christ's voluntary, self-humiliating death on the cross shows that God takes sin seriously. This can foster the realization of how pride and self-will obstruct deep friendship with God. The cross also helps expose the distortion of values brought on by sin, revealing the rightness of what God values over against our own idolatries.

Though it's just for God to punish sinners, we sinners are better served when Christ graciously, voluntarily takes our punishment instead:

- God's willingness to suffer punishment and curse demonstrates how seriously he takes sin, the divine human relationship, and the importance of reconciliation.

- Unlike us, who might be bitter and overwhelmed, Christ bears the punishment perfectly; thus we can respond in gratitude.
- In contrast to finite humans being punished, Christ's punishment is an adequate expression of God's holiness and what God truly values. The result can be our own moral education and transformation; even apart from our personally appropriating Christ's death, it still objectively reveals the stark contrast between a good, self-giving God and rebellious sinners.[5]

2. Christ is humanity's/Israel's representative, taking on our curse by hanging "on the tree" (Gal. 3:13) and fulfilling what humankind/Israel failed to. Sin brought the curse of exile and alienation. The cross reversed this, ushering in a new creation and a renewed covenant people under Christ's authority. So it isn't just any act of Christ, but a theologically rich and significant act on which forgiveness and reconciliation are based. While this reconciliation and other far-reaching benefits of Jesus' death are available to all (e.g., Jn. 3:16–17; 2 Pet. 2:1; 1 Jn. 2:2), they're, tragically, not appropriated by all.

3. The reason the innocent Jesus can take our punishment is that forgiveness is actually achieved through the "agreement" or willing participation between (a) the offenders, (b) the offended, and (c) the willing substitute (or surrogate)—namely, us, God, and the Son of God. Against some theologians who claim penal substitution is tantamount to theological child abuse, Jesus' being a voluntary substitute (Jn. 10:11–18) doesn't pit Father against Son. The entire Trinity is involved and together suffers in this experience. Nor is there injustice in this voluntary sacrifice. As Steven Porter has written, just punishment must always be directed toward wrongs deserving punishment. However, there isn't any injustice in someone else's voluntarily receiving that punishment if (a) "there are good reasons for such a transfer" and (b) "the victim agrees to accept such a substitution as fulfillment of the offender's debt."[6] In human societies, we *don't* make this kind of transfer for serious crimes because *we typically do not have any good reasons—and usually quite bad ones—for transferring punishment.* We have *little hope* for thinking this would produce any important goods. Not so with Jesus' self-sacrifice!

Christ's death reveals both the triune God's love and justice. Though God is for us (*pro nobis*), he is in some ways *against us.* He loves the world (Jn. 3:16–17), but his wrath remains on it (3:36). Augustine said that Jesus is both *the priest* making the offering and *the oblation* itself. God is the *just* and the *justifier* (Rom. 3:26).

If the essence of sin is man substituting himself for God, the essence of salvation is God substituting himself for man.[7]

18

Jesus' Uniqueness and the Plurality of Religions

"And there is salvation in no one else; for there is no other name under heaven that has been given among men by which we must be saved." (Acts 4:12)

Our era's "tolerance" isn't the classic, robust tolerance that allows people to think differently–to put up with error, falsehood, or whatever else they may find disagreeable. We don't *tolerate* things we *enjoy*–like chocolate or J. S. Bach's music. But today's flawed view of tolerance calls for "accepting," even "embracing" or "celebrating," differences–*until* someone starts making exclusive truth-claims or, worse, *evangelizing!* The "tolerant" won't accept or celebrate "narrow" claims. Persuading people about faith is "arrogant" and upsetting. So people write books to persuade people that it's wrong to persuade others! Educator Allan Bloom described this mind-set well: "Conflict is the evil we most want to avoid."[1]

Christians claiming that "Jesus is the only way" or "unique Savior" are often perceived to be arrogant, imperialistic, harmful, and insensitive. Why just *one* way of salvation that appears to leave untold millions, through no fault of their own, cut off from salvation in their ignorance?

Understanding Religious Pluralism

"I observe that you are very religious in all respects." (Acts 17:22)

The gospel is no stranger to religiously pluralistic environments; it was first proclaimed throughout the religiously mixed Mediterranean world with its many gods and temples, Greek philosophies, and emperor worship. Today's *religious pluralism,* however, offers an appealing approach to the liberal democratic Western societies: all religions are equally capable of salvation or liberation, none being superior to another.[2] Some pluralists view the different religions as different manifestations of the Ultimate Reality or the Transcendent—*God, Brahman,* the *Tao, Nothingness.* Like a three-dimensional hologram, just one film or picture underneath projects a different image depending on the angle and distance from which one observes it. So, one person might view the same underlying Ultimate Reality differently than another person. Or the religions could be likened to gold or silver (representing the underlying Ultimate Reality). These metals can be (a) solid, shaped, and polished; (b) a molten liquid; or (c) a rough, unrefined ore (representing the various world religions).

"All roads lead to the top of the mountain," we're told. Another analogy is of six Indian blind men before an observer: each touches different parts of the elephant, drawing dogmatic conclusions about the elephant based on his limited experience; the observer thinks such rigid beliefs rather comical. Applying this scene to "theologic wars," poet John Godfrey Saxe (1816–1887) writes of religious disputants with their exclusivistic claims; they "[r]ail on in utter ignorance" and "prate about an elephant not one of them has seen!"[3]

Pluralist John Hick calls for a "Copernican revolution of religions." Cosmology has shifted from a *Ptolemaic* geocentric (earth-centered) view of the universe to a *Copernican* heliocentric (sun-centered) one. Similarly, we must replace a christocentric view—the triune God's revelation in Christ as central with all other religions revolving or orienting themselves around it—with a "God"-/Reality-centered view, in which all the religions, including Christianity, "revolve" around *It.*

Beginning with philosopher Karl Jaspers (1883–1969), thinkers have made distinctions between three stages of religious development:

1. Ancient *pre-axial* religions are characterized by being tribalistic, mythical, nature-bound, and primal.

2. *Axial-age* religions arose in two stages: (a) first, significant "saving" or "liberating" ethical-religious ideas emerged in *India* (ritual-to-philosophical, or Vedic-to-Upanishadic, Hinduism, and then Buddhism); *China* (Confucianism, Taoism); and the "*West*" (Zoroastrianism, prophetic Judaism, Greek philosophy) around 800–200 B.C.E. (b) Then, springing from Judaism, two offshoot "Abrahamic" religions of Christianity and Islam arose.

3. The more pluralistic *post-axial* religious thinking around 1600–1800 (rooted in a departure from established religious authority) affirms that there are "different ways of experiencing, conceiving, and living in relation to the ultimate divine Reality which transcends all our varied versions of it," as Hick affirms.[4]

Hick doesn't naïvely insist that "all religions are basically the same." They can't all be true in what they affirm since their fundamental differences are *massive*. Buddhism's Dalai Lama puts it plainly: "Among spiritual faiths, there are many different philosophies, some just opposite to each other on certain points. Buddhists do not accept a creator; Christians base their philosophy on that theory."[5] By definition, truth excludes something–error or falsehood. Christians *and* Buddhists can't both be right on this matter; either God exists, or he doesn't. Muslims and Christians can't both be right about Jesus' death. Muslims reject his death on a cross (Sura 4:157–58); if correct, then the Christian faith crumbles (1 Cor. 15:13–19).

All the world's religions differ significantly about the nature of *Ultimate Reality* (a personal God; an impersonal, undifferentiated consciousness; or Nothingness), the *human condition* (sin, ignorance, or craving/desire), its *solution* (salvation, enlightenment, or the elimination of desire), or the *afterlife* (personal enjoyment of/separation from God, reincarnations or rebirths followed by personal extinction). Except for these massive differences, sure, all religions are "basically the same"! Sophisticated pluralists recognize these (a) *genuine, significant irreconcilable differences*.

For Hick and his ilk, (b) *religious belief is the result of culturally conditioned attempts to get at the Ultimate Reality*. The nomadic Muslim Tuareg or the Krishna devotee will be oriented to "the Real" through the filter or "baggage" of his particular religious and cultural background. Religious beliefs are *true* in the sense that they're oriented toward the Ultimate Reality, but *false* in another, due to cultural conditioning. There are different ways of conceiving, experiencing, and responding to this Ultimate Reality. Its *reality* is different from the *experience* of It. This resembles what Kant asserted: we can't have direct access to the *noumenal* realm (the thing in itself) but only to the *phenomenal* realm (as it appears to us). This position itself, however, raises questions about how Kant or Hick could *know* that this thing-in-itself or the Real is *unknowable*.

Another aspect of religious pluralism is that (c) *all the world's religions are equally capable of bringing salvation or liberation–not just one*. Salvation is the transformation from *self*-centeredness to *Reality*-centeredness, and no particular religion has a monopoly on such a transformation.

Religious pluralists typically claim that (d) *the realization of liberation is evidenced by the producing of morally upright "saints" in different religions*. The major world religions produce moral fruits in their devotees–in particular, treating others as they want to be treated. Christians have Jesus or Mother Teresa; Hindus Mahatma Gandhi; and Buddhists the Dalai Lama. No religion has the moral high ground over another.

Responses to Religious Pluralism

...how will we escape if we neglect so great a salvation? (Heb. 2:3)

The Christian maintains that the Christian faith is true and that the sacrificial death of Jesus is the basis of genuine salvation, whereas other religions are not savingly effective. Where other religions disagree with the Christian revelation, *at that point* they would be in error. This view is *particularlistic* or *exclusivistic,* but, as we'll see, *all* religious truth-claims are exclusionary. Before addressing problems with religious pluralism, we ought to keep four things in mind.

1. *All truth is God's truth—whether within the Christian faith or outside it.* In Acts 17, Paul cited pagan (Stoic) thinkers who spoke of God as the Creator and Sustainer who isn't contained by human temples. We likewise should pay attention to commonalities and bridges with other religionists, affirming the God-originated truth where we come across it. Buddhists or Confucians believe in honoring parents or in religious freedom; Muslims maintain that an eternally existent God created the universe. Because all humans are God's image-bearers, Christians can affirm that the poor or illiterate should be helped without making basic aid or education contingent on receiving the gospel.

2. *Non-Christians who consider Christians "narrow-minded" for believing in Jesus' uniqueness should remember that he spoke of it first.* Non-Christians who are offended by claims that Jesus is the only Savior should know this originated with Jesus; Christians aren't making this up (e.g., Jn. 14:6; cp. Acts 4:10). The critic must ultimately contend with the authoritative and staggering identity claims of Jesus himself.

3. *Religious dialogue requires equal respect, not equality of belief.* Here's a common "interfaith" scenario: Christians are invited to prayer breakfasts, dialogues, and panel discussions; but they're told they can't pray in Jesus' name or mention Jesus' uniqueness—this might "offend" Jews or Muslims. But isn't that restriction offensive to *Christians*? Why is it all right to offend Christians but not Jews and Muslims? Christians don't know how to pray *except* in the name of Jesus. So the Christian invited to such events should be allowed to pray *as a Christian,* not a Deist to some generic deity. In dialogue, one should graciously speak *as a Christian* rather than accept a lowest-common-denominator approach in discussion.

While Christians, Jews, and Muslims share an "Abrahamic faith," this doesn't mean they're equal. So if discussants approach the religious roundtable assuming religions are equally legitimate and true, they're not doing so *as* Christians, Muslims, or Hindus. Religious dialogue must begin with the equality of *persons,* not *belief. All* participants can discuss their particular views and experiences openly, and all sides can benefit from empathetically listening to clarify views and prevent the creation of caricatures and stereotypes (Jas. 1:19).

4. *Religion—including idolatrous conceptions of God within "Christendom"—may actually prevent people from knowing the living God.* As with many religious leaders in Jesus' day, "religiosity" may hinder people from truly and savingly encountering God. In India, I've witnessed Hindu festivals in which people cut and gouge their bodies. Rather than being "happy as they are," many live in bondage to evil spirits, oppressed by karma, bound by superstition,

and paralyzed by fear of death. I heard of one Muslim convert to Christ who declared, "The more I see of the world's religions, the more beautiful Jesus appears to me."

Religious Pluralism's Problems

With these preliminaries in mind, let's consider religious pluralism's problems.

First, religious pluralism from the outset eliminates the possibility of specific, historical divine revelation. Religious pluralism seeks to begin "from the ground up" by observing what goes on in mosques, church buildings, synagogues, temples, and Sikh gurdwaras. Many pluralists believe Jesus was just a God-conscious human being who certainly didn't rise from the dead; his later followers would *ascribe* divinity to him, as some of the Buddha's followers did to him. The pluralist, if correct, ultimately undermines the historic Christian faith; it's not just one of many legitimate ways of finding salvation or liberation.

While God begins with the particularities of Abraham or the Incarnation, he has the *universal* in mind—to bless all the families of the earth (Gen. 12:1–3). Like ripples from a *particular* stone tossed into a pond, so Christian mission to the *world* flows from the Incarnation; it offers salvation to all through God's enabling Spirit. Pluralism, however, leaves us with a property-less, content-less Ultimate Reality. How should we respond to It? Should we *love* It or *pray* to It or just "live ethically"? Can we know It even *exists*?

Second, religious pluralism is logically just as exclusivistic as the Christian—or any other—faith. The pluralistic-sounding Dalai Lama has declared that Tibetan Buddhism is "the highest and complete form of Buddhism";[6] indeed, "only Buddhists can accomplish"[7] what's necessary for liberation. More generally, religious pluralism itself is just as non-neutral and exclusivistic regarding the status of religious truth-claims. The religious pluralist believes that her view is true and the exclusivist—Christian, Muslim, Buddhist—is wrong for rejecting her view. She believes she has a virtue the Christian or Muslim doesn't. Indeed, pluralism implies that Christians ought to abandon belief in Jesus' deity, atoning death, and resurrection—beliefs she takes to be literally *false* and more like mere inspiring *metaphors*. Though the Christian faith is a *particular* exclusivism, however, religious pluralism turns out to be a *generic* exclusivism.

While pluralists may appeal to those roads-up-the-mountain or elephant analogies, we could ask how they *know* all religions' roads lead to the top and why those who disagree are *wrong*. How is it that *they* have the correct vantage point? Besides, such analogies don't actually *prove* a point; they only *illustrate* it. If Jesus is the only way, we can just *change* the analogy to something more appropriate: perhaps religions are like a labyrinth or a maze with only one way out. Here Jesus proves to be an advantageous starting point: What do we do with Jesus, who claims to reveal God to us and that our destiny is bound up with our response to him personally?

Third, even if religious belief is largely shaped by geographical and historical circumstances, this fact in itself doesn't entail religious pluralism's truth. Pluralists raise the geography objection: "If you'd been born in Saudi Arabia, you'd likely be a Muslim—or if in India, a Hindu." Though statistically true, this statement hardly proves the pluralist's point. The geography of a belief neither establishes nor neutralizes its truth. While a Marxist, monarchist, or conservative Republican would likely have joined the Hitler Youth had he grown up in Nazi Germany, we don't conclude that all political systems are equally legitimate (perhaps because they move persons from self-centeredness to political-centeredness!). Independent reasons exist for preferring certain forms of government over others.[8]

The same applies to beliefs about Ultimate Reality and the human condition: we rightly reject profoundly incoherent beliefs; we correctly question claims that depend heavily on phony documents or the character of a charismatic, womanizing charlatan who founds a religion—*even if* his followers turn out to be morally decent people. Indeed, if the Christian faith more readily explains many features of the universe and of the human condition than, say, various Eastern religions or other secular alternatives, then its greater plausibility shouldn't be trumped by the geography objection. Hardly neutral observers of the religious landscape, pluralists who reject Jesus' bodily resurrection or his remarkable authority claims as historically unreliable are taking quite a gamble. Not only would Jesus' radical uniqueness completely undermine pluralism; orthodox Christian tradition is buttressed by very strong historical support.

In addition, we can turn the tables on the pluralist: If *he* had been born in Madagascar or medieval France, *he probably wouldn't have been a pluralist!*[9] If all religions are "culturally conditioned attempts" to get at the Ultimate Reality, then pluralism is *just as culturally conditioned* as Christian or Hindu beliefs. How has the pluralist risen above his cultural conditioning to see things more clearly than the rest of us? Does the religious pluralist think that *he's* just another blind man touching *his* part of the elephant? No, he takes the view of the onlooker who sees the whole elephant and thinks the blind men to be foolish for their narrow-minded dogmatism!

Fourth, a religion's moral fruitfulness isn't necessarily the ultimate test of its legitimacy. What do we make of "moral atheists" who help their neighbors but reject the transcendent and even strongly oppose traditional religion as delusional and full of false promises? Should pluralists carry on "religious dialogue" with them—and to what end? Or what of religions that include ritual human sacrifice or racist beliefs? Are these also legitimate, culturally conditioned attempts to get at the Ultimate Reality?[10]

If no observable moral difference exists between adherents of the different religions, then the common pluralistic conclusion—that *all the great religions are equally capable of saving*–isn't more obvious than the conclusion that *it's not the case that all these religions are equally capable of saving.* In fact, it's quite reasonable to conclude that *we have no idea whether all religions are or aren't equally capable of saving.*[11]

Fifth, the Christian's motivation to live humbly, gratefully, graciously, and self-sacrificially is connected to Jesus' authority as God's Son; such motivation will lose much of its force if, as the pluralist contends, Jesus was a mere man. If Jesus isn't God incarnate, this would effectively take the wind out of historic Christianity's sails and seriously undermine our devotion to Christ. Yes, this is admittedly a pragmatic consideration, but the Christian faith is bound up with historical events such as Jesus' death and resurrection: if these never occurred, then Paul urges us to consider hedonism since a merely earthly hope in Christ is delusional.

Sixth, if Jesus is God's Son, this effectively undermines religious pluralism. Despite the above points, pluralism could logically still be true. However, if Jesus is God incarnate, then pluralism is false. We've noted reasons for taking seriously Jesus' uniquely divine status. Jesus wasn't just "another great religious teacher." (a) He was radically different from the *founders* of other great religions: *Jesus made unique claims that no other world religious leader did*–to forgive sins, hear prayers, be the judge of all, be always present with his followers, give rest to one's soul, have authority over angelic/demonic beings, receive worship. By contrast, Muhammad would have thought Jesus' personal claims blasphemous; Buddha was a metaphysical agnostic.

(b) *The earliest Christians–fiercely monotheistic Jews–bore witness to an exalted Jesus who shared in the divine identity,* which we've already noted. Such a conviction, buttressed by Jesus' own resurrection from the dead and postmortem appearances, vindicates those authoritative claims–that in him the kingdom of God, the new exodus, and the new creation had come. If there is salvation outside of Christ, then Jesus' coming to be a ransom for many (Mk. 10:45) was an ultimately misguided failure: if so, contrary to Jesus' Gethsemane impressions, the bitter cup *could have* been removed from him.

In the end, religious pluralism won't let Jesus be Jesus. If it did, it would undermine itself.

The Question of the Unevangelized

And thus I aspired to preach the gospel, not where Christ was already named. (Rom. 15:20)

If Jesus is the unique Savior, what of those who've never heard of him? A simple response is that *our good and wise God has the question of the unevangelized figured out and won't act unjustly.* If Jesus is truly God's incarnate Son, the "question of the heathen" is *secondary*; we should begin with what is clear and then work out the implications from there. So if Jesus has reliably revealed God to us, we can even take an *agnostic* position: "I *don't know* what the answer is to this challenging question of the unevangelized, but I do know a trustworthy God who has acted dramatically and remarkably in Christ, and this true, life-changing message must be proclaimed! Presumably this God isn't caught off guard on such matters." Also, no one will be condemned for never having heard of Christ: the more relevant question is: *How do the unevangelized respond to pervasive Spirit-promptings and divine clues?* God won't judge unjustly (Gen. 18:25).

Besides the agnostic and "exclusivist" or "particularist" views,[12] consider some of the following variants.[13]

1. *Inclusivism (wider-hope view):* While God's grace in Christ is the *actual* (ontological) basis for *every* person's forgiveness, inclusivists insist that *knowing* about Jesus of Nazareth (epistemological) isn't necessary to be saved: Christ's death is *ontologically* (actually) necessary for salvation, not *epistemologically* necessary. Those dying as infants and the mentally handicapped haven't *done* anything to incur God's judgment and thus, many Christians agree, would still be saved. And Old Testament saints like Abraham and David who cast themselves on God's mercy were saved by what Christ would one day accomplish (Heb. 10:4; cp. 9:13–14)–though they didn't know of Jesus.

Despite its merits, inclusivism has been criticized. (a) Its over-optimism about untold multitudes who cast themselves on God's mercy seems to go against the negative assessment of Romans 1–3. (b) Inclusivism doesn't really deal with the problem that many people don't respond to general revelation, yet respond to the preaching of the gospel–which isn't surprising since the gospel is the power of God for salvation (Rom. 1:16). (c) Inclusivism still has its own question of "injustice" to deal with: Many could complain that they were "born in the wrong place at the wrong time," having only the dim light of natural revelation, while others no more worthy were fortunate enough to be born in a time and place where they were able to hear the gospel and be saved. That's the problem inclusivism has been trying to solve in the first place.

2. *Postmortem evangelism:* Some Christians believe the unevangelized– and even the mentally handicapped and those who died as infants–will have a postmortem opportunity to personally encounter Jesus, hear the gospel, and either embrace it–and enjoy God's presence–or reject it and be removed from God's presence. The offer of salvation isn't limited to an earthly existence. While an intriguing possibility, this view is sometimes based on highly disputed biblical passages (e.g., 1 Pet. 3:18–22).

3. *Accessibilism (middle-knowledge view):* Building on the divine foreknowledge–human freedom discussion, I'll summarize a view I've defended elsewhere.[14] Assuming our good, wise God isn't willing that any perish but rather find salvation (2 Pet. 3:9), we could infer that ours is a world in which *no* person is born at the wrong place or time. Salvation is *accessible*

through God's pervasive grace to whoever would *want* it. Though most reject the light of God's general revelation (Rom. 1–3), this graciously-given knowledge is *adequate* for people to turn to God and be saved—based on Christ's redemptive work (as with Old Testament saints): God's "righteous judgment" will give to each person according to his deeds—"to those who by perseverance in doing good seek for glory and honor and immortality, eternal life" (Rom. 2:5–7).

Perhaps God, knowing what free creatures would do in an array of possible worlds he could create, has brought about a world in which *the maximal number of persons is saved and the minimal number of persons condemned.* Despite the workings and wooings of God's gracious Spirit, many will freely resist God in *any* world God placed them—*whether or not* they would hear the gospel. Those who are lost in *actuality* are those who would be lost in *any* world God placed them in. Despite God's grace toward them, their freely self-created condition of *transworld depravity* prevents them from embracing God. But why should God refrain from bringing many into his family simply because others, like the prodigal's older brother, refuse to enjoy the festivities? *God isn't unjust or unkind* if people he creates freely refuse his grace; so why should he be blamed? *What if, in the end, there is just no person who, having rejected the light of revelation that he does have, would have believed had he received more?* No unevangelized person is (justly) condemned simply because he *would* freely reject God's salvation no matter what possible world he might be placed in, but because he *does reject God's saving grace in his actual circumstances.*

While accessibilism the middle knowledge view may not be *the* resolution to our problem and another view on the unevangelized may well be true, its very logical possibility suggests the defensibility of God's just, merciful character toward all. Our topic ultimately goes beyond making inferences from scattered biblical verses and themes to *trusting in a good God to do no wrong.* Can the covenant-making, salvation-desiring God, whose self-expression—Jesus of Nazareth—died for the sins of the world, be trusted with such perplexing questions? *Can't we trust God, who loves all without exception and desires their salvation, to do his utmost so that none is prevented from experiencing salvation who truly desires it?* We shouldn't think about the unevangelized apart from *God's character, motives, and good purposes.*[15]

Beyond this, God has ways of revealing himself to Cornelius-like figures (Acts 10) who haven't yet heard the gospel. In a remarkable affirmation of Yahweh's working among the nations, Yahweh asks Israel, "Are you not as the sons of Ethiopia to Me, O sons of Israel?" and, "Have I not brought up Israel from the land of Egypt, [a]nd the Philistines from Caphtor and the Arameans from Kir?" (Am. 9:7). Angelic messengers might appear; Muslims in remote areas may have visions of Jesus and find salvation.[16] God is able to do far more than we can ask or imagine—even when it comes to the unevangelized. They're in good hands with him.

PART V

RE-CREATION

"For behold, I create new heavens and a new earth;
And the former things will not be remembered or come to mind."
(Isa. 65:17)

So if anyone is in Christ, there is a new creation: everything old has passed away; see, everything has become new! (2 Cor. 5:17 NRSV)

19

Body, Soul, and Resurrection

"Truly I say to you, today you shall be with Me in Paradise."
(Lk. 23:43)

Biblical Considerations

If Christ hasn't been raised from the dead, our faith is pointless. But because Christ "the first fruits" has been raised, this guarantees our own bodies will be "raised immortal" (1 Cor. 15:52). The immortality of the soul is a *Greek* philosophical view; it's not a *biblical* doctrine. *Immortality (aphtharsia, athanasia)–the immunity from decay and death because of our participation in the eternal life of the triune God*–is used in 1 Corinthians 15 in connection with the physical resurrection *body (soma)*, not the *soul (psyche)*. As the Nicene Creed affirms, "We look forward to *the resurrection of the body and the life of the world to come*"–not *"going to heaven after death."* Let's reflect on this below.

First, orthodox Christianity rejects the soul's permanent disembodiment but affirms a transformed physicality. Theologian Oscar Cullmann once said that if the soul is immortal, Easter is rendered unnecessary.[1] Simply "going to heaven when I die" implies there's no new creation; death hasn't been defeated. But this is precisely the point of Jesus' bodily resurrection. Our resurrection bodies *will* be part of the new heavens and earth in God's perfected re-creation. Christ won't return to take us away from earth, but will establish us on the new earth. Rather than abandoning creation, God renews it, affirming the goodness of the material world.[2] In 1 Corinthians 15:44–46, this new still-physical but transformed body with new capacities is called *spiritual* (that is, animated by the Holy Spirit) as opposed to the *natural* body ("soul-animated [*psychikos*] body"—as opposed to the misleading translation, "physical body" [e.g., RSV, NRSV]).

So Paul isn't contrasting the physical and the immaterial (the first-century Jew understood *resurrection* to involve *physical bodies*) but rather *two types of physical body*—one *naturally* animated by the human *soul* and the other *supernaturally* animated by God's *Spirit*. That's why Paul declares elsewhere that we long for "the redemption of our body" (Rom. 8:23), and that Christ "will transform the body of our humble state into conformity with the body of His glory" (Phil. 3:21)—a *transformed physicality*.

We thus have *newness* as well as *historical continuity* between the soul-animated body and the spiritual/Spirit-animated body: like a seed that is sown perishable and in dishonor and weakness, it is raised imperishable and in glory and power (15:42–44). This continuity doesn't require atom-for-atom replacement, which might present problems for bodies of missionary-eating cannibals who become Christians! God is able to use whatever bodily matter remains. And even if the body is, say, vaporized in an explosion, God is able to *create an immortal body suitable to each particular believer*.

Second, though body and soul function as an integrated whole ("functional holism"), the soul is able to survive bodily death ("substance dualism"). Scripture affirms a deep body-soul integration—despite the "hiccup" of the intermediate state of incompleteness when God graciously sustains the soul between death and future resurrection. The soul's separability is implied when Jesus tells the criminal on the cross: "*Today* you will be with me *in paradise*" (Lk. 23:43). After Lazarus' death, Jesus declares that "everyone "who believes in me shall live, even if he dies" (Jn. 11:25; cp. 8:51). *Though we may experience bodily death*, we can survive bodily death and continually experience spiritual life. Jesus corrects the resurrection-denying Sadducees: the God of the patriarchs is the God of the living; though their bodies be dust and bones, they "live to Him" (Lk. 20:38). Paul desires to depart—at death—and be with Christ (Phil. 1:23-24). In the intermediate state (2 Cor. 5:3–8), death brings an unnatural, temporary "naked" state with the "unclothed" soul apart from the body; then we "put on" or are "clothed" with a resurrection body—*life-after-life-after-death*, as one has said. Death, the soul's absence from the body, brings the soul into Christ's heavenly presence. The *souls* of martyred saints in heaven haven't yet received resurrection bodies (Rev. 6:9–10).

Ultimately, Scripture suggests, I *am not* my body. My soul—my *self* or "*I*"—doesn't perish at death, thanks to God's sustaining it in existence. The soul gives me my personal identity, despite bodily changes—or even my body's obliteration in an explosion. If, at Christ's return, the dead "will be raised imperishable" and "will be changed" (1 Cor. 15:52), then it must be the soul, not the decayed/destroyed body that gives me my identity in the meantime.

So, the soul is a unified immaterial substance that endures changes but gives me my ongoing personal identity, making me conscious and alive. According to Genesis 2:7, a human is "a living being" or "soul [*nephesh chayah*]"). The human soul is not only a center of awareness (which is true of animals, as we'll see). Because humans have been made in God's image, the human soul possesses freedom and moral responsibility; it has the capacity to be self-aware, believe, choose, reason, intend, emote, imagine, remember, and know and relate to God (spirit is the soul's spiritual, God-ward aspect).

Third, body and soul function as an organic, mutually interactive whole. My headache affects my soul's well-being; worry in my soul causes my stomach to churn. The soul is "present" at every point in the human body, directing it to grow and develop from conception to adulthood and "informing" it to carry out actions determined by the soul, the "I." Some of the soul's capacities may not be realized, however. A physical handicap—Alzheimer's disease, Down's syndrome—*blocks* or *prevents* the soul from thinking clearly. Or my eyeballs may work fine, but *my soul may not be paying attention or focusing*; so I'll miss seeing what's before me. Although my soul *uses* my brain, it isn't the same as the brain.

Fourth, having been made in God's image, humans are markedly distinct from animals. As we've briefly noted, animals *do* have souls that animate and direct their bodies; in Genesis 1:24, 2:19, and elsewhere, *animals* are also called *living creatures/beings* (*nephesh*); still, their soulish capacities are diminished where it really counts: they *don't* have intrinsic dignity, the capacity to relate to God, to make free choices (they simply act according to instinct and environment), to be morally responsible agents, to think self-consciously (thinking about their own thinking), to pursue truth rather than just survive.[3]

Scripture affirms an integrated, holistic "substance dualism," despite detractors within the Christian community.[4] This view is theologically significant in that (a) persons are capable of surviving death while retaining personal identity, and (b) the Incarnation is possible: God, who is spirit, becomes man; the *person* of Jesus *isn't identical* to his body.

Additional Considerations

Besides Scripture, we can offer other reasons for thinking that humans are more than their bodies and that the soul can survive death. These reasons suggest another argument for God's nature and existence—*the argument from mind*: consciousness and other soulish capacities make better sense in the context of a conscious, spiritual Creator rather than purely mindless material.

First, matter, by definition, doesn't include the concept of consciousness or other mental features. "What is matter? Never mind. What is mind? No matter!" So the joke goes. Because consciousness or other mental activity belongs to the "non-matter" category, we have very good reason for thinking that humans are more than their bodies. No physics textbook defines *matter* using *psychological, subjective, mental* characteristics, but rather spatial location, spatial extension, weight, texture, color, shape, size, density, mass, atomic, chemical composition. Brains have weight; thoughts don't. Brains can be dyed red or blue, not souls/minds. I can think about pain without being in pain. Beliefs can be true or false—matter can't be; it just is: "to talk about one bit of matter being true of another seems to me to be nonsense,"[5] Lewis wrote. Beliefs are more than just material brain states. Since brains have different properties than souls, they can't be identical to each other. Even if a *correlation* exists between brain functions and soulish capacities (e.g., a drug for the body may result in depression in one's soul), that doesn't entail the soul is *nothing more* than the brain. We should *expect* such correlations given the deep, organic connection between body and soul. But *correlation* doesn't equal *reduction* (the soul as "nothing more" than the brain).

Naturalists wonder how an immaterial soul and a physical body could interact. But just because we don't know *how* two things can interact, this doesn't mean they don't. Philosopher of science Bas van Fraassen asks, "Do concepts of the soul...baffle you? They pale beside the unimaginable otherness" of baffling phenomena in contemporary physics.[6] Also, theists have ready examples of how an immaterial substance (God) can interact with the physical world; he creates and sustains it in existence. Ironically, materialists have their own "interaction problem." Jaegwon Kim wonders how an immaterial entity could influence even *one* molecule, yet he admits to "our seeming inability to understand the phenomenon of consciousness as part of a world that is essentially physical" and to not knowing how we would even achieve such an understanding.[7] No wonder naturalist Jerry Fodor remarks: "Nobody has the slightest idea how anything material could be conscious. Nobody even knows what it would be like to have the slightest idea of how anything material could be conscious."[8]

Second, many people throughout history and across civilizations have held that the soul's separation from the body is quite intelligible. This doesn't necessarily show that the soul can exist apart from the body, but such widespread belief suggests that the notion of disembodiment may not be all that incoherent or counterintuitive.[9]

Third, if the soul's disembodied existence is even logically possible, the implications are enormous. Without logical contradiction, we can conceive of being disembodied, imagining ourselves in the body of another, living at another time in another culture, and having another person's skin pigmentation. So long as such metaphysically plausible scenarios are logically possible, the fabric of reality may not be all that naturalistic.

Fourth, the strong evidence for near-death experiences (NDEs) or out-of-body experiences (OBEs) suggests the soul can potentially exist without the body. Paul wrote that he may have had an OBE himself (2 Cor. 12:1–6). More recently, atheist philosopher A. J. Ayer saw an "exceedingly bright and also very painful" red light during four clinically dead minutes. He concluded that "death does not put an end to consciousness."[10] Patients revived from clinical death have given credible, documented descriptions of what happened while they were dead, suggesting the credibility of the soul's (temporary) separation from the body.[11]

Sixth, if human beings have libertarian freedom, this would strongly support the existence of a soul over materialism. This type of freedom means that it's up to the person/agent to do the choosing; the buck stops with the agent. While environment, genes, motives, or even character *influence* our choices, they don't *determine* them. Now, most naturalists reject a robust libertarian view of human freedom because it implies the soul's existence, that our decisions aren't tied to our material make-up.[12] We've noted how naturalist philosophers Nagel and Searle acknowledge our strong intuitions of freedom and moral responsibility. We should take these seriously, not reject them, since the fabric of our lives presupposes the following:

- *freedom:* we have strong intuitions of being self-movers, that our choices matter; our difference-making decisions are up to us, even though *influenced* by external inputs or even internal dispositions and motives;
- *moral accountability:* our legal and penal systems generally assume we're not just products of our biology or sociology; we know not to simply blame our genes or environment;
- *future-oriented decisions* and *truth-directed choices:* despite strong influences, by God's available grace we don't have to be stuck in the swamp of our past; we can be motivated by future possibilities and by hope. Also, we recognize that our decisions go beyond survival and should align with what's true.

If the determinist believes that our past dictates the decisions we make and beliefs we hold, then isn't *that* belief determined because of *his* past? If he believes that our motives dictate what we do, what about *his* motives in asserting this? For it is by accident that he is correct, not the result of reasoning power, lest any determinist should boast! In spite of themselves, determinists regularly assume—along with the rest of us—they're free, morally responsible agents.

Sixth, mechanistic cause-and-effect explanations aren't always preferable to personal, goal-directed ones, which would suggest the soul's existence. If the naturalist believes his choices and beliefs are physically and mechanistically determined by the workings of a nervous system, then that belief must itself be mechanistically determined. Explaining my joy at Valerie's and Kristen's vocal performance in neuro-physiological terms is fairly unhelpful and obtuse. More fruitful is the basic, commonsense, goal-oriented (intentional) explanation. This explanation isn't the result of mere physical operations, and this implies a nonphysical soul's existence.[13]

Seven, my entire body's cells are constantly being renewed every seven years. This suggests a non-physical soul gives me my identity over time. If all my body's cells, including brain cells, are completely replaced again and again, then, given naturalism, we should be completely different persons. How could I be held responsible for a crime committed twenty years ago since "I" didn't exist back then? Also, why fear an event in the distant future since "another person" will be experiencing it? A simpler explanation is that a soul gives each person her personal identity that remains though the body constantly changes. Such identity better supports the existence of a soul than various forms of materialism.

The soul's existence and ability to be temporarily separated from the body is quite supportable scripturally, but *the soul's disembodiment isn't the final state*: the one "who raised Christ Jesus from the dead will also give life to your mortal bodies through His Spirit who dwells in you" (Rom. 8:11). And if God raised Jesus from the dead, then Eastern views such as reincarnation are incorrect. As Hebrews 9:27 suggests, it's death and then judgment. Practically speaking, we're wiser to assume we have only one earthly life than to bet on many future lives to get life "right." Though some Westerners may see reincarnation as another nifty opportunity for self-improvement, the Hindu often finds it quite depressing and burdensome; paying for wrongs from a previous life compounded by ongoing failures in the present one creates a sense of despair. What relief God's grace in Christ could bring!

We can't address here the difficulties with reincarnation (e.g., if we've lived an enormous number of lives already, why haven't we reached perfection by now?).[14] However, given reincarnational views, we will ultimately be snuffed out, undergo a personal extinction into nothingness (*sunyata*), or lose our personal identity like a drop into the ocean of the pure, undifferentiated consciousness (Brahman). How different from being raised immortal, being forever in God's presence without obliterating our personal identity!

20

Faith, Doubt, and Hope

And have mercy on some, who are doubting. (Jude 22)

Faith and Doubt

Toward the end of her life, Thérèse of Lisieux experienced a deep, ever-worsening darkness of soul:

> It is worse torment than ever; the darkness itself seems to borrow, from the sinners who live in it, the gift of speech. I hear its mocking accents: "It's all a dream, this talk of a heavenly country, bathed in light, scented with delicious perfumes, and of a God who made it all, who is to be your possession in eternity….[D]eath will make nonsense of your hopes; it will only mean a night darker than ever, the night of mere non-existence."[1]

In hope and desperation, she scratched on the door of her cell, "Jesus is my only love." Centuries before, the reformers Luther and Calvin endured terrorizing anxieties.

Scripture itself is full of doubters. The lament psalmists wonder why God is absent. Thomas refuses to believe unless he sees Jesus' hands and side–and Jesus graciously accommodates him, although he should have believed his fellow disciples who had visited the empty tomb and seen Jesus. The "greatest" prophet, John the Baptist, had doubts about "the Lamb of God" he had announced (Jn. 1:29). Probably anticipating the fierce apocalyptic horned lamb of Jewish apocalyptic literature,[2] John assumed Jesus would "take away the sins of the world" by wiping out evildoers (Mt. 3:10–12). Should he now expect another? Jesus lovingly reminded the imprisoned John that the messianic promises were being fulfilled–the blind see, the lame walk, lepers are cleansed, the dead are raised, the good news is proclaimed to the poor (Mt. 11:1–11).

Doubts may often serve as faith's stumbling block or stepping stone; doubt can deepen one's despair *or* one's faith. The Christian heritage offers rich resources for grappling with pressing questions and anxieties. To help buttress our faith in times of doubt, we should investigate important questions and learn lessons from fellow-saints who, in John Bunyan's terms, have been locked up in Doubting Castle by Giant Despair. At many points, the Christian faith goes *beyond* reason, though it need not be viewed as being *against* reason. Biblical faith–personal commitment and trust–is directed toward God/Christ. Its personal nature (like marriage commitment) goes beyond the facts to personal embrace.

We're wise to recognize we're not always well-positioned to resolve our questions. At times we may need to release our doubts, confess "I don't know," learn to live with unanswered questions. Admitting our finitude isn't as bad as we imagine! So doubt and faith need not be opposed; faith implies perseverance and steadfastness–not giving up when soul-searching questions arise.

Some Christians fall into the rut of always asking, "*But what if* our faith isn't true?" They dig themselves into an ever-deepening hole of corrosive doubt that saps their spiritual vitality. While certain doubts may be *intellectual,* they are often *emotional,* and the constant what-if questions will likely never be satisfied by mounds of evidence. Doubt may also involve *spiritual warfare,* as the Accuser desires to destroy our confidence in Christ and make us spiritual casualties (1 Pet. 5:8; Rev. 12:10). Doubt can also stem from a *moral* problem. When believers have unconfessed sin in their lives, it can wreak havoc on the intellect, raise serious doubts, and produce all kinds of rationalizations.

In addition to our rich intellectual resources, believers have the grace of prayer, the creeds and liturgies across the ages, a community of fellow-pilgrims to share our burdens and to strengthen us on the journey. We fix our eyes on Jesus, who shows us what God is like (Jn. 14:9) and who is able to protect and rescue us fully (Heb. 7:25). We ourselves should have mercy on those who doubt (Jude 22). Certain doubts, however, come from a *failure* to fully love and trust God. In this case the doubter doesn't need more arguments but to devote himself wholly to God rather than be "double-minded" (Jas. 4:8; cp. 1:8). Further down the spectrum are the arrogant doubters who seem to make doubting a profession. Yet they seem to have such faith in themselves that they alone seem to know what's right for themselves; ironically, they refuse to doubt their own self-confidence.[3]

In the end, any ultimate assurance that we belong to God or that Jesus is the true and living way comes by the working of God's Spirit. Even though God can use evidences and arguments, we truly know we're children of our heavenly Father through the presence of Christ's Spirit (Rom. 8:15; Gal. 4:6; cp. Mt. 16:17)–not the writings of Thomas Aquinas or C. S. Lewis. Our greatest need isn't simply having intellectual answers (though this is important), but tasting and seeing God's goodness (Ps. 34:8) and knowing his living presence.

Faith and doubt needn't be completely at odds with each other. Faith can be steadfast, full of conviction, and persevering despite doubts and questions.[4] Just as we trust a surgeon's skilled hands, despite our anxious thoughts, so we can rely on God's promises in Christ, confidently placing ourselves in the hands of a faithful, covenant-keeping God, who is for us and who rewards those who diligently seek him (Heb. 11:6).

Wagering on God

"...choose for yourselves today whom you will serve." (Josh. 24:15)

The *ordinary* agnostic says, "I'd *like* to know if God exists, but because the evidence is equally balanced, I can't decide." Then there's the *ornery* agnostic, who says, "I don't know if God exists, and you can't know either"–the "*militant* agnostic" of bumper-sticker fame. The *ornery* agnostic actually *does* make a claim to know, but how does he *know* that no one can know God exists? Perhaps *he* doesn't think one can know, but why rule that out for others? His insistence basically amounts to atheism.

Even the *ordinary* agnostic can't live a consistent agnosticism her whole life. Since God is no armchair topic, an agnostic can't simply defer making a decision about God or Christ. She will repeatedly have to make choices that reflect either Christ's uniqueness or non-uniqueness; she will live as though God exists or doesn't exist–for example, treating humans with intrinsic dignity or not, trusting the functions of her mind or not, living as though life has meaning or not. She will live either as a practical theist or practical atheist. To *defer* is to *decide*–against God.

Refraining is theoretically, not practically, possible. Consider the paradox of (Jean) Buridan's ass: a rational donkey starves to death looking at two equidistant, equally appetizing bales of hay because it can't decide between them. *Practically* speaking, though, the donkey will go for one bale over the other rather than starve to death. Likewise, we can't be neutral about God all our lives; we can't precariously balance our lives on the knife-edge that divides between the pros and the cons of believing in God. There are *risks on either side*. So besides *intellectual* reasons for belief, the ordinary agnostic must consider *practical* ones as well. The agnostic who finds herself living as a *practical* theist has additional reason for embracing God. The match-up between one's *philosophy* and *everyday life* itself is one important way of assessing the likely truth of one's views.

Blaise Pascal (1623–1662) stressed the inescapable practicality of belief. His own dramatic conversion experience–a "night of fire"–utterly transformed him. Though he died at thirty-nine, before finishing a defense of the Christian faith, he jotted down *thoughts* that have been compiled in the book *Pensées*. A cluster of thoughts, now called *Pascal's wager,* assert that the decision to choose or reject the biblical God is momentous. If the evidence appears evenly balanced, reason can't decide for us. Pascal urges the agnostic to make the *choice* to commit herself to God, as *suspending* belief is, in effect, to side with the atheist. If she *does* commit to God and turns out to be right, the results are *infinitely* spectacular. But if it turns out God doesn't exist, any loss would be *finite.* And if the agnostic incorrectly risks God's nonexistence, the postmortem consequences are devastating. Practically speaking, we're far better off embracing God than rejecting him, and to suspend belief is to reject God.

Pascal has been criticized for the following reason: What of personal commitment within *other* religions? Pascal certainly isn't calling for agnostics in India to personally embrace belief in Brahman. Though a good point, we shouldn't forget that in Pascal's France, pretty much the only religious options were embracing the triune God of the Christian faith *or* rejecting him. Pascal's historical context was much like Christian philosopher Søren Kierkegaard's (1813–1855). His essay "Truth Is Subjectivity" didn't affirm that what I *feel* makes it true for me. No, he believed the Christian faith is true for all. However, his home country of Denmark was a part of a "Christendom" where dogs and public property were also "Christian." God had become domesticated and tamed,[5] and many of Kierkegaard's contemporaries didn't embrace their faith with a passionate inwardness– "and this passion is precisely the truth," he wrote. Such nominal "belief" was really sub-Christian.

Similarly, Pascal's society was most familiar with the Christian worldview–a view Pascal took to be true for all people. He also assumed there's *evidence* for the biblical God, and such evidence would be irrelevant in most nontheistic religious traditions. Furthermore, he presents a *personal, seeking* God who reveals himself so that he might be known by human beings. However, such a personal God is nonexistent in Buddhist, Jain, Taoist, Shinto, Confucian, and most Hindu traditions.[6]

Pascal uses an "anthropological argument" based on both the creation and the fall of humankind. Humans are both *magnificent* and *wretched*–"deposed kings." The Christian faith best explains this paradoxical condition. Thus Pascal urges his contemporaries to wager in favor of this seeking God. In doing so, he tries to give his hearers an "existential" or practical jolt out of their complacency.[7]

The Devotional Experiment

"I do believe; help my unbelief." (Mk.9:24)

What do we do when certain persons recognize there's good evidence for belief in God, but they find themselves simply unable to believe accordingly? They may tell us they'd *like* to believe but can't turn on faith like flipping a switch; that's not under their control. Perhaps their lifelong habit of unbelief makes it difficult to get out of this rut. The idea that our beliefs tend not to be under our control is known as—get ready!—*non-doxastic voluntarism*: the *inability* ("non-") to *choose* ("voluntarism") to *believe* ("doxastic"—*doxa*, classical Greek for "belief" or "thought"). The opposite view—epistemic voluntarism—claims that I control my beliefs.[8] Philosopher Paul Griffiths distinguishes between (a) *assenting* to certain beliefs (that we find ourselves believing or we take to be true, though we have no control over this); and (b) *accepting* a belief by choosing to treat a claim as true.[9] *Accepting* a belief as true involves an extra step—*exercising the will.*

Consider the father of a demonized boy, desperate for Jesus' help. Hopeful but uncertain, he cries out, "I do believe; help my unbelief!" (Mk. 9:24). He casts himself on Jesus, longing for more than what his intellect was telling him. There is a certain *assent* to what he takes to be true ("I believe"), but he exercises his *will* by calling on Jesus to aid him further ("help my unbelief!"). Throughout the Scriptures, believers and unbelievers are exhorted to trust God *beyond* what they are thinking or feeling and not be ruled by their circumstances or emotions. *We're called to act in ways that may seem contrary to our inclinations*—to rejoice or to give thanks (when we're feeling overwhelmed by circumstances), to be sober-minded and alert (when we're lethargic), to believe the promises of God that we are forgiven (even when we feel guilty). God repeatedly tells us to "snap out of it" by taking certain actions and realigning our focus. The very first act is *humbling ourselves and repenting.*

Some might object: "Isn't this play-acting—pretending to believe that things are what they really aren't?" No, this is actually *adjusting our minds to reality.* Reality encompasses more than our feelings or present beliefs. God is greater than the present state of our hearts (1 Jn. 3:18–20). We're not only emotional and believing creatures; we're also volitional, relational, and spiritual beings who are to be transformed by the renewing of our minds (Rom. 12:2). We're regularly called on to deliberately trust God's character and promises. Though not going against reason or evidence, we must make choices that go beyond them, that put intellectual belief (even if shaky) into practice. If we've been created to belong to God's family, this means we can't reason everything out before deciding to trust God. Trusting in God's reliability, *accepting* and not merely *assenting,* can *renew* our thinking and *inspire* certain actions.

What then do we advise those who have difficulty believing in God though they'd like to? While we can't *choose* to change our beliefs instantaneously or *directly* control them, we *can* put ourselves into a position or create conditions so that embracing certain beliefs will be more likely. We can *choose to put ourselves into an environment that is conducive to producing, indirectly, new beliefs* (indirect doxastic voluntarism).[10] *Acceptance*—the act of the will—can lead to *assent.*

For example, the seeker could meet with serious-minded, godly Christians in community. He could read and meditate on the Bible. He could attempt to pray and regularly gather with worshiping Christians. After all, it's hard to move toward belief when one surrounds himself with *unbelief* and *skepticism* (Ps. 1:1–2) or when one constantly *ignores* the influence of the believing community (Heb. 10:24–25). The spiritual journey must be intentional, not haphazard or casual. We are to *love* and *seek* wisdom (Prov. 8:17), to seek God with *all* our heart (Jer. 29:13). Pascal declared, "My whole heart strains to know what the true good is in order to pursue it: no price would be too high to pay for eternity."[11]

Some professing seekers may not be *very diligent* in their search, may have a *very narrow view* of what is "reasonable" and "explanatory," or may be *looking in the wrong places*–like Soviet cosmonaut Yuri Gagarin who announced that God didn't exist because Gagarin didn't see him in space! The true seeker, though, will *never cease* or *be deterred in* pursuing an abiding passion to know God. Rather than calling off the search partway through life, the seeker sees the knowledge of God as a matter of the greatest importance, worthy of a *persistent* lifelong quest. He won't resort to cheap shots against belief in God or shoddy investigation but will be open to whatever glimmers of God's presence are available.

Even if seekers can't control their *beliefs* (which are involuntary), they can control their *actions*. Philosopher Douglas Henry writes:

> If one has control over his actions, one has voluntary control over some of the *conditions* that give rise to belief. Even if one's beliefs are outside of one's direct control, one can nevertheless control such things as looking for new evidence, attending more or less carefully to one's evidence, and associating with persons or environments committed to intellectual virtue. Thus, *even if one cannot be faulted for holding particular beliefs, one can be faulted for the actions giving rise to one's beliefs.*[12]

We may be disposed to believe one way rather than another, but a *disposition* doesn't mean *necessity*. We can *act* in ways different from our *beliefs* or *dispositions*; this can lead us to form *new* beliefs and dispositions. Our *emotions* can tell us one thing, but we often *choose* to do what we're really not inclined to do at all. We may *feel* discouraged, but we *determine* not to be beaten by it; so we set our minds and actions in the opposing direction.

In this "devotional experiment,"[13] the not-yet-believing seekers can *begin* to praise, worship, and thank God even if they aren't inclined to, even if they can't change their emotions on the spot. They can read Scripture and the Christian classics that have inspired and assisted believers throughout the ages. The context of the Christian community and the proclamation of the Word can assist them in sensing the reality and presence of God. They can read defenses of the faith by thoughtful believers. Having a "religious experience" may come not as a lightning bolt on an unsuspecting soul, but gradually as the result of a genuine, patient willingness to befriend and engage those who claim and show evidences of experiencing and knowing God.[14]

Death, Hope, and the New Creation

He will wipe away every tear from their eyes; and there will no longer be any death; there will no longer be any mourning, or crying, or pain; the first things have passed away. (Rev. 21:4)

...and hope does not disappoint, because the love of God has been poured out within our hearts through the Holy Spirit who was given to us. (Rom. 5:5)

Petrarch (1304–1374), who purportedly launched the Renaissance and the revival of classical learning in Europe, wrote *Secretum Meum* (*My Secret*). In it, he has an imaginary dialogue with the long-dead church father Augustine, confessing his love for the elusive Laura, whom he adored from a distance. Augustine's advice to him was to spend his life preparing for death. The great Roman senator and philosopher Cicero (106–43 B.C.E.) wrote: "The entire life of philosophers [*Tota philosophorum*] is a preparation for death." Actually, he was citing Plato's *Phaedo* dialogue, in which Socrates insists: "those who really apply themselves in the right way are directly and of their own accord preparing themselves for dying and death" (64a).

Death can indeed make cowards of us all, but anticipating it can also move us to live the "examined life" that Socrates exhorted. By God's grace, reflecting on our mortality can prompt us to recognize our moral failures, seek redemption and forgiveness, and cast ourselves on God's mercy and grace. The triune God assures us that death isn't the last word. Instead, we have a hope that "does not disappoint, because the love of God has been poured out within our hearts through the Holy Spirit who was given to us" (Rom. 5:5). Jesus is the "Yes" to all of God's promises (2 Cor. 1:20).

Hope is *not* optimism—a humanistic can-do spirit that seeks to overcome obstacles, but without any guarantees. The *Humanist Manifesto III* proclaims great confidence in human potential and scientific achievement, aiming for "our fullest possible development" with a "deep sense of purpose." The result, though, is that the majority of people in the world have been utterly cut off from anything remotely resembling the fullest possible development and a deep sense of purpose. If the humanist is right, most humans have lived purposeless lives.

The hope of the good news is more secure—not a mere wish or upbeat attitude, but a *confident expectation rooted in God's promises in Christ*: "because I live, you will live also" (Jn. 14:19). And the realization of this hope is *graciously available to all who would desire it*; no one is cut off from the God who is near us and for us. Moreover, this hope is sustained by trusting in God's promises that have not only enabled believers to quench the power of fire or to shut the mouths of lions, but also to endure imprisonment and persecution or to die courageously (Heb. 11:32–40).

Jesus' resurrection on the "first day of the week" signals that the new creation has begun. The first Easter, which has been called the "eighth day of creation," means hope for a new heaven and earth in which God's justice finally and visibly prevails (2 Pet. 3:13). God has created and, though humans have fallen and rebelled, he has also promised to deliver. Not only does he send his incarnate Son at the proper time–to vanquish Satan, sin, and death in his cross and resurrection–but he promises to make all things new. During this in-between stage of *already* having the fulfillment of God's promises but *not yet* all of them ("realized eschatology"), we have two guarantees of a new creation: (a) the Spirit's presence within the lives of God's new people, and (b) Jesus' bodily resurrection as a promissory note for our own immortality. God's Spirit won't only restore creation's literal plants, crops, trees–and resurrection bodies–but he even now produces spiritual fruit, Christ's image, within us (Gal. 5:22–23; cp. Isa. 32:10–18; 57:15–19).[15] One day we'll possess imperishable resurrection bodies in the company of God's people, who will enjoy the presence of the triune God everlastingly. This is our magnificent hope.

Building on Anselm's *faith seeking understanding* and his *I believe that I may understand,* German theologian Jürgen Moltmann suggests a *spes quarens intellectum* ("hope seeking understanding")–that is, *spero, ut ingelligam* ("I hope, that I may understand").[16] Throughout the book, we've spoken of the rationality of *faith,* but we must not forget the rationality of *hope*–a forward-looking confidence that our trust in Christ won't disappoint and will bring with it ample answers and unspeakable joy. The love of wisdom–true philosophy–has a place for hope; wisdom doesn't call for answers when the time isn't right for them.

Though we face doubts, distress, disease, and death, Jesus' glorious appearing will bring resolution to the puzzles and questions of our mind, the fulfillment of our vocation as priest-kings, and the satisfaction of our deepest longing–the immediacy of the triune God's presence.

Questions for Personal Reflection and Small Group Study

Introduction

1. What is *wisdom*? Why does true wisdom begin with "the fear of the LORD" (Ps. 111:10; cp. Prov. 1:7; 9:10; 15:33)?
2. What does it mean to do philosophy "under the cross"?
3. How would you distinguish between philosophy as it is professionally done and how Scripture approaches it?
4. Alvin Plantinga has argued that Christians be distinctive in "doing philosophy." What do you think about his advice?
5. What have been your previous impressions of philosophy, and how do they compare with this book's perspective?
6. What are some of the definitions or descriptions of "religion" you've come across? What are the merits and problems of each?
7. C. S. Lewis wrote, "I believe in Christianity as I believe that the Sun has risen, not only because I see it, but because by it I see everything else." What is your response to his statement?
8. What is the point and the value of doing philosophy "Christianly"?

Chapter 1: Kings and Priests

1. What definitions of "human" or "human nature" have you come across? Do these have any merit?
2. Summarize as best you can what it means to be made in "God's image." What functions or roles does this involve?
3. Following the flow of creation, fall, redemption, and re-creation, describe what Jesus does as our representative to restore us to our rightful vocation as God's image-bearers.
4. What is the significance of the new creation and new exodus in Christ?
5. In what ways can we daily carry out our vocation as God's image-bearers?

Chapter 2: The Need for God

1. What is the "psychological crutch" argument?
2. Have you ever heard versions of this argument? Explain.
3. What is the "genetic fallacy"? How does this fallacy apply to the crutch argument?
4. Why is it important to differentiate between the *rationality* of belief and the *psychology* of belief?

5. How do we turn the turn the tables on the crutch argument?
6. At the end of this chapter, we note C. S. Lewis's argument from desire. Do you find his argument persuasive? Why or why not?
7. List some of the other problems with the crutch argument. Can you think of any others?

Chapter 3: God Triune

1. The doctrine of the Trinity is central to the Christian faith yet ignored by many Christians. Why is the doctrine of the Trinity so important?
2. What is the doctrine of the Trinity? Try to describe it accurately. Note the distinction between the "is" of identity and the "is" of predication (the Mark Twain analogy).
3. What do you think of the Cerberus analogy? Is it helpful?
4. In what ways is God one? What is the doctrine of *perichoresis?*
5. How does the doctrine of the Trinity address concerns raised by philosophers who are religious pluralists, feminists, or panentheists?
6. How does the doctrine of the Trinity shape how you pray/worship, relate to others, do your work?

Chapter 4: Talking About God and Knowing God

1. What is "the problem of religious language"?
2. What are some suitable responses to this alleged problem?
3. What is the difference between cataphatic and apophatic theology?
4. Historically, what motivated apophatic theology? What are the benefits and drawbacks of apophatic theology's emphases?
5. Does "negative theology" seem to fit what the Scriptures teach? Why or why not?
6. The Westminster Confession says that our chief end or goal is to "glorify God and enjoy him forever." How do we move beyond knowing *about* God to knowing and enjoying him?

Chapter 5: The Attributes of God (I)

1. What is the difference between God's being *necessary* and *everlasting?* What is the significance of this distinction?
2. How would you answer someone's question, "If God made the universe, who made God?"
3. What is time? What do you think about the statement, "God is outside of time"? Do you think it is accurate? Has our discussion of God's relationship to time given any insights or raised any questions for you?
4. What does it mean that God is all-knowing (omniscient)? What are some misunderstandings about omniscience? How does God's omniscience influence the way I live?

5. What is the relationship of God's foreknowledge to human free choices? Can we affirm both of these without contradiction? How does this have a bearing on prayer or the unevangelized?

Chapter 6: The Attributes of God (II)

1. Read Psalm 139:1–18. What does the psalmist have to say about God's omnipresence? How would you articulate what omnipresence is?
2. Why is it significant that God is "spirit"? What are your thoughts on the discussion of divine incorporeality?
3. When we hear that God is all-powerful (omnipotent), what does it mean? What does it not mean? Can God do *literally* everything? Is it a problem if he can't?
4. How does God's immutability give focus to your life? What does it mean for God to be unchanging? How has this doctrine been misunderstood? In what ways does God repent, and in what ways does he not repent?
5. What does it mean that God suffers? What scriptural instances of divine suffering stand out to you?
6. What were your impressions on the topic of divine humility? What are the implications of divine humility for your daily life, your relationships, communicating the gospel?
7. Summarize the doctrine of divine simplicity. What are its merits and/or shortcomings?

Chapter 7: The God of Truth

1. What are the key differences between premodernism, modernism, and postmodernism? What is the appeal–right or wrong–of postmodernism? What lessons can postmodernism teach us? What are some problems with it?
2. What is wrong with defining knowledge as having 100 percent certainty? Why is it important to think in terms of *degrees* of knowledge?
3. Why are (a) truth-denial, (b) knowledge-denial, and (c) total (global) skepticism impossible positions to take? What does this reveal about how we are designed/"wired"?
4. Which guidelines could we use to assess competing worldviews?
5. What does it mean that Jesus is "the truth" (Jn. 14:6)? How can we be people of truth? What does this encompass?

Chapter 8: Proofs or Pointers?

1. In what two major ways does God reveal himself? Why should Christians keep this in mind when talking to their non-Christian friends?
2. What do people mean when they say the world is "religiously ambiguous"? How do you respond to such a claim?

3. What is natural theology? Is this a valuable endeavor to undertake? Why or why not?

4. What is the problem with giving "proofs" to "demonstrate" God's existence? What is a wiser and more fruitful approach?

5. What is the difference between "thin" theism and "thick/robust" theism? Why is it important to go beyond thin theism? How do we do so?

6. What are the implications for non-theistic alternatives if natural theology is even minimally successful?

Chapter 9: Arguments for God's Existence

1. What is the cosmological argument for God's existence discussed in this chapter? How is this argument helped by contemporary science?

2. What does the design (teleological) argument try to show? How does contemporary science support such an argument? What are some challenges to the design argument? Can they be overcome?

3. Why does the existence of moral obligations, human dignity, and human rights connect us to a Source of supreme goodness? Are God and goodness necessarily connected? How might the non-theist argue against this, and what are your responses?

4. The aesthetic argument is not frequently used, but do you think it has merits? Why might an argument from beauty appeal to the non-theist over a cosmological or teleological argument?

5. Is there any merit to the religious experience argument? Do people from non-Christian religions possibly experience God remotely (even if not savingly)?

6. Which of the arguments more strongly resonates or connects with you? Why?

Chapter 10: God—The Best Explanation

1. When people say, "There isn't enough evidence for God," how do you respond? What do people need to consider besides "evidence"?

2. Why is the "inference to the best explanation" so important in discussing God's existence and attributes?

3. Describe the approach taken in the naturalism-theism chart. Do you find this more helpful than simply looking at individual arguments for God? Why or why not?

4. How do admitted problems (to account for consciousness, beauty, human rights, or the universe's beginning and fine-tuning) cited by naturalists offer assistance to the believer in God?

Chapter 11: Science, Nature, and the Possibility of Miracles

1. What is the difference between science and scientism?

2. What's wrong with the demand to "prove that scientifically"?

3. What philosophical assumptions do scientists begin with? Why should we keep this in mind?
4. What is the "God-of-the-gaps" claim? Does it have any merits?
5. How do you respond when people talk about the "warfare" between science and religion?
6. What are miracles? Are they "violations" of natural laws? Do you find helpful the distinction between (a) ordinary providence, (b) extra-ordinary providence, and (c) miracles? How does this discussion help us understand Scripture's emphasis on prayer's effectiveness?
7. What do we make of miracle claims in other religions?
8. What are some other arguments used to undermine miracles, and how do you answer them?

Chapter 12: The Problem(s) of Evil

1. We distinguished between the emotional and intellectual problems of evil. What are the appropriate responses to each? In what concrete ways can the Christian community respond to the evil in society?
2. Why should we first understand what evil is before responding to certain criticisms of belief in God based on evil in the world?
3. What is the logical problem of evil? Is it a problem? Why or why not?
4. What is the probabilistic or evidential problem from evil? How can we respond to it?
5. Why should we consider "principalities and powers" in a philosophical discussion of evil?
6. How does the cross of Christ address the problem(s) of evil? How should this shape the believer's thinking about evil? How does God's revelation in Christ offer responses to the problem of evil that will elude the naturalistic philosopher grappling with this issue?

Chapter 13: The Hiddenness of God

1. What is the problem of divine hiddenness? Have you struggled with this issue? What has encouraged you along the way?
2. Why are signs and abundant evidence by themselves insufficient to turn people to God? How do the Scriptures support this?
3. What is the place of miracles or evidence in the process of coming to trust in/embrace God?
4. What should our attitude be in light of God's existence—even if God appears hidden?
5. Can God be both a hidden God and a revealing God? Explain.

Chapter 14: Original Sin

1. What is original sin? Why is it a problem?
2. Explain in what way humans are both good and evil.

3. What is the difference between the "guilt" and "damage" interpretations of original sin? What are the implications of each? Which do you find more satisfying morally and biblically?
4. We noted that our fallenness doesn't give a complete picture of who we are. How does the second Adam inform our understanding of the first Adam?
5. What is "the moral gap," and how may original sin be a kind of grace to us?

Chapter 15: Hell

1. What is hell? What are some common misconceptions about hell?
2. What are some reasons for taking hell's fire and darkness to be figurative?
3. How can the doctrine of hell be squared with the character of God? Is the punishment disproportionate to the crime?
4. Why is the freedom of the will so crucial in coming to terms with hell?
5. Which objection to the doctrine of hell do you find most challenging? How do you respond to it?

Chapter 16: The Incarnation

1. What does the doctrine of the Incarnation affirm? Why is this so crucial for our salvation?
2. How does Scripture affirm both Jesus' divinity and humanity? How does the image of God help our understanding of the coherence of the Incarnation?
3. We noted three important distinctions to better understand the reasonableness of the Incarnation: (a) Jesus' *person* and *nature,* (b) being *fully* vs. *merely* human, (c) Jesus' *human* and *divine* consciousness. Explain each distinction. Did you observe any helpful analogies to better understand the Incarnation?
4. If Jesus was God, how could he be tempted? What do you think of the claim that the Son of God temporarily surrendered having access to certain capabilities–including knowledge that it was impossible to deviate from the Father's will–in order to accomplish his mission?
5. Why was Jesus not play-acting in his temptation? How does Jesus' weakness and temptation encourage you in your own struggle against sin and learning submission to God?

Chapter 17: The Cross of Christ

1. What is the difference between *objective* and *subjective* "theories of the atonement"? Which should receive priority and why?
2. What did the atonement achieve *corporately*–not simply individually? (Keep in mind Jesus' representative exile for Israel, as the true Son of God, and for humanity, as the second Adam.)

3. What did the atonement achieve *cosmically?*
4. Is there something morally problematic with an innocent person's taking a guilty person's punishment?
5. Is the charge of "divine child abuse" (God's sending Christ to die on the cross for us) a fair one? How do you respond to this assertion?

Chapter 18: Jesus' Uniqueness and the Plurality of Religions

1. What is *tolerance,* and how has the definition changed? What is the problem with the current understanding of tolerance?
2. Define religious pluralism. What are its main features? Have you talked with religious pluralists about their views? What have your conversations been like?
3. Can all religions be "basically the same"? Why or why not?
4. How should Christians engage in religious dialogue? What guidelines should all parties set down from the outset before engaging in dialogue?
5. What are the shortcomings of religious pluralism?
6. How do you answer the question regarding the unevangelized? What should we keep in mind as we try to think through this issue?

Chapter 19: Body, Soul, and Resurrection

1. Compare the Greek doctrine of immortality with the Christian view. What are the significant differences?
2. What are the biblical and theological supports for the soul's surviving death before the final resurrection (i.e., the intermediate state)?
3. Why does it make better sense to say that the soul–not the body–gives a person his ongoing identity?
4. What are some philosophical reasons for believing that a soul exists? Which do you find most persuasive and why? Why does naturalism fail to account for important "soulish" capabilities of humans?
5. What is the theological significance of bodily resurrection? Would it make a difference if our bodies died and our souls just "went to heaven" (end of story)?
6. What does the robust physicality of the new heavens and new earth suggest? Do many Christians need to revise their understanding of the afterlife?

Chapter 20: Faith, Doubt, and Hope

1. How should Christians think about doubt? How do we deal with intellectual doubt? with emotional doubt ("but what if I'm wrong?")?
2. Describe the ordinary agnostic and the ornery agnostic. How do you respond to each of these positions?
3. What is Pascal's "wager"? Does Pascal make an important point in encouraging the wager?

4. What is the difference between assent to a belief and acceptance of it? Should we advise the ordinary agnostic to undergo "the devotional experiment"? Why or why not?

5. Why is hope so important? How does it differ from optimism? How does hope shape how you live your life?

Notes

Preface

[1]Alvin Plantinga, "Twenty Years Worth of the SCP," *Faith and Philosophy* 15 (April 1998): 153.

[2]Alvin Plantinga, "Advice to Christian Philosophers," *Faith and Philosophy* 1 (July 1984): 255.

[3]Biblical scholar John Goldingay asserts, "If one starts from biblical narratives and asks after their theological freight, the vast bulk of their theological implications does not emerge within a trinitarian framework." From "Biblical Narrative and Systematic Theology," in *Between Two Horizons,* ed. Joel B. Green and Max Turner (Grand Rapids: Eerdmans, 2000), 131. However, we have triune glimmers in the Old Testament, with subtle, but rich themes of Wisdom, Word, and Spirit, and sufficient indications in the New Testament. This doctrine is a legitimate–and very fruitful–theological inference. Biblical scholar Richard Bauckham comments that the 325 C.E. Council of Nicea's *homoousion* (Christ's sharing the same nature as the Father) "functions to ensure that this divine identity is truly the identity of the one and only God. In its own way, it expresses the Christological monotheism of the New Testament." *God Crucified: Monotheism & Christology in the New Testament* (Grand Rapids: Eerdmans, 1998), 78–79.

[4]A term used by Hans Urs von Balthasar and, more recently, Kevin Vanhoozer, *The Drama of Doctrine* (Louisville: Westminster John Knox Press, 2005).

Introduction

[1]Graham Tomlin, *The Power of the Cross: Theology and the Death of Christ in Paul, Luther and Pascal* (Carlisle, UK: Paternoster, 1999), 154–65.

[2]See Peter Simpson, "The Christianity of Philosophy," *First Things* 113 (May 2001): 32–36.

[3]Bruce K. Waltke, *The Book of Proverbs: Chapters 1-15,* New International Commentary on the Old Testament (Grand Rapids: Eerdmans, 2004), 65, 101. Abraham assumes worshipers of the true God weren't in Gerar: "I thought, surely there is no *fear of God* in this place" (Gen. 20:11).

[4]Ben Witherington III, *Jesus the Sage: The Pilgrimage of Wisdom* (Minneapolis: Augsburg Fortress, 1994).

[5]"Take My Life," verse 4, in *Chalice Hymnal* (St. Louis: Chalice Press, 1995), no. 609.

[6]Thomas Nagel, *The Last Word* (New York: Oxford University Press, 1997), 130.

[7]Ibid., 131.

[8]Keith Yandell, "How to Sink in Cognitive Quicksand: Nuancing Religious Pluralism," in *Contemporary Debates in Philosophy of Religion,* ed. Michael L. Peterson and Raymond J. VanArragon (Oxford: Blackwell, 2004), 191.

[9]See James Davison Hunter's essay, "Religious Freedom and the Challenge of Pluralism," in *Articles of Faith, Articles of Peace,* ed. James D. Hunter and Os Guinness (Washington: Brookings, 1988).

[10]Paul J. Griffiths, *Problems of Religious Diversity* (Oxford: Blackwell, 2001), 7; see also 2–12.

[11]William Wainwright, *Philosophy of Religion,* 2d ed. (Belmont, Calif.: Wadsworth, 1999), v.

[12]Alvin Plantinga, "Advice to Christian Philosophers," *Faith and Philosophy* 15 (April 1998): 253–71.

[13]Alvin Plantinga, "Natural Theology," in *Companion to Metaphysics,* ed. Jaegwon Kim and Ernest Sosa (Malden, Mass.: Blackwell, 1995), 347. On Christian philosophers whose faith has proved intellectually satisfying, see Kelly James Clark, ed., *Philosophers Who Believe* (Downers Grove, Ill.: InterVarsity, 1995) and Thomas V. Morris, ed., *God and the Philosophers* (New York: Oxford University Press, 1995).

[14]C. S. Lewis, "Is Theology Poetry?" in *The Weight of Glory and Other Addresses* (New York: Macmillan, 1965), 140.

[15]G. Walter Hansen, "The Preaching and Defence of Paul," in *Witness to the Gospel: The Theology of Acts,* ed. I. H. Marshall and David Peterson (Grand Rapids: Eerdmans, 1998), 295–324. Compare Plato's *Apology,* 19, 23, and 24.

[16]This was from a 1994 Barna Group poll (with Nehemiah Institute and Josh McDowell Ministries): http://www.epm.org/pdf/03winter.pdf#search=%22josh%20mcdowell%20nehe miah%20institute%2055%25%22. Accessed 15 October 2005.

[17]J. Gresham Machen, "Christianity and Culture," *Princeton Theological Review* 11 (1913): 7.

Chapter 1: Kings and Priests

[1]This command/blessing is extended to Abraham (Gen. 17:2, 6, 8; 22:16–17), Isaac (26:4, 24), Jacob (35:9, 11–12; cp. 28:3), Joseph (48:3), and the nation of Israel in Egypt (47:27; Ex. 1:7).

[2]The patriarchs, God's earthly priests, also offer sacrifices to God wherever they go (Gen. 12:6–9; 13:3–4, 19; cp. esp. Gen. 22, the sacrifice of Isaac; etc.).

[3]John Sailhamer, "Genesis," in *Expositor's Bible Commentary,* ed. Frank E. Gaebelein (Grand Rapids: Zondervan, 1990), 4. These rarely combined verbs appear later in the Pentateuch as *serve* and *guard,* referring to *priestly/levitical service* and *guarding the tabernacle/sanctuary.* See Numbers 3:7–8; 8:25–6; cp. also Numbers 18:5–6; 1 Chronicles 23:32; Ezekiel 44:14.

[4]John Goldingay, *Old Testament Theology: Israel's Story,* vol. 1 (Downers Grove, Ill.: InterVarsity, 2003), 100.

[5]G. K. Beale, *The Temple and the Church's Mission* (Downers Grove, Ill.: InterVarsity, 2004), 81–87.

[6]N. T. Wright, *Climax of the Covenant* (Minneapolis: Fortress, 1995), 23.

[7]R. T. France, "Jesus the Baptist?" in *Jesus of Nazareth: Lord and Christ,* ed. Joel B. Green and Max Turner (Grand Rapids/Carlisle, UK : Eerdmans/Paternoster, 1994), 94–111.

Chapter 2: The Need for God

[1]Ludwig Feuerbach, *The Essence of Christianity,* trans. George Eliot (New York: Harper and Brothers, 1957), xxxix.

[2]Sigmund Freud, *Future of an Illusion,* ed. and trans. J. Strachey (New York: Norton, 1961), 30.

[3]Ibid.

[4]Peter Railton, "Some Questions About the Justification of Morality," *Philosophical Perspectives* 6 (1992): 45.

[5]Richard Dawkins, "Viruses of the Mind," *Free Inquiry* (Summer 1993): 34–41.

[6]Peter Berger, *A Rumor of Angels,* 2d ed. (New York: Doubleday, 1990), 51.

[7]John Calvin, *Institutes of the Christian Religion,* 1.3.1.

[8]See Paul C. Vitz, *Faith of the Fatherless* (Dallas: Spence, 1999), 8–9.

[9]See, for further discussion, ibid.

[10]C. S. Lewis, "The Weight of Glory," in *The Weight of Glory and Other Addresses* (New York: Macmillan, 1965), 6–7.

[11]Ibid., 7.

Chapter 3: God Triune

[1]David Bentley Hart, *The Beauty of the Infinite: The Aesthetics of Christian Truth* (Grand Rapids: Eerdmans, 2003), 174.

[2]J. P. Moreland and William Lane Craig, *Philosophical Foundations of a Christian Worldview* (Downers Grove, Ill.: InterVarsity, 2003), 593–95.

[3]On the Trinity's biblical foundations, see Paul Copan, *That's Just Your Interpretation* (Grand Rapids: Baker, 2001).

[4]Cornelius Plantinga, "The Threeness/Oneness Problem of the Trinity," *Calvin Theological Journal* 23 (1988): 51; Cornelius Plantinga, "The Perfect Family," *Christianity Today* 28 (Mar. 4, 1988): 27.

[5]Plantinga, "The Perfect Family," 27.

[6]Hart, *The Beauty of the Infinite,* 182.

[7]Frank G. Kirkpatrick, *A Moral Ontology for a Theistic Ethic: Gathering the Nations in Love and Justice* (Burlington, Vt.: Ashgate, 2003), 56.

[8]Colin Gunton, *The One, the Three, and the Many* (Cambridge: Cambridge University Press, 1993).

Chapter 4: Talking about God and Knowing God

[1]Lewis Carroll, *Alice in Wonderland & Through the Looking Glass* (Kingsport, Tenn.: Grosset & Dunlap, 1946), 240.

[2]David Hume, *An Enquiry Concerning Human Understanding* (New York: Liberal Arts Press, 1955), 173.

[3]Stephen Davis calls Phillips' assumption—"*objects* are necessarily contingent"—arbitrary. Why not make up a new term, *lobject*, which refers to anything that's *both* (a) *existent* and (b) *noncontingent*? *God, Reason, and Theistic Proofs* (Grand Rapids: Eerdmans, 1997), 50–59.

[4]J. L. Mackie, *The Miracle of Theism* (Oxford: Clarendon Press, 1982), 1–4.

[5]William Alston, "Referring to God," *Philosophy of Religion* 24 (1988): 116, 120. If we need to perfectly define or describe God before he can be evaluated, then we shall have to use *words* constantly, which *also* must be analyzed or defined perfectly—*ad infinitum* (113).

[6]For example, see K. A. Kitchen, *On the Reliability of the Old Testament* (Grand Rapids: Eerdmans, 2003).

[7]Thomas Aquinas, *Summa Theologica,* 1a.3.

[8]William Cowper, "Light Shining out of Darkness," hymn 15 in *Olney Hymns* (London: W. Oliver, 1779).

[9]Some ideas in this chapter are from Colin E. Gunton, *Act and Being: Towards a Theology of the Divine Attributes* (Grand Rapids: Eerdmans, 2003).

[10]Ibid., 63.

[11]Richard John Neuhaus uses this phrase in *Freedom for Ministry* (Grand Rapids: Eerdmans, 1992), ch. 1.

Chapter 5: The Attributes of God (I)

[1]E.g., Michael Martin and Ricki Monnier, eds., *The Impossibility of God* (Amherst, N.Y.: Prometheus Press, 2003); Jordan Howard Sobel, *Logic and Theism: Arguments for and Against Belief in God* (Cambridge: Cambridge University Press, 2004).

[2]In this regard, see Stephen T. Davis's defense of the ontological argument in *The Rationality of Theism,* ed. Paul Copan and Paul K. Moser (London: Routledge, 2003), 93–111.

[3]Paul Davies, "The Birth of the Cosmos," in *God, Cosmos, Nature and Creativity,* ed. Jill Gready (Edinburgh: Scottish Academic Press, 1995), 8–9.

[4]Paul Copan and William Lane Craig, *Creation Out of Nothing: A Biblical, Philosophical, and Scientific Exploration* (Grand Rapids: Baker, 2004).

[5]In Bertrand Russell, "Why I Am Not a Christian," in *Why I Am Not a Christian and Other Essays on Religion and Related Topics* (New York: Simon and Schuster, 1957), 6.

[6]This cantata (BWV 211) expresses a passion for coffee: "Ah, how sweet the coffee's taste is!" and, "Coffee, coffee, I must have it."

[7]Stephen Hawking and Roger Penrose, *The Nature of Space and Time* (Princeton, N.J.: Princeton University Press, 1996), 20.

[8]In a Feb. 1754 letter to John Stewart in *The Letters of David Hume,* 2 vols., ed. J. Y. T. Greig (Oxford: Clarendon Press, 1932), I:187.

[9]See Greg Ganssle, ed., *God and Time: Four Views* (Downers Grove, Ill.: InterVarsity, 2001); William Lane Craig, *Time and Eternity* (Wheaton, Ill.: Crossway, 2001).

[10]James Barr, *Biblical Words for Time* (London: SCM Press, 1962), 80.

[11]The *dynamic* (tensed) view is called the A-theory of time, and the *static* (tenseless) view is the B-theory.

[12]Jay Wesley Richards, *The Untamed God* (Downers Grove, Ill.: InterVarsity, 2003), 202–7.

[13]Jaroslav Pelikan observed that the idea of "an entirely static God" was a Greek philosophical concept adopted by a number of Christian theologians—without much biblical support. *The Emergence of the Catholic Tradition: 100-600: The Christian Tradition,* vol. 1 (Chicago: University of Chicago Press, 1971), 52–53.

[14]God could have created angels prior to the space-time universe, and this would have marked the beginning of time. Or God, anticipating creation, could have counted down in his mind, "Three, two, one...let there be light!" Again, this would be sufficient to ground time as well.

[15]Doesn't God's "foreknowledge" of the creation or redemption of humans suggest a future for God without creation? Scripture uses this term non-technically/-philosophically. It would be more precise to say that upon creation, God's tenseless knowledge of all truths would then become "indexed"–ordered according to his awareness of tensed truths. With creation, God becomes aware of future-tensed truths and thus has foreknowledge. William Lane Craig, "Response to Critics" in *God and Time,* ed. Gregory Ganssle, 175–86; William Craig, *God, Time, and Eternity* (Dordrecht: Kluwer, 2001), 271–75.

[16]Daniel Dennett, "Conditions of Personhood," in *The Identities of Persons,* ed. Amelie Oksenberg Rorty (Berkeley: University of California Press, 1976), 175–96. I'm following William Craig's analysis in *God, Time, and Eternity,* 43–55.

[17]E.g., Michael Martin, "A Disproof of God's Existence," *Darshana* 10 (1970): 22–24.

[18]Michael Martin, "A Disproof of the God of the Common Man," in *The Impossibility of God,* ed. Martin and Monnier, 234.

[19]Exodus 13:17–18; 19:21; 1 Samuel 16:2–3; 2 Kings 21:8; Jeremiah 18:7–10.

[20]Aquinas, *Summa Theologica,* 1.14.13, *ad* 3.

[21]William Craig notes: "I should go so far as to say that the implicit assumption of the perceptual model underlies virtually all contemporary denials of the possibility of divine foreknowledge of free acts." *The Only Wise God* (Grand Rapids: Baker, 1987), 121.

[22]Augustine, *On the Free Choice of the Will,* 3.3.6.

[23]Even if, say, backward causation is possible, the past is still unchangeable. *Changing* the past is different from *causing* the past. If a person prays about an event that has already taken place without knowing the outcome, it could be that his prayers to a foreknowing God causally effect what has already taken place. Craig, *The Only Wise God,* 76–77.

Chapter 6: The Attributes of God (II)

[1]For a philosophical summary of various divine attributes, see William Lane Craig and J. P. Moreland, *Philosophical Foundations of a Christian Worldview* (Downers Grove, Ill.: InterVarsity, 2003), 501–35; William Lane Craig, ed., *Philosophy of Religion: A Reader and Guide* (New Brunswick, N.J.: Rutgers University Press, 2002), 203–15.

[2]Cf. ch. 10 in William Lane Craig, *Time and the Metaphysics of Relativity* (Dordrecht: Kluwer Academic Publishers, 2001).

[3]Kai Nielsen in J. P. Moreland and Kai Nielsen, *Does God Exist?* (Nashville: Nelson, 1990; repr. Prometheus Press, 1993), 53.

[4]Bede Rundle, *Why Is There Something Rather Than Nothing?* (Oxford: Oxford University Press, 2004), 11.

[5]C. S. Lewis, *The Problem of Pain* (New York: Macmillan, 1962), 27–28; cf. George Mavrodes, "Some Puzzles Concerning Omnipotence," in *Readings in the Philosophy of Religion,* ed. Baruch Brody (Englewood Cliffs, N.J.: Prentice-Hall, 1974), 340–42.

[6]This expression is mentioned by Miracle Max (Billy Crystal) in the MGM film *The Princess Bride* (1987), directed by Rob Reiner.

[7]Anselm, *Proslogion* 7.

[8]Anselm, *Why God Became Man* 2.10. Thomas Morris writes that God's inability to sin "only indicates a necessarily firm directedness in the way in which God will *use* his unlimited power." *Our Idea of God* (Downers Grove, Ill.: InterVarsity, 1991), 80.

[9]Aquinas, *Summa Theologica,* I.25.3 *ad* 2.

[10]Michael Martin, *Atheism* (Philadelphia: Temple University Press, 1990), 309.

[11]Charles Taliaferro, *Contemporary Philosophy of Religion* (Malden, Mass.: Blackwell, 1998), 80–81.

[12]The following list is from Thomas P. Flint and Alfred J. Freddoso, "Maximal Power," in *The Existence and Nature of God* (Notre Dame: University of Notre Dame Press, 1983), 81–113.

[13]Taliaferro, *Contemporary Philosophy of Religion,* 75.

[14]See William Lane Craig's interesting discussion on tachyons and time travel and their relationship to philosophy of religion: "Tachyons, Time Travel, and Divine Omniscience," *The Journal of Philosophy* 85 (1988): 135–50. Even if backward causation is theoretically possible via tachyons (from the Greek *taxis,* "swift"–i.e., particles made to travel faster than the speed of light) and time travel, there is still the question of practical feasibility (i.e., saying that backward causation *won't* occur, not that it *can't*). In any event, such scenarios

wouldn't entail fatalism as they are distinct from human free choices and hardly undermine the compatibility of divine foreknowledge and human freedom.

[15]Colin E. Gunton, *Act and Being: Towards a Theology of the Divine Attributes* (Grand Rapids: Eerdmans, 2003), 126.

[16]Jay Wesley Richards, *The Untamed God* (Downers Grove, Ill.: InterVarsity, 2003), 196. See Richards' more detailed discussion of immutability.

[17]Jaroslav Pelikan, *The Emergence of the Catholic Tradition: 100-600: The Christian Tradition*, vol. 1 (Chicago: University of Chicago Press, 1971), 52–53.

[18]H. Van Dyke Parunak, "A Semantic Survey of *NHM*," *Biblica* 56 (1975): 512–32; R. B. Chisholm, "Does God 'Change His Mind'?" *Bibliotheca Sacra* 152 (Oct.–Dec. 1995): 387–99.

[19]This meaning of "repent" (*nacham*) in the Niphal is found in Exodus 32:12, 14; 1 Samuel 15:29; Psalm 110:4; Isaiah 57:6; Jeremiah 4:28; 15:6; 18:8, 10; 26:3, 13, 19; Ezekiel 24:14; Joel 2:13-14; Amos 7:3, 6; Jonah 3:9-10; 4:2; Zechariah 8:14.

[20]D. A. Carson, *How Long, O Lord?* (Grand Rapids: Baker, 1990), 186, 187–88.

[21]Pelikan, *Emergence of the Catholic Tradition*, 52–53.

[22]Richard Creel, "Immutability and Impassibility," in *A Companion to Philosophy of Religion*, ed. Philip Quinn and Charles Taliaferro (Malden, Mass.: Blackwell, 1997), 118.

[23]Alvin Plantinga, "A Christian Life Partly Lived," in *Philosophers Who Believe*, ed. Kelly James Clark (Downers Grove, Ill.: InterVarsity, 1993), 71.

[24]Gunton, *Act and Being*, 128–29.

[25]Rundle, *Why Is There Something?* 18 (citing Hume's *Dialogue Concerning Natural Religion*). I draw from C. S. Lewis, *Reflections on the Psalms* (New York: Harcourt Brace Jovanovich, 1958); idem, "The Weight of Glory" in *The Weight of Glory and Other Addresses* (New York: Macmillan, 1965); and idem, "The Great Sin" in bk. 3, ch. 8 of *Mere Christianity* (New York: Macmillan, 1952); Charles Taliaferro, "The Vanity of God," *Faith and Philosophy* 6 (April 1989): 140–54.

[26]See Paul Copan, "Divine Narcissism? A Further Defense of God's Humility," *Philosophia Christi* n.s. 8/2 (Winter 2006): 336–46.

[27]N. T. Wright, *For All God's Worth: True Worship and the Calling of the Church* (Grand Rapids: Eerdmans, 1997), 7.

[28]Richard Bauckham, *Bible and Mission: Christian Witness in a Postmodern World* (Grand Rapids/Carlisle, UK: Baker/Paternoster, 2004), 37.

[29]E.g., Exodus 20:5; 34:14; Deuteronomy 4:24; 6:15; 29:20; 32:16, 21; Joshua 24:19; 1 Kings 14:22; Ezekiel 8:3 (a graven "image of jealousy"); 16:38, 42–43; 39:25; Joel 2:18; Nahum 1:2; Zephaniah 1:18; 3:8; Zechariah 1:14; 8:2; 1 Corinthians 10:22.

[30]Frank G. Kirkpatrick, *A Moral Ontology for a Theistic Ethic: Gathering the Nations in Love and Justice* (Burlington, Vt.: Ashgate, 2003), 61–76.

[31]Some people may object to this point by bringing up passages such as Isaiah 43:21 ("The people whom I formed for Myself, will declare my praise") or Psalm 8:2/Matthew 21:16 (God's ordaining praise from the mouths of infants). See also Ephesians 1:6, 12, 14. But these passages can easily be reconciled with the point I have made.

[32]C. S. Lewis, *Reflections on the Psalms*, 94–95.

[33]C. S. Lewis, "The Weight of Glory" in *The Weight of Glory and Other Addresses*, 4–5.

[34]Colin E. Gunton, *The Christian Faith: An Introduction to Christian Doctrine* (Oxford: Blackwell, 2002), 181.

[35]Richards, *The Untamed God* (ch. 9) gives a nicely nuanced presentation and assessment of these versions. I borrow from some of his insights.

[36]Though we may not accept the classic understanding of simplicity, we can speak of, say, God's knowledge as being simple. Cf. William Alston, "Does God Have Beliefs?" *Religious Studies* 22 (1986): 287–306.

[37]Though *not* in the Aristotelian (and Thomistic) sense, which sees potency and actuality as creaturely.

[38]Cf. Paul Copan and William Lane Craig, *Creation Out of Nothing: A Biblical, Philosophical, and Scientific Exploration* (Grand Rapids: Baker, 2004), 173–80.

Chapter 7: The God of Truth

[1]Friedrich Nietzsche, *Human, All Too Human* (Cambridge: Cambridge University Press, 1986), 13.

²See Kevin Vanhoozer, *Is There a Meaning in This Text?* (Grand Rapids: Zondervan, 1998).

³Huston Smith, "The Religious Significance of Postmodernism: A Rejoinder," *Faith and Philosophy* 12 (July 1995): 415.

⁴John R. Searle, *Mind, Language and Society: Philosophy in the Real World* (New York: Basic, 1998), 17.

⁵Dallas Willard, "Toward a Phenomenology for the Correspondence Theory of Truth," *Discipline filosofiche* 1 (1991): 125–47. Found online at www.dallaswillard.com.

⁶Toby Lester, "What Is the Koran?" *Atlantic Monthly* (January 1999): 44; W. St. Clair-Tisdall, *A Manual of the Leading Muhammedan Objections to Christianity* (London: n.p., 1904).

⁷F. F. Bruce, *The New Testament Documents: Are They Reliable?* (Downers Grove, Ill.: InterVarsity, 2003 [repr. ed.]).

Chapter 8: Proofs or Pointers?

¹E.g., Jeffery L. Sheler, *Is the Bible True?* (San Francisco: HarperSanFrancisco, 1999); Kenneth A. Kitchen, *On the Reliability of the Old Testament* (Grand Rapids: Eerdmans, 2003); F. F. Bruce, *The New Testament Documents: Are They Reliable?* (Downer's Grove, Ill.: InterVarsity, 2003 [rev.ed]).

²E.g., John Hick, *An Interpretation of Religion* (London: Macmillan, 1989), 73–74 (2d ed., 2004).

³Thomas Aquinas, *Summa Theologica,* I.2.3.

⁴Stephen T. Davis, *God, Reason, and Theistic Proofs* (Grand Rapids: Eerdmans, 1997), 4.

⁵"My Pilgrimage from Atheism to Theism: A Discussion between Antony Flew and Gary Habermas," *Philosophia Christi* n.s. 6/2 (2004): 197–211.

⁶Dallas Willard, "Language, Being, God, and the Three Stages of Theistic Evidence," in J. P. Moreland and Kai Nielsen, *Does God Exist? The Great Debate* (Nashville: Thomas Nelson, 1990), 207.

⁷Stephen T. Davis, *God, Reason, and Theistic Proofs,* 5.

⁸"A Conversation with the Dalai Lama," *TIME* (Asia) 18 (October 2004), http://www.time.com/time/asia/magazine/article/0,13673,501041025-725176,00.html. Accessed Jan. 30, 2006.

Chapter 9: Arguments for God's Existence

¹I'm skipping over the fascinating, (I think, illuminating) abstract, and often-elusive ontological argument—a conceptual or *a priori* ("prior to experience") argument for God's existence. It argues from the definition of God to his necessary existence. It's an argument that can contribute to the cumulative case for God's existence. I'll be focusing, however, on some of the main *a posteriori* theistic arguments ("in light of experience"). However, see Stephen Davis's "Ontological Argument" in *The Rationality of Theism,* ed. Paul Copan and Paul K. Moser (London: Routledge, 2003); William Lane Craig, "The Ontological Argument" in *To Everyone an Answer,* ed. Francis Beckwith, et al. (Downers Grove, Ill.: InterVarsity, 2004); Daniel Dombrowski, *Rethinking the Ontological Argument* (Cambridge: Cambridge University Press, 2006).

²In John Hick, ed., *The Existence of God* (New York: Collier, 1964), 175.

³Michael Martin, *Atheism* (Philadelphia: Temple University Press, 1990), 106.

⁴William Lane Craig has done fine work on this topic; see his *Kalam Cosmological Argument* (New York: Macmillan, 1980).

⁵See Alexander R. Pruss, *The Principle of Sufficient Reason: A Reassessment* (Cambridge: Cambridge University Press, 2006).

⁶Some of these insights are taken from Stephen T. Davis, "The Cosmological Argument and the Epistemic Status of Belief in God," *Philosophia Christi* n.s. 1 (1999): 5–15. I won't be addressing the *Thomistic* argument here.

⁷Ibid., 13.

⁸Ibid. Empiricist John Locke still recognized that "man knows by an intuitive certainty, that bare nothing can no more produce any real being, than it can be equal to two right angles" (*Essay in Human Understanding,* 4.10).

[9]Paul Williams, *The Unexpected Way: On Converting from Buddhism to Catholicism* (Edinburgh: T & T Clark, 2002), 27–30. Cf. Harold Netland, "Natural Theology and Religious Diversity," *Faith and Philosophy* 21 (Oct. 2004): 503–18.

[10]Charlotte Brontë, *Jane Eyre*, III.28.9.

[11]Stephen C. Meyer, "A Scopes Trial for the '90s," *Wall Street Journal*, December 6, 1993, A14.

[12]See Del Ratzsch, *Nature, Design, and Science: The Status of Design in Natural Science* (Albany, N.Y.: SUNY Press, 2001), from which I draw.

[13]John Leslie, *Universes* (London: Routledge, 1989), 103.

[14]Brandon Carter, "Large Number Coincidences and the Anthropic Principle in Cosmology," in *Confrontation of Cosmological Theories with Observational Data*, ed. M. S. Longair (Dordrecht: Reidel, 1974), 72.

[15]Leslie, *Universes*, 99.

[16]Ibid., 102.

[17]John Barrow and Joseph Silk, *The Left Hand of Creation*, 2nd ed. (New York: Oxford University Press, 1993), 227, 26, 227, 38.

[18]Stephen Hawking, *A Brief History of Time* (New York: Bantam, 1988), 121–22.

[19]Roger Penrose, *The Emperor's New Mind* (New York: Oxford University Press, 1989), 344.

[20]Paul Davies, *The Mind of God* (New York: Simon and Schuster, 1992), 169.

[21]John Earman, "The SAP Also Rises: A Critical Examination of the Anthropic Principle," *American Philosophical Quarterly* 24 (1987): 312.

[22]Paul Davies, *Are We Alone?* (New York: Basic, 1995), 96.

[23]Immanuel Kant, *The Critique of Pure Reason*, trans. Norman Kemp Smith (New York: St. Martin's Press, 1929, 2nd ed.), 521 (A 625-26/B 653-54).

[24]Ratzsch, *Nature, Design, and Science*, 24.

[25]Ibid., 58.

[26]See Psalm 104:21, 29; Job 39:28–29; 41:1, 10, 14; cp. 1 Corinthians 10:25–26; 1 Timothy 4:3–4. John Goldingay reminds us: "Animal inclination to kill and eat other animals is built into their nature as animals and is part of the 'goodness' of creation, yet holding them back from doing that is part of humanity's vocation." *Old Testament Theology: Israel's Story*, vol. 1 (Downers Grove, Ill.: InterVarsity, 2003), 111.

[27]See Mark S. Whorton, *Peril in Paradise* (Waynesboro, Ga.: Authentic Media, 2005).

[28]Paul Davies, "Physics and the Mind of God," *First Things* (Aug./Sept. 1995): 34.

[29]C. S. Lewis, *The Abolition of Man* (San Francisco: HarperSanFrancisco, 2001), appendix.

[30]Kai Nielsen, *Ethics Without God*, rev. ed. (Buffalo: Prometheus Books, 1990), 10–11.

[31]E.g., Russ Shafer-Landau, *Moral Realism: A Defence* (New York: Oxford University Press, 2005).

[32]The necessity of moral truths doesn't make God irrelevant; such truths *still* require grounding in a personal God's good character: he necessarily exists in all possible worlds, is the source of all necessary moral truths, and is explanatorily prior—more basic—to these moral values. They would stand in asymmetrical relation to his necessity—like a pendulum, whose period (completed swing) can be deduced from the pendulum's length, but not vice versa (i.e., the pendulum's length explains its period, not the reverse). William E. Mann, "Necessity," in *Companion to Philosophy of Religion*, ed. William Quinn and Charles Taliaferro (Malden, Mass.: Blackwell, 1997).

[33]T. L. Carson, *Value and the Good Life* (Notre Dame: University of Notre Dame Press, 2000), 194.

[34]Derk Pereboom, *Living Without Free Will* (Cambridge: Cambridge University Press, 2001), xiii–xiv.

[35]J. L. Mackie, *The Miracle of Theism* (Oxford: Clarendon Press, 1982), 115.

[36]Letter to W. G. Down, 3 July 1881, in *The Life and Letters of Charles Darwin Including an Autobiographical Chapter*, ed. Francis Darwin (London: John Murray, Abermarle Street, 1887), 1:315-16.

[37]John Hare, *The Moral Gap: Kantian Ethics, Human Limits, and God's Assistance* (Oxford: Clarendon Press, 1996).

[38]John Rist, *Real Ethics* (Cambridge: Cambridge University Press, 2001), 1.

[39]Paul Draper, "Seeking But Not Believing," in *Divine Hiddenness: New Essays*, ed. Daniel Howard-Snyder and Paul K. Moser (Cambridge: Cambridge University Press, 2002), 204.

[40]Alvin Pantinga, as quoted in Rupert Shortt, *God's Advocates: Christian Thinkers in Conversation* (Grand Rapids: Eerdmans, 2005), 44.

[41]Uwe Siemon-Netto, "J.S. Bach in Japan," *First Things* 104 (June/July 2000): 15–17.

[42]Eugene P. Wigner, "The Unreasonable Effectiveness of Mathematics in the Natural Sciences." Found online at http://www.dartmouth.edu/~matc/MathDrama/reading/Wigner.html. Accessed 18 Aug. 2006.

[43]Steven Weinberg, *Dreams of a Final Theory* (New York: Vintage Books, 1992), 250.

[44]From Jonathan Edwards' *Personal Narrative* (c. 1740). PDF available through http://edwards.yale.edu/.

[45]Cf. George Appleton, ed., *The Oxford Book of Prayer* (Oxford: Oxford University Press, 1985).

[46]Cf. G. W. Hansen, "The Preaching and Defence of Paul," in *Witness to the Gospel: The Theology of Acts*, ed. I. H. Marshall and David Peterson (Grand Rapids: Eerdmans, 1998).

[47]Rudolf Otto, *The Idea of the Holy* (New York: Oxford, 1958). We won't deal here with sensory or visionary experiences, given their greatly varied nature.

[48]For some qualifying remarks on Otto, see Winfried Corduan, *The Tapestry of Faiths* (Downers Grove, Ill.: InterVarsity Press, 2002) 204–5.

[49]Richard Swinburne, *The Existence of God* (Oxford: Clarendon Press, 1979), 254. William Alston shows that "mystical perception" is parallel to sense perception in his *Perceiving God: The Epistemology of Religious Experience* (Ithaca, N.Y.: Cornell University Press, 1991). While not equivalent, they're *somewhat* alike, and the principle of credulity can aptly be applied to both.

[50]See R. Douglas Geivett, "The Evidential Value of Religious Experience," in *The Rationality of Theism,* ed. Paul Copan and Paul K. Moser (London: Routledge, 2003); Keith Yandell, *The Epistemology of Religious Experience* (Cambridge: Cambridge University Press, 1993).

[51]Also William Wainwright, *Philosophy of Religion,* 2nd ed. (Belmont, Calif.: Wadsworth, 1999), 120–38. Cf. J. P. Moreland's nice summary in *Scaling the Secular City* (Grand Rapids: Baker, 1987). Some people object to religious-experience arguments because they can't be "cross-checked"—presumably by sense experience or "scientific" criteria. But since *religious experience* provides us with our primary access to *divine* reality, and since God reveals himself when and as he pleases, we shouldn't expect that there necessarily *has* to be independent justification for religious experience (Wainwright, *Philosophy of Religion,* 132).

[52]From Geivett, "Evidential Value of Religious Experience."

Chapter 10: God–The Best Explanation

[1]John R. Searle, *Mind, Language and Society: Philosophy in the Real World* (New York: Basic, 1998), 36.

[2]Alvin Plantinga, "Natural Theology," in *Companion to Metaphysics,* ed. Jaegwon Kim and Ernest Sosa (Malden, Mass.: Blackwell, 1995), 347.

[3]Ninian Smart, "Religion as a Discipline," in *Concept and Empathy,* ed. Donald Wiebe (New York: New York University Press, 1986), 161.

[4]Jaegwon Kim, "Mental Causation and Two Conceptions of Mental Properties." Paper presented at the American Philosophical Association Eastern Division Meeting (December 1993), 2–23.

[5]Edward O. Wilson, *Consilience: The Unity of Knowledge* (New York: Knopf, 1998), 266.

[6]Ned Block, "Consciousness," in *A Companion to the Philosophy of Mind,* ed. Samuel Guttenplan (Malden, Mass.: Blackwell, 1994), 211.

[7]John Searle, "The Mystery of Consciousness: Part II," *New York Review of Books* (Nov. 16, 1995): 61.

[8]Jaegwon Kim, "Mind, Problems of the Philosophy of," s.v. *The Oxford Companion to Philosophy,* ed. Ted Honderich (New York: Oxford University Press, 1995), 578.

[9]Colin McGinn, *The Mysterious Flame* (New York: Basic Books, 1999), 14.

[10]Colin McGinn, *The Problem of Consciousness* (Oxford: Basil Blackwell, 1990), 10–11.

[11]David Papineau, *Philosopical Naturalism* (Oxford: Blackwell, 1993), 119.

[12]Thomas Nagel, *The View from Nowhere* (New York: Oxford University Press, 1986), 111, 113.

[13]Jane Goodall, *Through a Window* (Boston: Houghton Mifflin, 1990), 109.

[14]John Searle, *Minds, Brains, and Science* (Cambridge, Mass.: Harvard University Press, 1986 repr.) 87, 88, 92.

[15]Francis Crick, *The Astonishing Hypothesis: The Scientific Search for the Soul* (New York: Charles Scribner's Sons, 1994), 3.

[16]Richard Rorty, "Untruth and Consequences," *The New Republic* (31 July 1995): 32–36.

[17]Simon Blackburn, *Being Good: A Short Introduction to Ethics* (New York: Oxford University Press, 2001), 133, 134.

[18]Bertrand Russell, *Human Society in Ethics and Politics* (London: Allen & Unwin, 1954), 124.

[19]Derk Pereboom, *Living Without Free Will* (Cambridge: Cambridge University Press, 2001), xiii–xiv.

[20]Edward O. Wilson, *Consilience* (New York: Knopf, 1998), 268, 269.

[21]James Rachels, *Created From Animals: The Moral Implications of Darwinism* (Oxford: Oxford University Press, 1990), 77.

[22]J. L. Mackie, *The Miracle of Theism* (Oxford: Clarendon Press, 1982), 115.

[23]Stephen Hawking and Roger Penrose, *The Nature of Space and Time* (Princeton, N.J.: Princeton University Press, 1996), 20.

[24]Cited in John D. Barrow, *The World Within the World* (Oxford: Clarendon Press, 1988), 226.

[25]John Barrow and Joseph Silk, *The Left Hand of Creation,* 2nd ed. (New York: Oxford University Press, 1993), 38, 209.

[26]Anthony Kenny, *The Five Ways* (New York: Schocken, 1969), 66.

[27]Kai Nielsen, *Reason and Practice* (New York: Harper & Row, 1971), 48.

[28]Francis Crick, *Life Itself: Its Nature and Origin* (New York: Simon & Schuster, 1981), 88.

[29]Jacques Monod, *Chance and Necessity* (London: Collins, 1972), 134–35.

[30]See Charles B. Thaxton, Walter L. Bradley, Roger L. Olsen, *The Mystery of Life's Origin* (New York: Philosophical Library, 1984).

[31]Paul Davies (a Deist of sorts) makes this claim in *The Fifth Miracle* (New York: Simon & Schuster, 1999), 272.

[32]Bernard Carr and Martin Rees, "The Anthropic Principle," *Nature* 278 (1979): 612.

[33]Fred Hoyle, *The Intelligent Universe* (London: Michael Joseph, 1983), 220.

[34]See the introduction to Antony Flew's *God and Philosophy,* 2nd ed. (Amherst, N.Y.: Prometheus, 2005).

[35]John Wheeler, cited in Gerald Schroeder, "Can God Be Brought into the Equation?" Review of *Science and Religion: Are They Compatible?* ed. Paul Kurtz and Barry Karr, in the *Jerusalem Post,* May 23, 2003, 13B. See Paul Davies, *The Fifth Miracle,* 272.

[36]Richard Dawkins, *The Blind Watchmaker* (New York: Norton, 1986), 1.

[37]Francis Crick, *What Mad Pursuit* (New York: BasicBooks, 1988), 138.

[38]Dawkins, *Blind Watchmaker,* 6.

[39]Charles Darwin, *The Origin of Species,* corr. ed. (New York: Thomas Y. Crowell, n.d.), 459, 460.

[40]Paul Draper, "Seeking But Not Believing," in *Divine Hiddenness: New Essays,* ed. Daniel Howard-Snyder and Paul K. Moser (Cambridge: Cambridge University Press, 2002), 204.

[41]Paul A. M. Dirac, "The evolution of the physicist's picture of nature," *Scientific American* 208/5 (May 1963): 47.

[42]Bertrand Russell, cited in Eugene Wigner, "The Unreasonable Effectiveness of Mathematics in the Natural Sciences." Found online at http://www.dartmouth.edu/~matc/MathDrama/reading/Wigner.html. Accessed 18 Aug. 2006.

Chapter 11: Science, Nature, and the Possiblity of Miracles

[1]Richard Dawkins, *River Out of Eden: A Darwinian View of Life* (New York: BasicBooks, 1995), 33.

[2]Richard Lewontin, "Billions and Billions of Demons," *NY Review of Books* (Jan. 9, 1997): 28–32.

[3]Del Ratzsch, *Philosophy of Science* (Downers Grove, Ill: InterVarsity, 1986), 15.

[4]Stanley Jaki, *The Savior of Science* (Washington: Regnery Gateway, 1988).

[5]John Post, *Metaphysics: A Contemporary Introduction* (New York: Paragon House, 1991), 85.

[6]Carl Sagan, *Cosmos* (New York: Random House, 1980), 4.

[7]See Robert C. Koons, "Theism and Science," in *The Rationality of Theism*, ed. Paul Copan and Paul K. Moser (London: Routledge, 2003).

[8]Cited in Mark Noll, *The Scandal of the Evangelical Mind* (Grand Rapids: Eerdmans, 1994), 205–6.

[9]Del Ratzsch, *Nature, Design, and Science: The Status of Design in Natural Science* (Albany, N.Y.: SUNY Press, 2001), 142–43.

[10]Cited in Jaroslav Pelikan, *Jesus Through the Centuries* (New York: Harper & Row, 1985), 190.

[11]I myself have experienced and have known trustworthy people who have witnessed specific indicators of divine involvement in their lives and remarkably precise answers to prayer. For a sampling, note the personal experiences recounted in J. P. Moreland and Klaus Issler, *The Lost Virtue of Happiness* (Colorado Springs: NavPress, 2006), 113–14, 172–75; J. P. Moreland, *Kingdom Triangle* (Grand Rapids: Zondervan, 2007), ch. 7. Helen Roseveare's story about a dying baby, a hot water bottle, and a doll in *Living Faith* (Minneapolis: Bethany House, 1987); Tom Morris's story of the beach ball in *Philosophy for Dummies* (New York: IDG Books, 1999), 233–36; A. T. Pierson, *George Müller of Bristol* (Grand Rapids: Kregel, 1999 [repr.]) or George Mueller's autobiography; the story of Sadhu Sundar Singh's dramatic conversion in Charles E. Moore, *Sadhu Sundar Singh: Essential Writings* (Maryknoll, N.Y.: Orbis, 2005), 11–15; Pauline Selby, *Persian Springs: Four Iranians See Jesus* (London: Elam Ministries, 2001); David H. Greenlee, *From the Straight Path to the Narrow Way: Journeys of Faith* (Waynesboro, Ga.: Authentic Media, 2005); Craig S. Keener, *Gift and Giver* (Grand Rapids: Baker, 2001), esp. 175–76. While some may explain many of these testimonies and answers to prayer as coincidental or otherwise ambiguous, I think the activity and concern of God offer a more plausible context to explain them.

[12]Technically, supernatural acts alone don't establish any religious claim but must be understood by the broader religious and theological backdrop (Deut. 13:1–5; 2 Thess. 2:9–10; Rev. 13:13; 16:14).

[13]I've (co)edited three books on this topic; scholars such as William Craig, N. T. Wright, Stephen Davis, and Gary Habermas have done much good work on Jesus' resurrection.

[14]Richard Dawkins, *A Devil's Chaplain* (Boston: Houghton Mifflin, 2003), 150.

[15]Frank G. Kirkpatrick, *A Moral Ontology for a Theistic Ethic: Gathering the Nations in Love and Justice* (Burlington, Vt.: Ashgate, 2003), 55.

[16]Rudolf Bultmann, *Kerygma and Myth* (New York: Harper, 1961), 4–5.

[17]C. S. Lewis, *Miracles* (New York: Macmillan, 1960), 3.

[18]John Earman, *Hume's Abject Failure* (New York: Oxford University Press, 2000).

[19]See Gary R. Habermas, "Resurrection Research from 1975 to the Present: What Are Critical Scholars Saying?" *Journal for the Study of the Historical Jesus* 3/2 (2005): 135–53.

[20]Efforts to find parallels between Christianity and these mystery religions "have failed, as virtually all Pauline scholars now recognize," and to do so "is an attempt to turn the clock back in a way now forbidden by the most massive and learned studies on the subject." N. T. Wright, *What Saint Paul Really Said* (Grand Rapids: Eerdmans, 1997), 172, 173. Historian Michael Grant notes that Judaism was a milieu to which doctrines of deaths and rebirths of mythical gods seem so entirely foreign that the emergence of such a fabrication from its midst is very hard to credit. And *no* dying-and-rising-god cults existed in first-century Palestine. *Jesus: An Historian's Review of the Gospels* (New York: Scribner's, 1992), 199.

[21]N. T. Wright, *The Resurrection of the Son of God* (Minneapolis: Fortress, 2003), 710.

[22]James D. G. Dunn, *Jesus Remembered* (Grand Rapids: Eerdmans, 2003), 855.

[23]Earman, *Hume's Abject Failure,* 43.

[24]See Charles Taliaferro and Anders Hendrickson, "Hume's Racism and His Case against the Miraculous," *Philosophia Christi* n.s. 4 (2002): 427–41.

[25]Rundle, *Why Is There Something Rather Than Nothing?* (Oxford: Oxford University Press, 2004), 28.

[26]Even Harvard scholar Helmut Koester notes that it is never claimed that Osiris rose from the dead. *Introduction to the New Testament (I): History, Culture, and Religion of the Hellenistic Age* (Philadelphia: Fortress, 1982), 190.

[27]Gary Habermas, "Resurrection Claims in Non-Christian Religions," *Religious Studies* 25 (1989): 167–77.

[28]See David K. Clark's excellent essay, "Miracles in the World Religions," in *In Defense of Miracles,* ed. R. Douglas Geivett and Gary R. Habermas (Downers Grove, Ill.: InterVarsity, 1997), 199–213.

[29]Available from the Smithsonian's Department of Anthropology in Washington, D.C.

Chapter 12: The Problem(s) of Evil

[1]N. T. Wright, *Evil and the Justice of God* (Downers Grove, Ill.: InterVarsity, 2006), whose insights are reflected throughout this chapter.

[2]Richard Dawkins, *River Out of Eden: A Darwinian View of Life* (New York: BasicBooks, 1995), 132–33.

[3]C. S. Lewis, *The Problem of Pain* (New York: Macmillan, 1962), 10.

[4]Daniel Howard-Snyder, "God, Evil, and Suffering," in *Reason for the Hope Within,* ed. Michael J. Murray (Grand Rapids: Eerdmans, 1999), 78–79.

[5]R. Douglas Geivett, "A Neglected Aspect of the Problem of Evil." Paper at the Evangelical Philosophical Society meeting, Orlando, Fla. (November 1998); cp. Bill Anglin and Stewart Goetz, "Evil Is Privation," *International Journal for Philosophy of Religion* 13 (1982): 3–12.

[6]C. S. Lewis, *Mere Christianity* (New York: Macmillan, 1952), 45–46.

[7]J. L. Mackie, "Evil and Omnipotence" in *Readings in the Philosophy of Religion: An Analytic Approach,* ed. Baruch Brody (Englewood Cliffs, N.J.: Prentice-Hall, 1992).

[8]Richard Swinburne, "Why God Allows Evil," in *Contemporary Philosophy of Religion,* ed. Steven Cahn and David Shatz (Oxford: Oxford University Press, 1982), 8.

[9]Howard-Snyder, "God, Evil, and Suffering," 84.

[10]Peter van Inwagen, "The Problem of Evil, the Problem of Air, and the Problem of Silence," in *The Evidential Problem from Evil,* ed. Daniel Howard-Snyder (Bloomington, Ind.: Indiana University Press, 1996), 150.

[11]William L. Rowe, "The Problem of Evil and Some Varieties of Atheism," *American Philosophical Quarterly* 16 (October 1979): 41n.

[12]E.g., Howard-Snyder, ed., *The Evidential Problem from Evil.*

[13]Peter van Inwagen, "The Magnitude, Duration, and Distribution of Evil," in *God, Knowledge and Mystery: Essays in Philosophical Theology* (Ithaca, N.Y.: Cornell University Press, 1995).

[14]Lewis, *The Problem of Pain,* 93.

[15]See chapters 16 and 17 in Paul Copan, *"That's Just Your Interpretation"* (Grand Rapids: Baker, 2001); and chapter 9 in Paul Copan, *"How Do You Know You're Not Wrong?"* (Grand Rapids: Baker, 2005).

[16]Howard-Snyder, "God, Evil, and Suffering," 93.

[17]M. Scott Peck, *People of the Lie* (New York: Simon and Schuster, 1983); and idem, *Glimpses of the Devil* (New York: Free Press, 2005).

[18]See Gordon Graham's brilliant book, *Evil and Christian Ethics* (Cambridge: Cambridge University Press, 2001).

[19]In Dahmer's last public interview, he affirmed: "I've since come to believe that the Lord Jesus Christ is truly God, and I believe that I, as well as everyone else, will be accountable to him." *Dateline NBC* (29 Nov. 1994).

[20]See Richard Bauckham, *God Crucified: Monotheism and Christology in the New Testament* (Grand Rapids: Eerdmans, 1998).

[21]Alvin Plantinga, "A Christian Life Partly Lived," in *Philosophers Who Believe,* ed. Kelly James Clark (Downers Grove, Ill.: InterVarsity, 1993), 71.

[22]Martin Hengel, *Crucifixion* (London: SCM Press, 1977), 1.

Chapter 13: The Hiddenness of God

[1]Friedrich Nietzsche, *Daybreak,* trans. R. J. Hollingdale (Cambridge: Cambridge University Press, 1982), 89–90.

[2]N. R. Hanson, *What I Do Not Believe and Other Essays* (New York: Humanities Press, 1971), 313–14.

[3]John R. Searle, *Mind, Language and Society: Philosophy in the Real World* (New York: Basic, 1998), 36. See the introduction to chapter 10 above.

[4]Thomas Nagel, *The Last Word* (New York: Oxford University Press, 1997), 130 (my emphasis).

[5]Sara Teasdale, "Mastery," in *The Collected Poems of Sara Teasdale* (New York: Macmillan, 1939), 121.

[6]Some of these comments are taken from Paul K. Moser's essay, "Divine Hiddenness, Death, and Meaning" in *Philosophy of Religion: Classic and Contemporary Issues,* ed. Paul Copan and Chad V. Meister (Oxford: Blackwell, 2008).

[7]Pascal, *Pensées,* #430.

[8]Furthermore, we should carefully guard ourselves against the spirit-dulling, deperson-alizing dangers of modernity. Modern society's automation and technology promote instant gratification and a greater sense of control over our lives. Our sense for God, too, may be sufficiently dulled. Modernity can easily make practical atheists of us all. See Craig M. Gay, *The Way of the (Modern) World* (Grand Rapids: Eerdmans, 1998).

[9]See Paul K. Moser's *Why Isn't God More Obvious? Knowing the God Who Hides and Seeks* (Atlanta, Ga.: RZIM, 2000). I am indebted to Moser for a number of points in this chapter.

[10]Pascal, *Pensées,* 38 (#99).

Chapter 14: Original Sin

[1]For a more expanded discussion, see Paul Copan, "Original Sin and Christian Philosophy," *Philosophia Christi* n.s. 5/2 (2003): 519–41.

[2]Edward T. Oakes, "Original Sin: A Disputation," *First Things* 87 (1998): 16.

[3]Colin E. Gunton, *The Triune Creator: A Historical and Systematic Study* (Grand Rapids: Eerdmans, 1998), 203.

[4]Henri Blocher, *Original Sin* (Downers Grove, Ill.: InterVarsity, 2000), 128.

[5]James Leo Garrett, Jr., *Systematic Theology,* vol. 1 (Grand Rapids: Eerdmans, 1990), 493.

[6]Douglas Moo, *The Epistle to the Romans,* New International Commentary on the New Testament (Grand Rapids: Eerdmans, 1996), 328n.

[7]Alvin Plantinga, *Warranted Christian Belief* (New York: Oxford University Press, 2000), 206–7.

[8]Though he denies the doctrine of original sin, Richard Swinburne argues that "bad desires incline," but "they do not (as such) necessitate." *Responsibility and Atonement* (Oxford: Clarendon Press, 1989), 138.

[9]Moo, *Romans,* 331. On various theories of how sin is transmitted, see Charles Sherlock, *The Doctrine of Humanity* (Downers Grove, Ill.: InterVarsity, 1996), 233–38.

[10]We could add that fallen human *society* or *culture*–"the world"–requires redemption; its idolatrous, oppressive, and unjust structures and lifestyles undermine human flourishing.

[11]Millard Erickson, *Christian Theology* (Grand Rapids: Baker, 1983–85), 639; Gordon R. Lewis and Bruce A. Demarest, *Integrative Theology,* 3 vols. (Grand Rapids: Zondervan, 1996), 2:235

[12]G. K. Chesterton, *Orthodoxy* (Garden City, N.Y.: Image/Doubleday, 1959, repr. ed.), 15.

[13]Michael Ruse, "Darwinism and Christianity Redux: A Response to My Critics," *Philosophia Christi* n.s. 4/1 (2002): 192.

[14]See Arthur Koestler, *The Lotus and the Robot* (New York: Macmillan, 1961), 273–74.

[15]Cf. Gordon Graham, *Evil and Christian Ethics* (Cambridge: Cambridge University Press, 2001); Karl Menninger, *Whatever Became of Sin?* (New York: Hawthorn Books, 1973).

[16]Paul C. Vitz, *Psychology as Religion* (Grand Rapids: Eerdmans, 1977), 104.

[17]O. Hobart Mowrer, *The Crisis in Psychiatry and Religion* (Princeton: Van Nostrand, 1961), 40.

[18]Vernon Grounds, "Called to Be Saints–Not Well-adjusted Sinners," *Christianity Today* (Jan. 17, 1986): 28.

[19]Gary Anderson, *"Necessarium Adae Peccatum*: The Problem of Original Sin," in *Sin, Death, and the Devil,* ed. Carl E. Braaten and Robert W. Jenson (Grand Rapids: Eerdmans, 2000), 38.

[20]Stephen J. Duffy, "Our Hearts of Darkness: Original Sin Revisited," *Theological Studies* 49 (1988): 618.

[21]John Hare, *The Moral Gap: Kantian Ethics, Human Limits, and God's Assistance* (Oxford: Clarendon Press, 1996).

[22]Terence Penelhum, *Christian Ethics and Human Nature* (Harrisburg, Pa.: Trinity Press International, 2000), 22, 41.

[23]Joel B. Green and Mark D. Baker, *Recovering the Scandal of the Cross* (Downers Grove, Ill.: InterVarsity, 2000), 54–55, 95.

[24]Cf. Lk. 18:11.

Chapter 15: Hell

[1]See William Lane Craig (debate with Ray Bradley), "Can a Loving God Send People to Hell?" Debate found at http://www.leaderu.com/offices/billcraig/docs/craig-bradley0.html.

[2]C. S. Lewis, *The Great Divorce* (London: Geoffrey Bles, 1946).

[3]Peter Kreeft and Ron Tacelli, *Handbook of Christian Apologetics* (Downers Grove, Ill.: InterVarsity, 1994), 300.

[4]Stephen Travis, "The Problem of Judgment," *Themelios* 11 (Jan. 1986): 53.

[5]C. S. Lewis, *The Screwtape Letters* (New York: Macmillan), 38.

[6]George MacDonald, as quoted in C. S. Lewis, *George MacDonald: An Anthology* (New York: Macmillan, 1948), 85.

[7]William Crockett says, "The precise nature of the resurrected bodies [of the wicked] is not always clear" ("The Metaphorical View," in William V. Crockett, ed., *Four Views on Hell* [Grand Rapids: Zondervan, 1996], 69). Murray Harris speaks of the "silence of Paul and the other New Testament writers about the nature of that embodiment for the wicked for judgment" ("Resurrection and Immorality in the Pauline Corpus," in *Life in the Face of Death*, ed. Richard N. Longenecker [Grand Rapids: Eerdmans, 1998], 151).

[8]J. I. Packer, "The Problem of Eternal Punishment," *Crux* 26 (September 1990): 25.

[9]Evangelicals who have held to conditional immortality include John Stott, John Wenham, Philip E. Hughes, Stephen Travis, and Clark Pinnock.

[10]William Lane Craig, "Politically Incorrect Salvation," in *Christian Apologetics in the Postmodern World*, ed. Timothy R. Phillips and Dennis L. Okholm (Downers Grove, Ill.: InterVarsity, 1995), 88.

[11]Joel B. Green and Mark D. Baker, *Recovering the Scandal of the Cross* (Downers Grove, Ill.: InterVarsity, 2000), 54–55; cp. 95.

[12]D. A. Carson, *How Long, O Lord?* (Grand Rapids: Baker, 1990), 103.

[13]William Lane Craig, "Politically Incorrect Salvation," 88.

[14]Ibid.

[15]Carson, *How Long, O Lord?*, 102.

[16]Stephen Davis, "Universalism, Hell, and the Fate of the Ignorant," *Modern Theology* 6 (January 1990): 179.

[17]Carson, *How Long, O Lord?*, 102.

[18]Charles Seymour, *A Theodicy of Hell* (Dordrecht: Kluwer, 2000).

[19]See discussion in Robin A. Parry and Christopher H. Partridge, eds., *Universal Salvation? The Current Debate* (Grand Rapids: Eerdmans, 2004).

[20]C. S. Lewis, *The Problem of Pain* (New York: Macmillan, 1962), 118–19.

[21]James Sennett, "Is There Freedom in Heaven?" *Faith and Philosophy* 16 (January 1999): 69–82; Michael J. Murray, "Heaven and Hell," in *Reason for the Hope Within*, ed. Michael J. Murray (Grand Rapids: Eerdmans, 1999), 287–317.

[22]This point taken from N. T. Wright, *Evil and the Justice of God* (Downers Grove, Ill.: InterVarsity, 2006), 92, 96.

[23]Lewis, *The Problem of Pain*, 122.

[24]Travis, "The Problem of Judgment," *Themelios* 11 (January 1986): 53.

[25]Lewis, *The Problem of Pain*, 127.

Chapter 16: The Incarnation

[1]John Hick, *The Fifth Dimension: An Exploration of the Spiritual Realm* (Oxford: One World, 1999), 234–36.

[2]In Marcus J. Borg and N. T. Wright, *The Meaning of Jesus: Two Visions* (San Francisco: HarperSF, 1999), 149.

[3]C. S. Lewis, "Fern Seed and Elephants" in *Fern-Seed and Elephants and Other Essays on Christianity*, ed. Walter Hooper (London: Collins, 1975), 106–7.

[4]See Larry Hurtado's landmark book, *Lord Jesus Christ: Devotion to Jesus in Early Christianity* (Grand Rapids: Eerdmans, 2003).

[5]E. K. Simpson and F. F. Bruce, *The Epistles of Paul to the Ephesians and to the Colossians,* New International Commentary on the New Testament (Grand Rapids: Eerdmans, 1957), 194.

[6]Gerald O' Collins, *Christology* (Oxford: Oxford University Press, 1995), 233.

[7]If humans are *created* or *finite,* did Jesus become a creature? No, he *took on* human nature and a human body. While both *are* God's creations, this doesn't mean that they are *necessary* to being human. Are humans *necessarily* finite? We can deny that both *creaturehood* and *being finite* are *necessary* or *essential* characteristics of human beings since God couldn't become something contrary to his nature. Thomas Senor, "The Incarnation and the Trinity," in *Reason for the Hope Within,* ed. Michael J. Murray (Grand Rapids: Eerdmans, 1999), 247. Also, I borrow much from Thomas V. Morris, *The Logic of God Incarnate* (Ithaca, N.Y.: Cornell University Press, 1986).

[8]Gerald Hawthorne, *The Presence and the Power* (Dallas: Word, 1991), 218.

[9]R. T. France, "The Uniqueness of Jesus," *Evangelical Review of Theology* 17 (Jan. 1993): 13.

[10]Gerald Hawthorne, *The Presence and the Power,* 212, 216. R. L. Reymond writes: "There is no confusion [in the crucifixion] of the divine and human natures of Christ. It is not the divine nature as such which is crucified; it is the divine person, because he is also human, who is crucified." "Incarnation" in *Evangelical Dictionary of Theology,* ed. Walter A. Elwell (Grand Rapids: Baker, 1984), 556–57.

[11]R. L. Reymond, "Incarnation" in *Evangelical Dictionary of Theology,* ed. Walter A. Elwell (Grand Rapids: Baker, 1984), 556–57. Cp. Acts 20:28: "…the church of God which He purchased with His own blood."

[12]Gerald O'Collins, *Interpreting Jesus* (Ramsey, N.J.: Paulist, 1983), 186.

[13]Ibid., 185.

[14]Morris, *The Logic of God Incarnate,* 149–50.

[15]O'Collins, *Christology,* 271.

Chapter 17: The Cross of Christ

[1]John Meier, "The Circle of the Twelve: Did It Exist During Jesus' Public Ministry?" *Journal of Biblical Literature* 116 (1997): 664–65.

[2]N. T. Wright, *Evil and the Justice of God,* 57. I borrow insights from ch. 3 of Wright's book.

[3]Ibid., 59.

[4]John Stott, *The Cross of Christ* (Downers Grove, Ill.: InterVarsity, 1986), 88.

[5]At certain points, I draw on John Hare, *The Moral Gap: Kantian Ethics, Human Limits, and God's Assistance* (Oxford: Clarendon Press, 1996); and Steven Porter, "Rethinking the Logic of Penal Substitution," in *Philosophy of Religion: A Reader and Guide,* ed. William Lane Craig (New Brunswick, N.J.: Rutgers University Press, 2002), 596–608.

[6]Porter, "Rethinking," 605.

[7]Stott, *Cross of Christ,* 160.

Chapter 18: Jesus' Uniqueness and the Plurality of Religions

[1]Allan Bloom, *The Closing of the American Mind* (New York: Simon and Schuster, 1987), 228.

[2]A helpful overview on religious pluralism is David Basinger, *Religious Diversity: A Philosophical Assessment* (Burlington, Vt.: Ashgate, 2002).

[3]John Godfrey Saxe, "Six Blind Men & the Elephant." Found at the "About Hinduism" website: http://hinduism.about.com. Accessed 1 December 2006.

[4]John Hick, *An Interpretation of Religion* (London: Macmillan, 1989), 235–36.

[5]Dalai Lama, *Kindness, Clarity and Insight* (New York: Snow Lion, 1984), 45.

[6]Ibid., 51.

[7]In José Ignacio Cabezón, ed. *The Bodhgaya Interviews* (New York: Snow Lion, 1988), 22.

[8]Peter van Inwagen, "*Non Est Hick,*" in *God, Knowledge, & Mystery* (Ithaca, N.Y.: Cornell University Press, 1995), 213–14.

[9]Alvin Plantinga, "Ad Hick," *Faith and Philosophy* 14 (July 1997): 295–302.

[10]Roger Trigg, *Rationality and Religion* (Oxford: Blackwell, 1998), 56–57.

[11]Paul Griffiths, *Problems of Religious Diversity* (Oxford: Blackwell, 2001), 149.

[12]*Exclusivist, inclusivist,* and *pluralist* are three standard categorizations that aren't always helpful and can overlap. Depending upon the context, these terms need further nuancing. For example, a Christian exclusivist *shouldn't* hold that truth can't be found outside the Christian revelation, and a Christian inclusivist believes that Christ *alone* is the basis of anyone's salvation. Harold Netland, *Encountering Religious Pluralism* (Downers Grove, Ill.: InterVarsity, 2001).

[13]See John Sanders, ed., *What About Those Who Have Never Heard?* (Downers Grove, Ill.: InterVarsity, 1995); Veli-Matti Kärkkäinen, *An Introduction to the Theology of Religions* (Downers Grove, Ill.: InterVarsity, 2003).

[14]See Part V in Paul Copan, *True for You, But Not for Me* (Minneapolis: Bethany House, 1998). On this, I follow the work of William Lane Craig.

[15]William Lane Craig, "Is 'Craig's Contentious Suggestion' Really So Implausible?" *Faith and Philosophy* 22/3 (July 2005): 361.

[16]Pauline Selby, *Persian Springs: Four Iranians See Jesus* (London: Elam Ministries, 2001); David Greenlee, *From the Straight Path to the Narrow Way: Journeys of Faith* (Waynesboro, Ga.: Authentic Media, 2005).

Chapter 19: Body, Soul, and Resurrection

[1]Oscar Cullmann, "Immortality of the Soul or Resurrection of the Dead?" in *Immortality and Resurrection*, ed. Krister Stendahl (New York: Macmillan, 1965).

[2]See N. T. Wright, *For All the Saints: Remembering the Christian Departed* (Harrisburg, Pa.: Morehouse, 2003).

[3]On the status of animals, see Paul Copan, *"How Do You Know You're Not Wrong?"* (Grand Rapids: Baker, 2005), 123–56.

[4]For a range of views, see Joel B. Green and Stuart L. Palmer, eds., *In Search of the Soul* (Downers Grove, Ill.: InterVarsity, 2005).

[5]C. S. Lewis, *Christian Reflections* (Grand Rapids: Eerdmans, 1967), 64.

[6]Bas van Fraassen, "Empiricism in the Philosophy of Science," in *Images of Science*, ed. Paul Churchland (Chicago: University of Chicago Press, 1985), 258.

[7]Jaegwon Kim, "Mind, Problems of the Philosophy of," s.v. *The Oxford Companion to Philosophy*, ed. Ted Honderich (New York: Oxford University Press, 1995), 578.

[8]Jerry A. Fodor, "The Big Idea: Can There Be a Science of the Mind?" *Times Literary Supplement* (3 July 1992), 5.

[9]Charles Taliaferro, *Contemporary Philosophy of Religion* (Malden, Mass.: Blackwell, 1998), 94.

[10]A. J. Ayer, "What I Saw When I Was Dead"—an appendix in Terry Meithe and Antony Flew, *Does God Exist?* (San Francisco: HarperCollins, 1991), 225.

[11]See J. P. Moreland and Gary Habermas, *Beyond Death: Exploring the Case for Immortality* (Eugene, Oreg.: Wipf and Stock, 2004); Michael B. Sabom, M.D., F.A.C.C., *Recollections of Death: A Medical Investigation* (New York: Harper & Row, 1982).

[12]Stewart Goetz, "Naturalism and Libertarian Agency," in *Naturalism: A Critical Analysis*, ed. William Lane Craig and J. P. Moreland (London: Routledge, 2000), 157.

[13]Victor Reppert, *C.S. Lewis's Dangerous Idea: In Defense of the Argument from Reason* (Downers Grove, Ill.: InterVarsity, 2003), 107–8.

[14]On Eastern monism and reincarnation, see Paul Copan, *That's Just Your Interpretation* (Grand Rapids: Baker, 2001).

Chapter 20: Faith, Doubt, and Hope

[1]"St. Therese of Lisieux: Quotations." At http://www.littleflower.org/learn/reflect/frjrquotations.asp.. Accessed 24 April 2006.

[2]"Lamb" in Jewish apocalyptic literature is at times a fierce horned lamb that destroys the enemies of Israel (*1 Enoch* 90:9; *Testament of Joseph* 19:8–9). Cp. "the wrath of the Lamb" in Revelation (6:16; also 17:14), who is also the slain Passover Lamb.

[3]Ruther A. Tucker, *Walking Away from Faith* (Downers Grove, Ill.: InterVarsity, 2002), 213.

[4] Nicholas Wolterstorff, "The Assurance of Faith," *Faith and Philosophy* 7 (October 1990): 396–417.

[5] C. Stephen Evans, "Is Kierkegaard an Irrationalist?" in *Kierkegaard on Faith and the Self* (Waco, Tex.: Baylor University Press, 2006), ch. 7.

[6] See Douglas Groothuis, "An Unwarranted Farewell to Pascal's Wager," *Philosophia Christi* n.s. 4/2 (2002): 501–8.

[7] See Thomas V. Morris, *Making Sense of It All: Pascal and the Meaning of Life* (Grand Rapids: Eerdmans, 1992).

[8] Some of these thoughts are taken from Louis J. Pojman, "Faith Without Belief," *Faith and Philosophy* 3 (1986): 157–76; Robert Audi, "Faith, Belief, and Rationality," *Philosophical Perspectives* 5 (1991): 213–39; William P. Alston, "The Deontological Conception of Epistemic Justification," *Philosophical Perspectives* 2 (1988): 257–99; Alexander Pruss, "Christian Faith and Belief," *Faith and Philosophy* 19 (2002): 291–303; Jay Wood, "Faith," in *The Routledge Companion to Philosophy of Religion*, ed. Paul Copan and Chad V. Meister (London: Routledge, 2007); James Sennett, *This Much I Know* (unpublished manuscript).

[9] Paul J. Griffiths, *Problems of Religious Diversity* (Malden, Mass.: Blackwell, 2001), 26–30.

[10] Some of these thoughts are taken from Douglas V. Henry, "Does Reasonable Nonbelief Exist?" *Faith and Philosophy* 18/1 (January 2001): 75–92. See also Jay Wood, *Epistemology* (Downers Grove, Ill.: InterVarsity, 1998), 27.

[11] Pascal, *Penseés*, #429.

[12] Henry, "Does Reasonable Non-Belief Exist?" 84.

[13] Caroline Franks Davis, *The Evidential Force of Religious Experience* (Oxford: Clarendon Press, 1989).

[14] Henry, "Does Reasonable Non-Belief Exist"? 84.

[15] Paul views the Spirit's fruit as the fulfillment of Isaianic prophecies (*righteousness, peace, confidence,* and *joy* [in 32:10–18]; *praise, peace, joy* [in 57:15–19]). See G. K. Beale, "The Old Testament Background of Paul's Reference to 'the Fruit of the Spirit' in Galatians 5:22," *Bulletin for Biblical Research* 15.1 (2005): 1–38.

[16] Jürgen Moltmann, *Theology of Hope,* trans. A. Leitch (London: SCM Press, 1967).